THE
LAST GREAT RACE

THE
LAST GREAT RACE
THE IDITAROD

TIM JONES

STACKPOLE BOOKS

Copyright © 1988 by Tim Jones

Published by
STACKPOLE BOOKS
Cameron and Kelker Streets
P.O. Box 1831
Harrisburg, PA 17105

Printed in the United States of America

10 9 8 7 6 5 4 3 2 1

Originally published in 1982 by Madrona Publishers, Seattle
Cover art © 1982 by Jon Van Zyle
Pen and ink drawings by Jamichael Henterly

Library of Congress Cataloging-in-Publication Data

Jones, Tim, 1942–
    The last great race.

    Originally published: Seattle : Madrona, 1982.
    1. Iditarod Trail Sled Dog Race, Alaska.
2. Iditarod National Historic Trail (Alaska) – History.
I. Title.
SF440.15.J66 1988   798'.8   88-12182
ISBN 0-8117-2233-3

For Ariel and all the children
who grow up with Alaskans for heroes

Preface

AT A PARTY DURING THE 1979 FUR RENDEZVOUS IN ANCHORAGE I WAS talking with Gareth Wright, a long-time sprint racer from Fairbanks who had won the World Championship Sled Dog Race three times. He asked how I was doing and I told him I'd started a book on the Iditarod but for one reason and another—mostly lack of money—the project, after about four months of part-time work, had come to a standstill. A man who had been sitting on the couch with us leaned around Wright and asked, "You want to write a book about the Iditarod?"

I said, "Yes."

"How much do you need?"

I named a figure I thought was high. He said, "I'll write you a check."

That was how I met Del Allison. In the two weeks left before the start of the Iditarod, he not only wrote a check, but hired an airplane and pilot to fly me along the trail. And the help didn't stop there. When my writing bogged down in the muddle of having to hold a job, he found a cabin in the woods where I could write and loaned me a dog team for traveling back and forth while the work progressed. Through it all, Del Allison provided the inspiration to keep me going, with his belief that the only limits a person has are the ones he imposes on himself. Simply, this book wouldn't exist without Del Allison, who put faith in a stranger and then followed up with immeasurable support, providing the will to keep going no matter how difficult the trail.

I recalled thinking after our talk at the party that even if the check didn't come through, just the thought of the offer had raised my spirits to the point where I felt anything was possible. This book is the result of a chance encounter that has grown into a life-long admiration for a man who refuses to accept limitations.

Because of that one encounter there were many more. One of the first was with pilot Ed Gurtler—Crazy Horse. From our first flight with our screaming dive earthward while I photographed a racer on the Burn, through a harrowing flight in the whiteout near Iditarod and on to the windy bluffs of the Seward Peninsula, we developed a relationship of respect. I don't think I'll ever get used to flying in turbulence in small airplanes, or even in big ones for that matter, but when I have to fly, there's no one I'd rather go with than Crazy Horse—for his abilities with the airplane, for his knowledge of wilderness flying and for the kind of trust that goes unspoken.

Many people helped, some with their expertise and some by feeding and housing a writer and pilot along the trail. For two weeks, I ate, mostly out of my pockets, beef jerky and Corn Nuts, so the hot meals here and there in the villages were most appreciated. Harry and Patty Lacey offered a place to sleep in Farewell as did Goog Anderson in McGrath. The big pile of spaghetti Erin and James Gerrin served up in McGrath was the first meal since Anchorage. Audra Forsgren's thick soup at Ophir stayed with us for more than a day. I'm sure we were part of Jim Flemings' headache at Iditarod, but the stew he made served well until our next stop, and his correspondence with me since, in which he describes a way of life I envy greatly, has served to keep my own dreams alive. Ernie and Barbara Chase in Grayling served us another hot meal—moose ribs and vegetables—and found us a place to stay. Ernie sold us airplane fuel even though his own limited supplies were dwindling and there could be no more until the barges came up the river after breakup.

In Kaltag Larry Thompson opened his house and offered another stew, this one beaver. Farther along at Shaktoolik, the Takak family put out a table full of food, and if I insulted their hospitality by not eating much, it was because I had a cold and was worried I'd infect the whole family. But their sandwich of reindeer meat was a lifesaver. We stayed in the school at Koyuk, and almost enjoyed reindeer stew with Ralph Willoya in Golovin.

In Nome Albro Gregory offered a place to stay at the Nome *Nugget*, but I ended up staying with Mark and Kitty Fuerstenau and slept in my first soft bed on the trail — though by that time I'd become so used to floors and ground I had trouble sleeping.

Those people along the trail helped keep a writer and pilot alive while others helped in a different way, providing insight and information. Gareth Wright, with his knowledge of care and feeding, helped me understand the complexities of a dog team. During the race, Dick Mackey, drawing from his own experience, unselfishly shared his extensive racing knowledge when I was hesitant to approach the mushers, who were more intent on running the race than talking with a writer who'd had eight hours' sleep and often had a full stomach as well.

Veterinarians Phil Meyer, Tony Funk and Derrick Leedy were free with their medical knowledge, even when they might have felt they were telling more than they should. Race marshal Pat Hurren, too, spoke candidly, telling me about the race and dog mushing and his job of monitoring fifty-four drivers and eight hundred dogs to make sure the race was run fairly.

One fellow I came to regard as a friend had long since passed from the scene. As I read through the newspapers from the city of Iditarod, I grew to appreciate George M. Arbuckle, journalist veteran of several gold stampedes, not only for his wit and insight into a gold camp, but for his use of language in a writing style that has been all but lost. Arbuckle chronicled what no history book could begin to present, from tea parties on Nob Hill to the death of C.C. Chittick to the robbery of the tramway.

A long list of others provided the kind of help that can't be tabulated. They were the friends who believed, put up with me, encouraged and supported and listened and read, and without them work on this book might have been a lot more discouraging.

Of course there would have been no book at all if men and women didn't accept the challenge of the Iditarod Trail Sled Dog Race across a thousand miles of Alaska. All of the mushers, even in their sleepless condition, tolerated curious eyes and ears, cameras, notebooks and tape recorders, and some, open to conversation, were able to add a lot to my understanding. For the solitary kind of person who tackles the Iditarod, the intrusions must have been annoying and distracting, yet everyone in one way or another was helpful. Just the fact that the mushers chose to run the Iditarod, to accept the challenge of Alaska for themselves and for all of us, was enough.

Perhaps the most fascinating aspect of Alaska is that its history and its heritage are so close. Memories of the frontier period in the rest of the country have faded into books and museums and park dedications, but in Alaska some of the people who pushed to the edges of that frontier still live. Here and there men and women still prospect for gold, trap and use dog teams for work. It wasn't until the 1970s that the U.S. Postal Service discontinued its last sled dog routes.

The Iditarod Trail Sled Dog Race is a link to what has come before: mushers and dogs face the same mountains, rivers, ocean ice, wild animals and capricious weather that were there in last year's race and in last century's mail run.

The Iditarod rekindles the light of adventure that's in all Alaskans while keeping us in touch with history. And the men and women who run it are some of the modern heroes of Alaska.

Contents

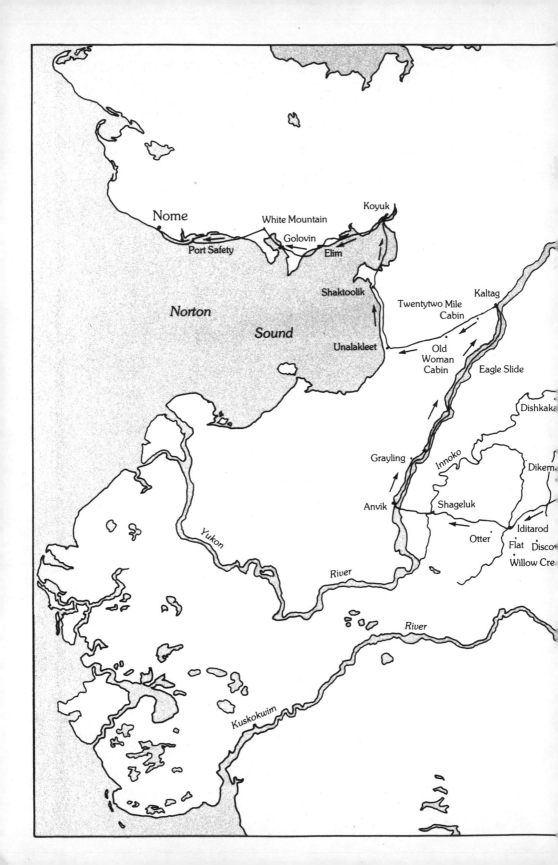

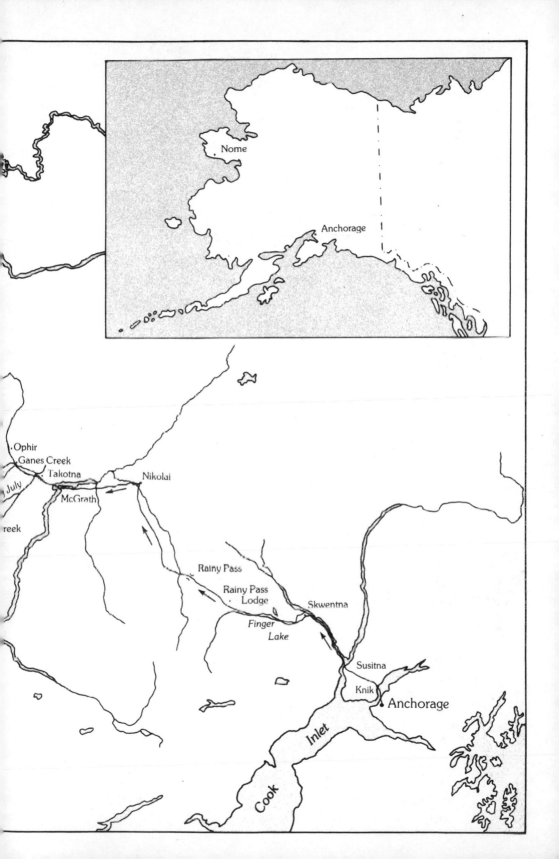

The Last Great Race

IDITAROD TRAIL RACE

★★ ANCHORAGE TO NOME ★ 1049 MILES ★★

START

1. Anchorage: The Starting Line

EIGHT HUNDRED SLED DOGS YIPPED AND HOWLED IN THEIR TRACES OUT-side Mulcahy Stadium in Anchorage. Along with their owners — quieter but just as keyed up — they captured much of the best of Alaska tradition: centuries of Eskimo and Indian culture, the mail drivers and freight haulers, the gold rush, the ability to survive in a rugged land, and the frontier spirit that carried the 1925 life-saving scrum from Nenana to Nome.

The annual Iditarod Trail Sled Dog Race from Anchorage to Nome was about to start.

Gathered here were fifty-five dog drivers fresh from lonely training trails that had taken them through spruce forests, across treeless tundra and onto frozen river ice — trails that had cut into the snows not only of Alaska but as far away as the farmland of Ohio. The drivers — mushers — were from the most predictable and unpredictable walks of life.

A lawyer had entered the race along with several who claimed trapping as a profession. There were two doctors and an Eskimo ivory carver and a millionaire real-estate developer as well as a couple of bush pilots. One of the mushers was a fisheries biologist, another an electronics technician. The field included truck driv-

ers, an insurance executive and a woman carpenter. Many lived in
bush Alaska working seasonally at any number of jobs to support
their true profession of sled dog racing, and described their occu-
pations as if in one word: trapper-prospector-fisherman-carpenter-
handyman-contractor-hunting-guide. Two were even Indian
chiefs — at least in the modern context as presidents of village corporations established under the Alaska Native Claims Settlement
Act of 1971. The youngest musher had turned eighteen three
months before the race; the oldest was a grandfather in his sixties.

They came to the starting line with only one aspect of their lives
in common — they all drove dog teams. All had spent at least a
year preparing for this race, and many had been at it, training,
learning, planning, talking, and experimenting, for longer than
that. Their motives differed. One of the drivers, Joe May, said,
"There are fifty-five guys racing for fifty-five different reasons.
Some are 100 percent competitive, some are 100 percent noncom-
petitive." For the competitive ones, the only goal was to finish
first, to outrun everyone else across Alaska. For others, the race
was an 1100-mile-plus camping trip, a wilderness adventure that
they took part in for the same reason that other people climb
mountains — the experience — and the accomplishment itself was
sufficient reward. Some of the mushers were preparing and learning; they had entered the race to pick up the knowledge and experience necessary to win a future race. Now in its seventh running, the race was past the day when a first-timer could win it.
Strategy, knowledge of the trail, and the care and feeding of dogs
had become so complex that the rookie racer could never expect to
beat those who had gone before.

The assortment of men, women and dogs was gathered outside a
stadium designed for baseball in the summer and high school foot-
ball in the fall. Surrounding the park on a circular lot cleared of
snow, the trucks of the mushers stood silent — but theirs was the
only silence. Dogs peeked through openings in the little doors of
home-constructed dog-box carriers in the beds of the trucks. Other
dogs stood outside, tied to the trucks by chains. Few of the dogs
were quiet for any length of time. Mushers checked their gear, piling it into long sleds or talking with spectators in the endless line
that walked by watching, asking questions, petting dogs or just
looking and dreaming. Some of the teams, the ones that would be

first to the starting line, were already in harness, now and then a dog jumping against the restriction of harness and sled, anxious to be going.

Inside the park a banner was suspended over the starting line, pronouncing that this was the start of the 1,049-mile Iditarod Trail Sled Dog Race. A trail had been carved out of the snow around the park's 440-yard running track and as many as two thousand spectators stood on the berm raised by the digging out of two feet of snow. The sky held clear and blue, but the midmorning temperature, ten degrees and rising, was too warm for the comfort of the dogs. An announcer raised a patter over a squeaky public address system, hyping the race, warning mushers it was half an hour, then fifteen minutes, then ten until race time.

As time grew short, the spectators left the trucks and walked to the perimeter of the track to watch the first quarter-mile of a race that could take three weeks or more to complete.

The dogs inhaled the excitement in the atmosphere as the announcer called for the first few mushers to prepare to approach the starting line. As the first team moved up, the dogs still anchored in the lot raised a chorus of yipping and yowling and plain old barking — in addition to the song that only an Alaskan husky can make, almost as if he's talking. If the dog kept his mouth still, it would be a howl, but in a high key he opens and closes his mouth, producing a soprano yow . . . owoo . . . oowoo that really means, "Hey, boss, they're leaving me behind."

The sounds and actions of the dogs seemed to charge the mushers as well. They were animated, confident, some jovial, some serious, many showing smiles and optimism as the months and months of preparation faded behind them and the time to hit the trail approached.

At precisely 10 A.M. February 24, 1979, the announcer called the first musher to the starting line, but no one came. The starting position, Number One, was reserved to the memory of Leonhard Seppala, one of the great mushers of the past, to whom the race was dedicated. Though the legendary Seppala had driven his last trail, his spirit lived on in the Iditarod, and the first two minutes at the starting line were reserved, in silence, for him. Seppala was perhaps the most famous of the old-time Alaska dog drivers and a hero of the relay that rushed desperately needed diphtheria serum to the children of Nome in 1925. Standing quietly near the starting line during the moments of silence for Number One were three other veterans of that serum relay: Edgar Kalland, Billy McCarty and Charlie Evans. Harry Pitka,·a fourth member of the relay, lay seriously ill in an Anchorage hospital nearby. The four served as living links with a part of the history and heritage of Alaska only recently past. As the two minutes of silence ended, the first of the modern legends answered the call to the starting line.

Joe May of Trapper Creek, Alaska, following the imagined runner tracks of Number One, pulled up to the starting line behind fourteen big Alaska huskies. If a movie director could create the face of an Alaska trapper, he'd come up with Joe May. Bearded, weather-saddened, with an expression of intelligence and humor, May looked like a combination of Abraham Lincoln and everybody's favorite grandfather. Seasoned in the merchant marine on the Great Lakes, he had made the transition from ship to sled. "I just wanted to go somewhere, move to Alaska. There's always a reason why you can't," he had said earlier. "All of a sudden one day the reasons went away. Took me about two weeks to get rid of everything I owned. I either gave it away, sold it or burned it." On this, his second attempt at the Iditarod, he followed the legendary Leonhard Seppala around the track and out of Mulcahy Stadium.

After May, the announcer called fifty-four more teams to the line at two-minute intervals. Later the differences in time would be accounted for when the mushers took mandatory twenty-four-hour layovers.

Among those called were three former winners. Emmitt Peters, an Indian from Ruby, had set the speed record for the race in 1975, running 14 days, 14 hours, 43 minutes and 45 seconds. A short, thin 38-year-old, he squinted into the sun through yellow-tinted glasses, his raven-black hair hidden under a peaked cap. He had finished first, third, fourth and fifth in four races.

Jerry Riley had won the race in 1976 and finished second in '75 and '77. He carried with him the reputation of being perhaps the toughest person on the trail and maybe the toughest on his dogs. He came from a family of dog drivers and could trace the lineage of his dogs to a breed his father developed almost fifty years ago. Reportedly he'd been warned by the trail committee about his treatment of dogs, but others pointed to Riley's successes and said he couldn't do that well mistreating animals. Many passed it off, saying he was no tougher on the dogs than he was on himself, and the tales surrounding him led to the conclusion that he could pull the sled to Nome himself if his dogs failed.

Right behind Riley, Rick Swenson's team pulled up to the banner. Swenson won the race in 1977, and in 1978 he lost to Dick Mackey by a lead dog's nose after an exciting chase down Nome's Front Street, the first close finish in the history of the race. Swenson, confident to the point of cockiness, said he had the best team he'd ever run. He wore a bulky burnt-orange parky that hung to his knees, rimmed on the bottom by a border of fur. He also wore a yellow hat with a black rectangular insignia that at first glance looked like the CAT logo of the Caterpillar Tractor Company. But Swenson's hat said DOG in an identical typeface.

His rival from the year before was not racing, but Mackey's son Rick had entered the race driving some of his father's dogs. This was the son's second attempt at the Iditarod.

The people in the race represented a broad spectrum of the Alaska population. There were the Eskimos. Isaac Okleasik from Teller had won a ceremonial running of the race in 1967. Herbie Nayokpuk, perhaps the most popular musher with the crowds, at fifty was in his fourth Iditarod. He'd always finished in the top five. He came from Shishmaref, on the Chukchi Sea, where he operated a general store. An ivory carver since boyhood, he used traditional Eskimo ivory toggles instead of brass snaps to attach his dogs to the lines — in one race he even experimented with ivory runners on his sled. In recent years, when snow machines replaced dogs in the arctic, Nayokpuk had continued to maintain dog teams and, along with the Iditarod Trail Race, had been an instrumental factor in the resurgence of sleds and dogs. Victor Katongan and Clarence Towarak, both from Unalakleet, crossed the starting line; later came another Eskimo, Joe Garnie of Teller.

Ken Chase and Don Honea, along with Peters and Howard Albert of Ruby, represented Alaska's Indian culture. Chase and Honea were presidents of their village corporations: Honea, of Dineega Village Corporation in Ruby, and Chase of the Ingalik Village Corporation in Anvik. Chase was now the only musher left who had run every race, and the call of his name caused a buzz through the crowd. The previous year he had shared that distinction with Dick Mackey, but Mackey, after he won the race, had accepted the duties of president of the race committee and was now serving as race umpire. To complement Chase's accomplishment, his lead dog Piper also had run every race. Proud of his heritage, Chase tried to adhere as much as he could to the Indian ways. At times, in response to a question on how or why he did something, Chase would smile a little lopsidedly and explain, "an old Indian trick." Chase's dogs weren't running as well as he would have liked. He'd had to leave the team for a day while he attended to some business in Anchorage just before the race, and while he was gone some of the dogs broke loose and joined in a massive dog fight that apparently went on for an hour or more. The fight had left them all drained and some injured, still licking wounds, both physical and psychological. Even Piper, though uninjured, was down — but Piper kept the rest of the team going.

Since 1974 when Mary Shields and Lolly Medley were greeted in Nome by a sign proclaiming, "You've come a long way, baby," women had competed regularly in the race. Susan Butcher had been the first to finish in the top twenty — in 1978 — and this year she was shooting for the top ten. But, like many racers, she'd had her problems on the training trails. Ill for the month of January, she had just recovered when most of her dogs suffered food poisoning. As her dogs regained their health, she caught the bug again and her training program suffered for a total of almost two months. As if that weren't enough, during a training run one day, her team took a tromping from a moose that had challenged them for the trail.

Patty Friend, a carpenter with the U.S. Bureau of Land Management, was also running the race. Earlier in the season she had won the Cantwell 200, the first woman in recent memory to win a long-distance sled dog race. Part of her BLM duties involved work on a management plan for the Iditarod Trail, which had been designated a national historic trail by Congress. She was a former instructor in the National Outdoor Leadership School. Her husband, Rod Perry, had run the race twice.

Joe Redington, Sr., in his sixties and the oldest musher in the race, reached the starting line to cheers and shouts and clapping. Patriarch of a dog-mushing family and a grandfather several times over, Redington had pushed, argued, dreamed, and cajoled to make the Iditarod Race a reality, eventually mortgaging his own homestead, and he accepted with pride and modesty the title Father of the Iditarod. He had run every race but the first, at which time he was involved with organization. As he waited at the starting line, a television crew scurried around him and his eighteen dogs until the timer shouted, "Go!"

Three eighteen-year-olds brought the age span of the racers to almost fifty years. Rome Gilman, wearing a Rome to Nome button, Karl Clauson and Mark Couch, all barely out of high school, came to the line to tackle the trail. Gilman's goal, in addition to the finish line, was money to start studying veterinary medicine.

Many of the drivers came from bush Alaska where they took at least part of their living from the land, hunting, gardening, trapping and fishing. Among them were Keith Jones, a fisherman from Ambler in northwest Alaska who had once climbed Mount McKinley; John Barron, who lived in a bush cabin along the Yentna River in southcentral Alaska; Terry McMullin, a trapper from Eagle; and Jerry LaVoie, who gave his address as the Anvik River and his occupation as "bush liver." Others who fell generally into the group were Steve Vollertsen, who lived in Takotna, one of the stops along the original Iditarod Trail early in the century; Dick Peterson, a guide from Chisana and a contender for the rookie-of-the-year award; and Walter Kaso, a native of Brooklyn who had lived north of Talkeetna along the Susitna River for the previous five years. Another of those from the bush was Gene Leonard, whose cabin at remote Finger Lake in the foothills of the Alaska Range had been a checkpoint since the first race. For six years he'd watched the race pass by until he finally decided to run it. Recalling his days as a bartender in Syracuse, New York, he'd named his dogs after drinks. His leaders, Gin and Tonic, led Leonard's team of booze hounds out onto the Iditarod Trail.

Another who gave one of those vague addresses was Sonny Lindner, who came from the Johnson River and worked as a carpenter and contractor in Delta. He had finished eleventh the previous year despite a training accident when he'd speared himself on a branch as he passed it on his sled. The accident broke three ribs and his sternum and he had started the race that year with his ribs bandaged and his arm strapped to his side to keep the breastbone from separating. Unassuming, almost shy in public, Lindner simply answered yes or no to the announcer's questions. A former Eagle Scout, Lindner had climbed Mount McKinley, using dogs much of the way. While he stood at the starting line with more than a thousand miles in front of him, his handler looked at him from the sled and asked, "Got the map?"

In 1978 Lindner had won the prize as rookie of the year. In this race, Dick Peterson wasn't the only one going after that title; Gary Hokkanen and Lee Gardino were planning to give Peterson a run for the money. Hokkanen, who fell into the trapper-guide-dog-driver-mechanic category, was a friend of '77 winner Rick Swenson and had come up to Eureka from Minnesota to live and to train for the Iditarod. He had brought six dogs with him from Minnesota, had bought a few more and had borrowed two from Swenson. Tall and thin with a wisp of a beard and wearing wire-rimmed glasses, he wore a blue parky similar to Swenson's that his wife had put together shortly before the race. Gardino, a pipe-fitter from Chugiak, was also entering the race for the first time with serious intentions. He would set the early pace for the rookie mushers.

Two doctors and a veterinarian were competing. Ron Gould, a physician from Clear, had attempted the trip once before but had been forced to drop out. As he lit the cigar clenched in his teeth he told the announcer, "My wife told me if I don't get to Nome, don't come home." The other physician, Jim Lanier, a pathologist at Anchorage's Providence Hospital, was taking pledges for so much a mile to help in the costs of a new thermal unit at the facility.

Terry Adkins had been the official veterinarian for the race in 1973. Since then he'd run it every time, even after his air force duties took him out of Alaska. He brought a depleted team to the starting line, having lost one of his leaders in a freak accident the week before. He had flown the team north from Wyoming by commercial airliner, and a friend had met him at the Anchorage airport with a pickup truck and dog box. While headed north to Willow, the truck had run into winds gusting through the Matanuska Valley at up to a hundred miles per hour. The wind blew the dog box off the back of the truck and Adkins' lead dog was killed. That was just the beginning of the wind problems that would plague the race.

Ron Brinker also came to the race from a military background.

A Vietnam veteran, Brinker was entering his first Iditarod. A quick glance led to a guess that he must have been one of those supply sergeants from all the war movies who manage to appropriate a few things for themselves — almost every article of clothing and much of his gear had the look of army issue. He'd even invented a special pressure cooker for dog food made from one of the army's thermal food cans. Wanting to enjoy the full experience of the race, he'd built his own sled as well. Riding in the sled as handler was seventy-four-year-old Norman Vaughan, whose experience in dog mushing dated back to 1929, when he drove dogs in support of Admiral Richard Byrd's assault on the South Pole. Vaughan had attempted the Iditarod three times and in his third try, in 1978, finally completed the race. Some of the dogs in Brinker's team belonged to Vaughan. As Brinker moved around the track, the grin on his face had to be one of the most infectious in the stadium. Throughout the race Brinker's humor never faded, and he approached the trail's difficulties with the attitude of a man who'd faced much worse dangers in his life.

From a remote checkpoint village had come Eep Anderson, who owned a piece of McGuire's Tavern in McGrath, and Ernie Baumgartner, who worked in the same village as an electronics technician with the Federal Aviation Administration. The only lawyer in the race, Myron Angstman, came from Bethel in southwestern Alaska, bringing with him a setter, Irish and English mixed, as his lead dog. Three mushers from the end of the trail, Nome, had entered the race: Jim Rowe, an air-taxi pilot; Brian Blandford, a carpenter; and Richard Burmeister, a schoolteacher who was leaving the starting line still suffering the effects of a training spill in which he had broken three ribs and dislocated his shoulder.

Bud Smyth was another who faced the race with a sense of humor. He probably had run the Iditarod four times previously — probably, because in 1977 there was a mysterious musher named Vasily Zamitkyn who claimed Ayak Island as home. Zamitkyn wore a dark hood throughout the race, which he had finished in last place. When he crossed the finish line in Nome he stopped only long enough to pick up a bottle of vodka and then head on toward Russia. Some said the masked musher really was Bud Smyth, but Zamitkyn kept his silence. Smyth tended to come up with innovations, and this time he had the idea he could cook his dog food while he was moving, and he had built a stove, complete with stovepipe, right into the sled. The contraption led race marshal Pat Hurren to ask Smyth if he could buy a bag of popcorn.

While several of the mushers, particularly those with good sponsors, had been able to take time off to concentrate on training their dogs, many more had had to hold down jobs, splitting their attention between their dogs and their work, running the race as a hobby. Among them were John Wood, an engineer who'd finished thirtieth the previous year; Bob Chlupach, a fisheries biologist who raced purebred Siberian huskies; Rick McConnell, running as the Red Baron, a name taken from the Anchorage bar sponsoring him; Mel Adkins, who'd loaned his dogs to his brother Steve, then found a sponsor, borrowed dogs for himself and was now running the race; and Bill Rose, a contractor from Palmer who'd had to drop out of the race the year before. Cliff Sisson, who worked for the state parks department on the Kenai Peninsula, had won a ninety-mile race from Soldotna to Hope earlier in the season and had a team outfitted in matching purple harnesses with pompons on them. Harry Harris worked in electronic communications in Fairbanks, and Kelly Wages was a general contractor in the same city. Don Montgomery, an insurance executive, had come all the way from Ohio to race.

Artist Jon Van Zyle, driving purebred Siberian huskies, had run the race in 1976 and afterward painted a series of twenty pictures of his trail experiences. This year he had done the official poster for the race. His motive wasn't the competition; it was the experience and vision and subject matter, plus the joy he took in the dogs.

Each driver had moments in the limelight before taking off down the long, lonely trail, and for some the trials, both humorous and serious, began right there in Mulcahy Park.

Ron Aldrich, who lived on a homestead at Montana Creek, was in his fifth running. An easygoing retired air force colonel who raised dogs and taught flying, he drove some of the biggest animals in the race. His wheel dogs, the ones directly in front of the sled, weighed in the neighborhood of ninety pounds apiece. Aldrich left the starting line and drove around the track, but just before he left the stadium, his leaders balked and the team bunched up. In the melee, a male that had been running behind a female in heat caught her and they hobbled out of the park on six legs. Aldrich lost twenty minutes waiting until the two disentangled themselves.

Del Allison had entered the biggest team in the race, or so he thought. He'd intended to set out with twenty-one dogs, apparently needing them to haul his six-foot-five frame and 250 pounds. But, when Allison, a real-estate developer from Willow, arrived at the starting line, he counted only nineteen dogs. In the confusion of a team that big being hooked up, two dogs had ducked under the truck and the handlers had missed them. Allison had to pull his team over to the side while his brother, John, went to collect the two missing dogs. If a team can't start on time the musher has to wait until all the others have left. Allison was near the end anyway, so he pulled his team over to the side and said, "Well, if I have to stand here longer, at least the announcer will say my name more often." John returned with the two errant dogs and Allison left after the last team.

If Allison's and Aldrich's problems were humorous, Gayle Nienhueser's was more serious. At the beginning of the race, his dogs were hyperactive. The excitement of the start and the crowds, coupled with the rest they'd probably had in the days just before, could bring any dogs to fever pitch and make them difficult to control. Because of this, each musher was required to carry in the sled a dog handler, who'd be dropped off later, to help control the excited dogs in the stadium and on the way out of town. Even with as much as five hundred pounds of driver, handler, and equipment on board, some mushers towed a large tire or two behind them to help slow and control the team. Even so, the dogs could go too fast, moving at a dead run instead of the trot they'd been trained for. As Nienhueser tore around the track with his son on top of the sled for ballast, the sled tipped on one of the curves, throwing musher and son into the berm, but Nienhueser held on, dragging, until he could control and right the sled. Somehow in the spill he hurt his arm, an injury that went unnoticed for a time in the excitement and confusion as he regained control and ran out of the stadium.

An hour and forty-eight minutes after Joe May drove his dogs out of the park, Del Allison followed. Their destination was Eagle River, first checkpoint on the Iditarod Trail, fifteen miles ahead.

2. The Trail, the Racers, the Dogs

FOR THE MUSHER STANDING ON SLED RUNNERS AT THE START OF THE race, those dogs stretched out in front of him pointing toward Nome represented at least a year of training, feeding, and buying and repairing gear, not to mention thousands of dollars — all for the chance to drive a dog team a thousand miles through the wilds of Alaska.

Behind were countless hours of preparation; ahead lay historic trails and at least two weeks of sleeplessness, tremendous physical effort, harsh winds and temperatures well below zero. Everything about the trail was steeped in history, from the dogs to the sled designs, from the mushers — a few of them descended from old-time drivers — to the cabins they'd stay in at some of the twenty-three checkpoints along the way.

The race trail generally would follow routes first blazed in the early part of the century by freighting teams and mail drivers. It follows first the Iditarod Trail itself, which was surveyed and brushed out in the winter of 1910 and 1911 to provide a link between the gold rush town of Iditarod in westcentral Alaska and the railhead at Kern Creek, south of Anchorage, connecting with the seaport of Seward.

Once it reaches the town of Iditarod the trail connects with a web of older trails established when prospectors spread across Alaska and built settlements where they'd found pay. In winter, before the advent of the airplane, those trails were the only link with the outside world, and the people who drove them — on their way Outside to get grubstakes for spring — became news-bearers and mailmen. The race follows alternate routes along the web. In even-numbered years the teams go north to the Yukon River at Ruby, then follow the river west toward Nome. In odd-numbered years the trail turns west to go through the almost abandoned town of Iditarod, then north to Nome. Even then the route varies from year to year because of the vagaries of weather and conditions, so no one's ever sure just how long the race is. Officials tag the distance officially at 1,049 miles: 1,000 because they know it's more than 1,000 miles, and 49 because Alaska was the forty-ninth state admitted to the union. Adding up the estimated distances between checkpoints for this race resulted in a more realistic sum of 1,137 miles.

The dogs who were running that trail evolved from breeds first used before the turn of the century. From the time the white man arrived in Alaska, dogs were at a premium and mushers would use almost any dog capable of pulling a sled, even bird dogs and hounds. Eventually the dogs brought north by gold prospectors mixed with the dogs used by Indians and Eskimos and even with wolves. Two breeds, malemutes, named for the Malmuit Eskimos of the Kotzebue area where the dogs were first encountered, and the Siberian husky, introduced to Alaska from Russia, eventually were recognized by the American Kennel Club as pure breeds.

The malemutes, generally big and tough, worked well with heavy freight but couldn't sustain the speeds needed for racing. The Siberians, smaller and faster but still tough enough for the long trail, became the more accepted racing breed.

The Siberian huskies are believed to have come to America with a Russian trader who brought a few to Nome in 1908. In 1909, after seeing the dogs work and race, Nome miner Fox Maule Ramsey journeyed to the Anadyr River area of Siberia and brought back as many as sixty of the dogs to Nome. He separated those dogs into three teams for the 1910 All-Alaska Sweepstakes and, despite the scoffs of onlookers, the smaller dogs took first and second places in the four-hundred-mile competition. Later, John "Iron Man" Johnson, also using Siberians, won the race in a record time that stood until the race was discontinued. A couple of years later, Leonhard Seppala entered the Nome racing scene with Siberian teams and won the last three sweepstakes races. Seppala later traveled to the East Coast with his dogs and joined the racing circuit there, popularizing the Siberian husky.

Though he was known principally as a dog racer, Seppala's most famous run with those Siberians came in 1925 when Nome's only doctor diagnosed an outbreak of diphtheria. The Nome hospital did not have enough serum on hand to treat all the patients, so relief agencies organized what would become the most famous sled dog race of all time. The serum was carried north by the Alaska Railroad to the railhead at Nenana, where a dog-puncher named Wild Bill Shannon picked it up, wrapped it in fur and headed west toward Nome. The serum was carried by a relay of nineteen mushers including Seppala before it reached Nome a little more than 170 hours later. The serum run caught the fancy of American newspapers and the story was carried all over the world, building a legend that has lasted to the present.

In the 1960s that legend and the tradition of the sled dog in Alaska led Joe Redington, Sr. of Knik to begin dreaming of a race from Anchorage to Nome. In time he managed to convince others the project was workable. In 1967, the hundredth anniversary of Alaska's purchase from Russia, Redington and his friends organized the first Iditarod Race, a two-day event run over twenty-five miles of the original trail. Seppala himself was invited to be honorary race marshal, but he died shortly before the race was run. His wife took his place, and while she was in Alaska she spread the ashes of the most famous of the old-time dog drivers along the Iditarod Trail.

Redington's dream grew and infected others. The first Iditarod Trail Sled Dog Race to Nome, dedicated to Leonhard Seppala, became a reality in 1973. In later years the race was dedicated to others of the mushers who had made that attention-getting relay to save the children of Nome.

When thirty-four teams left Anchorage in March 1973 they began an adventure that few people thought they had a chance of completing. No one had attempted a race across Alaska before, and there was a lot to be learned. Twenty-two teams eventually made it to Nome and the Iditarod Trail Sled Dog Race became a reality. With it began the experiences that would provide a body of knowledge about sled dogs and long-distance mushing.

Looking at the distance and the heavy equipment they'd have to carry, many of the mushers chose to use large dogs, more like the malemutes. A few of those dogs could trace their lineage all the way back to those that had run for Seppala fifty years before.

Few of the dogs fell into the purebred category, though. Over the years, mushers in general and Iditarod racers in particular crossbred dogs for specific traits, paying little attention to the purity of the breeds. Competition increased and the Iditarod mushers began looking at smaller and faster dogs, breeding for speed as well as toughness, stamina, good feet and happy, interested animals who could stand the rigors of a thousand miles both physically and psychologically. As knowledge and experience expanded and equipment became lighter and the trail better groomed, the mushers began to field dogs who could pull the load and still maintain a pace of ten or eleven miles an hour.

The key to the value of any dog is what the mushers call "head": attitude. Dogs, like people, have varying personalities. Some are happy, some distant, some spooky. Some get bored on the trail; others take to it as if there's nothing else in life, responding to the joy of the trail. The training and racing have to be done carefully; dogs have a psychological breaking point after which they just won't work. Part of the training of any dog team involves just keeping the dogs' spirits up, keeping them feeling good with what they're doing. Besides looking for inherent good head, mushers train for it. After hard training early in the winter, they ease up on the schedules in the weeks before the race, taking the dogs on short happy runs that are just enough to keep the interest up and the muscles in tone.

As he trains, the musher watches where each dog works best in the team. Dogs fall into four general categories as they're lined out in the team: leaders, swing dogs, team dogs and wheel dogs. Good leaders are essential. They have to stay out front, keeping the lines tight and the other dogs moving, and to do that they have to be faster than the others and accepted as the leaders. Many dogs need to follow another, but a leader has to be able to accept the responsibility of running out front. He has to stay on the trail, finding it with his feet by feeling the firmness of the snowpack and with his nose by scenting teams that have gone before. The leaders also have to take commands: *gee* and *haw*, old mule-skinner terms for right and left. Some will take *come gee* or *come haw* — commands to turn the team and sled completely around. A *whoa* calls for a stop, though the drag of the sled brake probably means more than the word. The word *mush*, supposedly the starting command, is part of the legend, not the reality. *Mush* probably came from the early French dog drivers in Canada shouting *marchez*, meaning *go*. Most often the word for getting started is *hike* or *go* or *come on*, but as the dogs get used to the routine of the trail, just shaking the sled will bring them up and moving, sometimes even when the musher doesn't want them to.

The two dogs directly behind the leaders are called swing dogs. Often leaders in training, they have an important job, particularly on turns. When the first dogs make a turn, the rest of the dogs in the team have a tendency to jump off in that direction without following around on the trail. Part of the swing dogs' duty is to make sure the team stays in the trail rather than jumping off into deep snow.

Behind the swing positions run the team dogs. That's the term for all the other dogs except the wheel dogs. The team dogs have one chore: to pull. They're the ones in the trenches and in them lie the power and stamina over the long haul. The generally accepted practice is to require a dog to pull no more than its own weight, but in reality the dogs are capable of pulling much more, at least for short distances.

Under the weight-to-weight ratio a team of fourteen fifty-pound dogs could handle seven hundred pounds easily. The early mail and freight drivers would pull four or five hundred pounds with just five or six dogs. The weight a team pulls during the Iditarod usually ranges from about three hundred pounds to something more than five hundred, which includes the driver.

The last two dogs in the team are the wheel dogs, another term taken from the mule skinners. If the leaders are the brains of the outfit, the wheelers are the brawn, often the biggest dogs in the team. They run right in front of the sled, and steering it is one of their main functions. The swing dogs have to keep the team in the trail on a curve; the wheel dogs have to keep the sled in the trail, hauling it around trees and stumps. The wheel dogs also provide the first oomph when the team starts. They have to break the sled loose and give it momentum when the musher hollers to go. Once started, they have the continuous pressure of that sled bouncing and pounding right behind them, chasing them down the trail. As the last dogs to go over the top, the wheel dogs also have the toughest chore on hills. Once the rest of the team clears a hill the dogs might relax and leave the sled hanging precariously, the only support coming from the musher, pushing from behind. At this point the wheel dogs, the last to have the pressure of the hill relieved, dig in to bring the load up.

The dogs in a team aren't necessarily assigned to fixed positions for the entire length of the race. Some leaders may be fast and good at finding the trail, but not able to take commands well. The command leaders will be put to work when there are trails to be crossed and towns to go through, where the driver needs more steering control. One dog might not go into the wind as well as another, or one might be more apt to chase a wild animal encountered on the trail. Sometimes a musher might put swing dogs or team dogs in lead for a while just to relieve the pressure on the dogs out front. Or he might just want to give one guy a rest and put him back in the team. Even wheel dogs end up in lead on occasion. Throughout the training and into the race itself the musher moves the dogs around, looking for the best combinations for particular conditions.

During that first race in 1973 the mushers had only a little idea of what to expect, and only one veterinarian traveled along with them to watch over the dogs. But with experience came better care and feeding for the most important element of the race — the dogs. As far as food and health care go, the dogs fare much better than the mushers. Race rules stipulate that a veterinarian examine each dog within seven days before the race and that each dog have had its rabies, distemper and parvovirus shots within a required period. No dog is allowed in the race if it fails to pass the vet check.

In addition, a veterinarian is stationed at each checkpoint along the trail to examine and treat the dogs, and the vet has the authority to require a musher to drop a dog if it's not up to par. During the race each musher is required to stop once for twenty-four hours at a checkpoint to rest his dogs. Booties are required to protect the dogs' feet along icy trails. In general, mushers have learned over the years that the better care they give the dogs the better their chances in the race.

The equipment the mushers use also has improved with experience, although in outward appearance it isn't much different from that used by the old-timers.*

The sleds, made from hardwood such as birch or ash, for the most part follow traditional designs and weigh between forty and a hundred pounds. Eight or ten feet seems to be the average length. Rawhide holds the wooden sections together so that the sled, instead of being rigid and breakable, has enough give to allow parts to move a bit on the bumps and curves of the trail. The load is carried in the basket. A limber curve of wood called the brush bow protects the front of the sled from obstructions and is intended to fend off trees and absorb the shock of collision. The driver's handhold is called the drive bow or, sometimes, the handlebar. Vertical stanchions support the basket on the runners. The runners, curved at the front of the sled, extend to three or four feet behind the basket, where the driver stands. The sections of runners that the driver stands on usually have pieces of cut-up motorcycle tires attached to the upper side to provide some purchase. The runners are made of wood, with a surface of hard plastic to slide easily over the snow and still withstand abrasion. Often the plastic has to be changed a couple of times during the race.

In recent years several mushers have used what's called a toboggan sled — a new design, lighter, for long-distance racing. Instead of being supported on raised stanchions, the basket on this sled rests on a sheet of plastic that extends the length of the sled on top of the runners, providing a lower center of gravity and eliminating the breakable stanchions while providing a more stable toboggan-like surface on the trail.

A gangline or towline of nylon or aircraft cable connects the dogs to each other and the sled. Along the gangline the dogs are tied in by necklines and tuglines. The necklines join the gangline to the dogs' collars, essentially to keep them in place and facing in the right direction. The power comes through the tugline. Each

*A drawing of a typical modern sled appears on page 246.

dog wears a harness of nylon webbing that circles the shoulders and runs under the chest and forelegs, with a diamond pattern of webbing across the back. Race rules require that the harnesses be padded around the shoulders and legs to prevent chafing. On a well-fitted harness, the diamond pattern ends in a loop just above the base of the dog's tail, and that's where the tugline is connected.

A dog's power goes through the tugline and into the gangline, which is connected to the sled through a bridle of nylon rope intertwined with the stanchions.

Into the musher's sled go all the supplies the driver will need over a thousand miles. Race rules require a musher to carry certain equipment: a cold-weather sleeping bag; a hand ax; a pair of snowshoes; one day's food for each dog — at least two pounds per dog; a day's food for the driver; eight booties for each dog; and a packet of envelopes postmarked in Anchorage and later to be postmarked in Nome and sold to raise money for the race. This required equipment is verified at each checkpoint. In addition to the required items, a musher usually carries a two-burner Coleman stove, often altered so there's a fuel tank for each burner; some sort of pot for cooking; a change of clothes; spare footgear including mukluks or vapor-barrier "bunny boots" for extremely cold weather, or lighter rubber-bottomed shoe-pacs for wet going in warmer temperatures; and repair tools, spare snaps and lines, and anything else that might come in handy on the trail.

They also might carry any number of other items needed in cold weather on a two-week trip: dog medicine; human medicine; hand warmers; snacks; lip balms; and, usually, some sort of firearm, mostly to protect the dogs in case of a chance encounter with moose or other animals on the trail.

Before the race, drivers and helpers may spend a week or more at their meat grinders preparing dog food. The food, carefully planned and packaged, is then bagged in gunny sacks and shipped to each of the twenty-three checkpoints. Into those sacks also goes the musher's food — and although drivers may spend hours and hours agonizing over exotic high-energy mixes for the dogs, often the food they ship for themselves leaves something to be desired. One musher sent Mexican food to each checkpoint; another went exclusively Chinese. Veterans of the trail have found certain foods that work well for them. Emmitt Peters ships packages of Kentucky Fried Chicken. Rick Swenson sends steak, pizza and cheese. These are in addition to the rich stews and soups and other meals people at the checkpoints offer. But three meals a day aren't enough; the rigors of the trail lead the mushers to eat a lot of snacks, which can range from high-energy commercially-produced trail snacks to homemade collections of nuts and fruits and candies, to quarter-pound sticks of butter.

The mushers' own health along the trail is mostly a matter of personal attention. Few of the villages have resident doctors, and none follows the race. The two doctors who happened to be running the race were the only professionals along the way.

As the stack of equipment grows and the bags are filled, a musher's bills begin to pile up. Sleds alone cost $500 to $600. Maintaining the twenty to forty dogs it takes to assure a team of twelve or fourteen runs into thousands of dollars annually. One musher estimated it cost $2,400 just to raise a puppy to the age when it could run in a team. With the costs of equipment, transportation and loss of time from work, the amount can reach discouraging proportions. Joe May once said he used to worry about every eighty-nine cents he spent for a brass snap until one day it didn't matter any more. "Everything just started going to the dogs and I stopped counting."

Costs vary according to the money a musher has available and what he hopes to accomplish. Rick Swenson, a serious racer, estimated it cost him $18,000 to run. Ron Brinker, in his first race and going for the experience, estimated he spent $10,000 — and he built his own sled and ran borrowed dogs. For most, the race involves more money than they can earn while training dogs on any kind of regular schedule, so almost all spend a good deal of time looking for sponsors.

It's a rare business in Alaska that hasn't been approached at least once to sponsor a dog musher. Some businesses support the race generously, paying all a racer's bills or giving $5,000 or $10,000. More often, however, a musher has several sponsors. Almost every meat market in the state saves meat trimmings for at least one musher's dogs. Some national outdoor-equipment manufacturers donate sleeping bags and clothing. Some of the sponsors use the mushers and their teams in advertising, others just like to see their names on sleds even though only a few people might notice, and many do it simply for the pride in knowing they've helped out and can feel at least a vicarious kinship with the adventure. Still, many teams go without any sponsorship and the musher ends up with a good-sized debt for his trouble. Even if a musher should finish in the top twenty and win money, chances are he won't cover his bills.

On race day, all the preparation, equipment, training, care and money come down to one consuming goal. The rest is forgotten in the heat of the adventure as the trail stretches out ahead for more than a thousand miles toward that one goal — the arch over Front Street in Nome.

3. Anchorage to Knik to Skwentna

UNDER SUNNY SKIES, WITH THE TEMPERATURE NEAR TWENTY DEGREES, THE fifty-five mushers and eight hundred dogs followed trails along snow-covered streets, bicycle paths and sidewalks, then out into the backwoods of Anchorage. For a few miles the dogs followed trails used the previous weekend during the Fur Rendezvous World Championship Sled Dog Race, a three-day sprint. As the Iditarod Trail left the Rondy Trail the mushers turned to cross the base of the 3,500-foot Chugach Mountains, through the Fort Richardson Military Reservation, and on to the Eagle River Valley, to connect with the original trail. The earlier trail had bypassed the Anchorage area, running from the rail terminus at Kern Creek through the Chugach Mountains via Crow Pass to the Eagle River Valley. Now the town of Eagle River would serve as the first checkpoint of the Iditarod Trail Race. Much of the way into town the trail paralleled nearby roads, and spectators jammed the highways to catch a glimpse of the adventurers just starting their long journey to Nome.

For the spectators, the warm day and even warmer sun were pleasant. For the dogs and the mushers, however, the story was different. Twenty degrees is uncomfortably warm for sled dogs,

24

especially when they're working hard. Although the Anchorage area had had a relatively mild winter, January and February temperatures in the interior of the state had hovered near fifty degrees below zero Fahrenheit. Where Sonny Lindner trained on the Johnson River near Delta Junction east of Fairbanks, the temperature descended one day to sixty-four degrees below. Although a musher wouldn't normally run dogs in that weather, nevertheless the dogs were outside, acclimating, and once used to such cold, they would find the move to Anchorage, with as much as an eighty-degree temperature change, devastating.

Picture a ten-degree day in New York City. Put on a fur coat, wool scarf, heavy gloves, warm hat and boots, then get on a plane for Miami Beach. When you arrive, the temperature's in the eighties, but you don't take your furs off — instead you go for a run on the beach. The consequences of such a run are easy to imagine, and that's what the dogs were facing, without the option of being able to take off their fur coats. Aware of the temperature problems, the mushers eased up, not pushing the dogs too hard, trying to relieve at least some of the mental and physical stress. By the end of the first day, when the race had passed through the trees at the end of Knik Lake and out of spectator country, most of the mushers planned to run at night when temperatures were colder, leaving the heat of the day for rest and easing life for the dogs and themselves. The mushers, also used to cold weather and exerting as much as the dogs, also felt the effects of the heat. Running a dog team is more than just riding the sled runners. All along the trail the driver has work to do — hopping off to push the sled up hills and stream banks, pumping with one foot to help the sled along, running forward to untangle a couple of dogs, shouting and encouraging. And the heat generated by the work behind the sled that day allowed few mushers to keep their parkas on as they passed through Anchorage and the warm weather.

The first leg of the trail took most of the mushers about two hours. At Eagle River the teams caught up with their trucks for a ride to Lake Lucille in Wasilla, about twenty-five miles farther on. During the first two years of the race the trail crossed the ice on the Knik and Matanuska rivers near where they empty into the north end of Cook Inlet, but in recent years Alaska's winters have been unusually warm — some people say the jet stream has

moved, others claim the planets are coming into line — in any
case, the rivers haven't frozen near their mouths. Since the dog
teams couldn't cross the open water, they had to be carried by
truck to restart on the other side. However, race organizers had
wanted to keep Anchorage involved in the race because Anchorage is the center of population and hence the center for raising
money, an important fact, considering that the race operates on a
budget of a quarter of a million dollars or more. So, no matter what
the difficulty, there's always a ceremonial start for the folks in Anchorage and then, at least for this race, a twenty-five-mile parade
of pickup trucks with dogs riding in straw-filled compartments on
the back, sleds riding on top, and signs everywhere proclaiming
the names and sponsors of the mushers, all heading to a restart
somewhere safely across the two open rivers.

The race began again on the ice of Lake Lucille in the afternoon.
The fickleness of Alaska weather had turned against mushers and
dogs and now they all felt the first bite of the winds that would
plague this race. Terry Adkins already had felt that bite when the
dog box flew off his truck and his lead dog was killed. During that
storm, wind damage had been so heavy in the Matanuska Valley
that the governor had designated the valley a disaster area. It had
been weeks since the worst of the storm, but the winds hadn't
abated much and as the sun sank over Lake Lucille, the winds
came up again, sending to shelter all who had any place to go.
Posts had been frozen into the ice of the lake in a semicircle, and at
each post was a dog truck, with a sled and team tied to the post
while mushers check their gear, packed their sleds and waited
their turns to leave, the turns determined by their positions coming into Eagle River. Winds howled across the lake at forty and
fifty miles an hour, blowing the light snow off the ice and leaving
virtually no purchase for the people and dogs moving across. Race
officials asked spectators to park their cars along the trail to provide a windbreak for the teams, and the onlookers took the opportunity to stay inside the warm vehicles. The trail passed into a
chute made of snow fence that went through a double line of cars
for about a quarter of a mile to the far side of the lake, where the
teams climbed a short bank and disappeared into the woods.

Joe May left first, just before 3:00 P.M., crossing the lake gingerly, watching the wind and the slippery footing, the dogs staying

close to the lee side of one row of automobiles. The wind had the dogs spooked a little and somehow they lost traction on the ice and the leaders crawled, or were blown, under the front of a Winnebago camper — one that was backing up. The driver didn't see the dogs and their lines, tangled on the front of his vehicle, and kept going backward as May chased and screamed at him. The driver, after an eternity for May, finally understood and stopped. May retrieved the front end of his team from under the front end of the camper with no apparent damage to either, then regathered and turned the dogs toward the woods at the other side of the lake and disappeared. The rest of the day proceeded much the same, with sleds being blown over, dogs losing their footing and as many as seven or eight volunteer handlers grasping ganglines to help the teams across the ice.

As darkness came and many spectators left, taking their windbreaking automobiles with them, the call went out for more people to help the teams across the ice. Onlookers joined in and quickly realized how difficult a quarter-mile of ice can be. Holding Harry Harris's gangline between two pairs of dogs, one group of spectators started down the ice. At the end of the snow fence another group joined them. The folks in the second group had learned the hard way; they didn't grab the gangline, they grabbed the people holding the gangline. There was enough wind, and so little purchase on the ice, that the holders needed holding. The combined groups took firm grips on each others' parkas and maneuvered while they tried to keep the dogs on their feet. Once out of the protection of the cars, they felt the full force of the wind and a couple of people went sprawling. Harris yelled. He didn't know any of the helpers, and they could be destroying his team and his chances. Soon, however, everybody was upright again and they made the woods and sent Harris on his way, one of the last mushers to cross the lake.

From Lake Lucille the trail headed about fifteen miles south to Knik, now a town of just a few people, directly across Knik Arm of Cook Inlet from Anchorage. At the turn of the century, Knik was the main settlement in northern Cook Inlet, a prospering village that served as a gateway to the Interior and a stopping point on the Iditarod Trail. The town had provided stores, hotels, and liveries for dog and horse, and served as the center for a small farming community developing on its outskirts, along with being a supply center for mining operations in the area. Anchorage at the time was just that, a place where boats anchored so passengers and freight could be lightered to Knik, which did not have a good harbor. However, when construction of the Alaska Railroad began in 1914, the Anchorage site was chosen as a main construction camp and the town grew from there, while Knik mostly faded into history. Still, it remains home for a small group of people and a center of Iditarod activity. Joe Redington, Sr. and his wife Vi live in Knik, where the Alaska Mushers Hall of Fame is maintained.

The teams passed through Knik quickly. Some drivers stopped to feed and rest their dogs after the harrowing day of crowds and excitement and heat and wind, but most hurried on. One who stopped was Joe Redington. His lead dog Feets had developed a problem and Redington decided to leave him at home. Most mushers have more than one leader but because of other business, Redington hadn't been able to do much training this year and as a result hadn't had time to develop another reliable lead dog. To the wags following the race, Susan Butcher became Joe's leader, since his team followed hers through much of the rest of the race.

Most of the mushers took their teams past Knik a ways to camp farther along the trail, happy to be out of the confusion of the Anchorage start, the Eagle River trucking, the Lake Lucille winds and the crowds that went along with all of it. For the most part, mushers are solitary persons more at home on the lonely trail than they can ever be even in small groups of strangers, and crowds make many of them at least as nervous as they make the dogs. On the trail again, events returned to something like normal and it must have been with relief that the mushers passed into the trees at the end of Knik Lake and felt they were truly on their way to Nome, that the day of Anchorage had ended.

While the mushers and their teams headed toward the first checkpoint at Susitna Station, about fifty miles to the west, most of the corps of people connected with the race headed back to Anchorage to hustle plane rides or wait until a previously hired airplane could be repaired for the flight down the trail.

The next day, as the leading mushers crossed the lake-dotted muskeggy swamplands of the Susitna River Valley past Flathorn Lake to Susitna Station on the Susitna River, race progress was checked for the outside world through a room in the Anchorage Westward Hilton Hotel, a disaster area called the Iditarod Race Headquarters. Running the show, mostly out of her head and sometimes her hip pocket, was Lois English. In almost one breath she complained about the "ricky racers" — those who had already fallen behind — explained to a new volunteer what her job was, told a reporter on the phone where the leaders were, made or took three phone calls, accepted a compass Gayle Nienhueser's wife brought in to send to him, tried to help find a tail wheel for a pilot who broke one in a landing, and accosted a writer — me — with "What do you want?" As one of the people lucky enough to be following the race from checkpoint to checkpoint, I was part of the keyed-up crowd surrounding Lois English. Without waiting for my answer, she asked someone how many calls had been on the Code-A-Phone. "When was it updated, did anybody find a tail wheel, have we got all the food up to Rainy Pass, has anybody heard where Gould, Nienhueser, Couch and Leonard are, and get this stuff down to Larry Thompson's igloos." She never seemed to stop even to breathe.

The mention of Larry Thompson brought a reaction, and I was one of those reacting. He was the official pilot for the race and more than likely a ticket out to the trail. "When will he be in? Can I go?"

"Yes. No. I don't know, where's the checksheet for Susitna, has anyone told the information table in the lobby about the new arrivals, somebody get that phone. Larry's coming in tonight and can take you in the morning. Is there any coffee left?"

"Great. Where do I meet him?"

"No coffee. Hello, yes, all that's on the Code-A-Phone, can you call that number, thanks. At the igloos, 8:00 A.M. I'll call you when he's on the way in — he dropped two dogs at Skwentna, we need fuel to Rohn River, will somebody make some coffee?"

"What igloos? Where?"

"We've got people coming into Rainy, take these checksheets down to the lobby. Hello, no, we don't have him into Skwentna yet, is there a radio guy at Rohn? Behind the Wien cargo at the airport, what am I going to do with this compass, please get that phone, are you done there yet? I'll call and tell you when he's coming in. Now we're out of sugar."

All the worry about the trials of the race had been about the dogs and mushers, but maybe somebody should have watched Lois English and the people around her as they attempted to keep the public informed, let wives and families know where the mushers were and how they were doing, get the equipment and people organized and shipped, and keep up with the logistics of a race the magnitude of the Iditarod. It was catching. Anybody in the vicinity became just about as hyper as she was; even down the hall her full-tilt boogie resounded, and all of us hoped she'd get her coffee soon, although at the pace she was flying she didn't sound as if she needed it. Fortunately, through selective translation, she passed on the information I needed; Larry Thompson would be at his igloos behind the Wien cargo terminal at eight in the morning.

The igloos are white cargo containers designed to fit inside Wien Air Alaska's Boeing 737 jets. Wien was helping out in the race by offering the mushers reduced rates to fly their bags of food and gear, in the igloos, to McGrath, Unalakleet, Nome and Anchorage. From those centers, Larry Thompson's air force of small Cessnas and Piper Supercubs would take over, flying the bags and other gear to the more remote checkpoints. The Thompson corps also picked up the dogs that mushers had left behind at the checkpoints and brought them to the collection centers. Eventually the dropped dogs, at least the ones from southcentral Alaska, ended up at the state correctional facility at Eagle River where inmates had volunteered to care for them until the mushers or their wives could retrieve them.

On the third day of the race, at about 8:30 A.M., a red and white Cessna 185 on skis, but with the wheels down for the asphalt runway, landed and taxied round the 747s and DC10s at Anchorage International Airport until it came up to the igloos and stopped. Out stepped Larry Thompson, a short, dark-skinned man wearing buckskin moccasin-type boots that reached his knees. He came over and smiled at me through his dark beard. "You're finally going to get to go, heh? Help me with this first, will you?"

He opened the door on the passenger side of the airplane and out tumbled seven dogs clipped together on a chain. He took them over to another chain where other dogs were resting while waiting for the people from Eagle River to pick them up.

The jumble of dogs made me wonder what Thompson did if the

dogs got nervous in the airplane or started fighting.

"Aw, I just flip it on its side or upside down. Jumbles 'em up and scares 'em and they stop real fast." He loaded up what was left in one of the igloos, threw in other gear and prepared for the flight to Rainy Pass. Thompson already had removed the passenger seats so he could carry more cargo, and what now served as a passenger seat was two bags of dog food and a sleeping bag to replace one lost by a musher. Shortly we were in the air, flying across Cook Inlet to the Susitna River Valley that most of the mushers already had crossed.

As the Iditarod Trail passes through Alaska it crosses three distinct cultural zones. This first, which includes Anchorage and the Susitna Valley and goes on up into the imposing Alaska Range, is the area of Alaska most influenced by the white man. There are areas of Alaska still the domain of Indian, Eskimo and Aleut, places where the white man is only an intruder, and the trail passes through some of them. But all the land below Thompson's plane now fell within an easy airplane hop from Anchorage, the lowlands and low hills leading to the Alaska Range, where the white man has taken over. Lakesides and stream banks are lined with cabins built by people from Anchorage or by the guiding and flying services that operate out of the state's largest city. Small settlements and homesteads are scattered across the area, leaving but little of the original Indian influence.

Later the trail would move out of the white man's area into what is still basically Indian country, and from there go on to Eskimo territory.

Through the frozen muskeg and swamp, over low hills and across creeks and rivers, the Iditarod Trail winds in a generally westward then northwest direction much as it did early in the century. The original trail has been difficult to locate but today's trail generally follows the original route, exactly on it in places where it could be located.

From the plane I could see where melting and freezing cycles had left the snow looking like wet plaster. Gray-blue dotted lines meandered here and there through the thickets and across frozen lakes, evidence of foraging moose. Now and then the dark shape of a feeding moose showed through the thick but leafless brush.

Below, on the trail, what we couldn't see was the drama that had already begun to unfold. The warm temperatures had held during the days, and the heat may have begun to exact a toll. Most of the mushers had been running at night when temperatures were lower, but still several teams had picked up an illness manifested in diarrhea. Several explanations of the cause had been offered, including the stress of the trail, especially on younger teams; the possibility of a virus left on the Rendezvous Trail out of Anchorage; poorly trained teams; and the possibility that teams new to the area had picked up a virus that had been making the rounds of the Matanuska Valley earlier in the winter. Race veterinarians treated the dogs with Vitamins B-12 and B-complex and antibiotics. Most, but not all, of the leading teams passed through without much trouble, though few teams got by without a dog or two feeling the illness.

Although starting position doesn't mean much in a thousand-mile race, Joe May, who started first, had stayed in front, setting an almost blistering pace. He ran on a schedule, moving for five and a half hours, stopping for four, moving again for five and a half, then stopping for nine. He had trained his dogs on this routine and from first snow worked with them until they could go a hundred miles on that twenty-four-hour schedule. When they reached that peak, which, as planned, came in early to mid-February, two to three weeks before the race, May eased off on the dogs, taking what he called "short, happy runs, down to get the mail." These might have been anywhere from five to fifteen miles, just enough to keep the dogs in condition both mentally and physically. Although the pace he wanted was about nine miles an hour, May later said he didn't consider that fast. "I can't run against the fast teams, but if I can be consistent I should be able to run as good on the last day as on the first day and on that schedule I can eat up a whole lot of dog teams, and if I get the right kind of conditions I can eat them all up." Others trained differently, looking for faster dogs, in the eleven- and twelve-mile-per-hour range, and counting on a well-groomed trail most of the way, where May would hope for what he called dirty weather and deep snow to slog through so his dogs would leave others behind.

The first part of the trail snaked through spruce, birch and alder until it reached Susitna Station. From there on the trail had been cut along the Yentna River fifty miles to Skwentna at the confluence of the Yentna and Skwentna rivers. May reached the Susitna River and checkpoint before midnight of the first day, staying six minutes, just time to sign in and out, and headed up the Yentna for the next checkpoint.

In that first fifty miles the mushers began to sort themselves out according to ability and the quality of their dogs and training. Gradually the strongest contenders worked their way toward the front or at least to positions they wanted to hold. For May, Herbie Nayokpuk, Eep Anderson and Victor Katongan, it was out front as far as possible. For others, the idea was to stay near the front but let others break trail and use up their lead dogs, but all stayed within striking distance, a couple of hours from the lead. Some fell behind by losing the trail, others because they hadn't trained their dogs well enough or were just learning feeding and care techniques. Some had other problems.

As the teams passed through the alders on the way to Su Station, some took wrong turns through the brush, their mistakes leaving confusing trails for those following. Del Allison's team of twenty-one took one, then another, of the side cuts and eventually ended up with lines and dogs wound around the bushes everywhere. With ten pairs of dogs plus a leader, the gangline put the leader as much as ninety feet in front of the sled. While Allison worked to untangle the dogs, Ernie Baumgartner came up behind him. Unable to pass, but not realizing how big a team Allison had tangled in the bush, Baumgartner started helping with the mess so he could pass and go on "It looked like it rained dogs on the bushes. I worked farther and farther from the sled," he later recalled. But the team kept disappearing ahead in the bushes. "I just had to ask, 'How many dogs do you have here?' "

The answer twenty-one didn't surprise him by this time and he wasn't surprised at all to hear Allison tell him there were times going through the brush when he couldn't see his leaders and that was how this tangle had happened in the first place.

Following along the same trail, Richard Burmeister, running his first Iditarod, suffered with a dog psychology problem he had not anticipated. Living in Nome, he naturally had trained near his home on the Seward Peninsula. However, the peninsula, at least the western portions of it, is virtually treeless. When Burmeister arrived in Anchorage to start the race, his lead dog Misty had seen very few trees and was unused to traveling through heavily-forested areas. Even on the trip out of Anchorage the dog balked everywhere along the trail. "She just caved in every time she saw a tree," Burmeister said. He finally had to drop her at Wasilla in order to continue.

Burmeister found another leader in his team and could keep going. Lee Gardino lost a lead dog along the same stretch with quite a different result. His leader aggravated an old injury and came up limping too badly to continue. Gardino had to drop the dog at Susitna Station. From there Gardino kept apace with the leaders for a time while he tried one dog after another in lead. But none of the dogs really took the responsibility and the team's progress was due mostly to the will of the musher.

Joe May covered the hundred miles into Skwentna in a bit more than twenty-four hours, just about right with his schedule. Not too far behind him were others who wanted to stay out front: Anderson, Nayokpuk and Katongan. Though the field still was sorting itself out, relationships already were becoming obvious and a group formed right behind the leaders. During the warm daytime hours a group that included former winners Rick Swenson, Emmitt Peters and Jerry Riley camped, though not together, near Lake Creek about fifteen miles from Skwentna. With them were Sonny Lindner, Isaac Okleasik, Joe Redington, Susan Butcher, Rick Mackey, Dick Peterson and Gary Hokkanen. Behind them the field thinned into groups of mushers and stragglers with May out front almost twenty-four hours ahead of last-place runner Mark Couch.

Most of the trail into Skwentna followed the Yentna River, but there were places where it crossed islands or went up on the bank. On one fifty-foot downhill slide Emmitt Peters' lead dog Digger stopped and dipped for a drink of snow while the rest of the team was moving. The action came too fast for the musher to react and brake the sled. Before Peters could bring the sled and team under control, several dogs had run over his leaders and dragged Digger a short distance tangled in the lines. By the time Peters could extract the dogs from the lines and straighten the whole group out again, Digger was limping. "You could see where the muscles crossed in front of the leg," he said later. "When I saw Digger was hurt I wanted to cry. I could have dropped Diamond but not Digger." He put the injured lead dog, the veteran of five previous races, in the sled and carried him on into Skwentna. There was no veterinarian at Skwentna so Peters fed and rested his dogs and headed on to Finger Lake, where a vet could look at the leg. The vet told him Digger had injured some tendons and gave Peters some medicine to ease any pain, and Digger continued in the race, but not without babying from the musher. As often as possible, Digger rode in the sled, saving his strength and healing the leg for when it would be needed.

Behind Peters, a dog in Bob Chlupach's team didn't fare so well. Moose, quite reasonably, like to walk the hard-packed trails rather than slog through deep snow. Occasionally a 1,500-pound moose is going to break through the crust of even the hardest-packed trails, leaving a deep and dangerous hole for the slender legs of dogs. One of Chlupach's registered Siberians stepped into a moose hole in the trail and broke a leg. The musher carried the dog into Skwentna where it was shipped back to Anchorage for treatment.

By the time the teams had crossed the relatively flat hundred miles into Skwentna, they were reaching the limits of southcentral Alaska. Above them now, visible from the trail on the rises where there were no trees, was the barrier, looking blue and white and impassable, the wall of mountains called the Alaska Range, including the tallest mountain in North America.

4. Skwentna to Rainy Pass

ATOP A FORTY-FOOT BANK ON A SLOUGH OF THE SKWENTNA RIVER, JOE
Delia presided over the Skwentna checkpoint, which was his own
large immaculate log house. Delia, a true Alaska bush character
thirty years out, traps, hunts, fishes, serves as postmaster and is
known affectionately as the mayor of the tiny settlement where he
raises two youngsters on his own. An imposing, dark man, he's always the center of the scene, either telling the stories for which
he's famous or listening to somebody else's. He opened his home
for the mushers, making them as comfortable as possible, even
relinquishing his upstairs sleeping loft to the women of the trail,
while the men slept on the carpeted floor downstairs.

A fixture in the race since its inception, Joe Delia was one of the
original trailblazers who packed trail from Skwentna to Rohn
River. In the early years of the race he drove a snow machine the
150 miles through the Alaska Range, up Ptarmigan Pass and down
a treacherous canyon called Hell's Gate to the lowlands of Interior
Alaska. In later years race officials moved the trail to Rainy Pass,
where the original Iditarod route had gone, shortening the
distance but leaving it no less dangerous.

Because Joe Delia broke trail up to Ptarmigan Pass, the race didn't follow the original Iditarod Trail through his area. He'd allow, now, as how he moved the trail to protect his livelihood. As a trapper, Delia was then spending much of the winter pursuing marten. But, as the days grew longer toward March and ice in the dammed ponds began to melt, the trapper turned to the beaver that began coming out of their lodges during the warmer, longer days as the water opened. By race time Delia had his traps set for beaver and lynx, which also hunt the water animals. His trapline ran along a portion of the old trail. Afraid mushers might inadvertently disrupt his traps, Joe moved the course a little to follow his by-this-time abandoned marten line rather than the working beaver line. He didn't break trail any more, nor did he trap full time, the responsibility of raising two children alone in the bush keeping him at home much of the time. Still, even part-time trapping brought him a few thousand dollars each year and with his salary as postmaster he was able to get by relatively comfortably. He's not one for town, traveling to Anchorage only infrequently, going as long as a year or two between visits.

He'd like to run the race someday, at least make the sled dog trip to Nome. But Joe Delia doesn't do things the way other men do. "Sure, I'd like to run the race," he says. "Only I'd take nuthin' in the sled; hunt and trap and fish my way to Nome. I can do it, you know. Might take a little longer." No one doubts him in the least.

Limited by time and expense, he has to trust a snow machine these days and doesn't run dogs any more. But dogs weren't completely out of the family. His daughter Christine maintained a team and a year earlier had won a junior race in Anchorage. At thirteen, she approached the dogs with all a teen-ager's enthusiasm, and with the Iditarod heroes right there in her own house, she kept the mushers busy answering questions.

Rick Swenson, before he left Skwentna, found he had an extra supply of choice lamb chops, his primary dog food. He gave the box to Joe Delia for Christine's dogs, but Joe had a different idea. Toward late winter after a steady diet of moose, when other supplies began to run a little thin, a few pounds of lamb chops could look mighty good — too good to feed the dogs. The meat went into the family's food cache and Delia somehow neglected telling Christine about Swenson's gift to her dogs.

People like Joe Delia who live along the trail live there at least

partially because they like the solitude and enjoy the quiet, unclut-
tered life. But during the race, Delia accepted the disruption ami-
ably, welcoming the company, although he was probably relieved
to see the last racer leave. But even after the racing crowd had
gone, the chores lingered, principal among them the care of
dropped dogs.

After the hundred miles from Knik, the first full day of the race,
the mushers had figured out which dogs were going to go on and
which needed to be left behind. The warm temperatures had
taken their toll along with the sickness and diarrhea; the mushers
dropped the sick dogs at Skwentna. Many of the mushers also had
dogs they had known all along wouldn't make it all the way. Such
dogs may have been good for one or two hundred miles but lacked
the stamina for the long haul to Nome. They were valuable in easing the burden along this initial part of the trail and saved valuable
energy in the other dogs. Once those extra dogs had served their
purpose, they ended up on the picket lines across the slough from
Delia's house. Also among the dropped dogs were the pets, maybe
a wife's favorite, one she had wanted to see run in the team, but a
dog the musher knew wouldn't go all the way to Nome. For one
reason or another, thirty-four dogs ended up tied in the woods at
Skwentna. Of the fifty-five teams in the race, twenty-three left
Skwentna with fewer dogs than they'd started with, but the front
runners, the possible winners like May, Peters, Swenson and
Nayokpuk, those who might seem to be pushing the dogs harder
to win, left with full healthy teams, as did twenty-eight others.

To Delia fell the responsibility of caring for the dropped dogs.
He used food the mushers had to leave behind to feed the drop-
outs until Larry Thompson and his air force could fly them back
to Anchorage. Not everything the mushers ship to the checkpoints
gets used, and like Rick Swenson with his lamb chops, many of the
mushers left the remainder for Joe Delia and his family. Those
leftovers were the only payment for the hospitality and work the
checkers provided.

Delia opened his home to the mushers for two days, but despite
the comforts, the leaders passed through quickly. Joe May made
the hundred miles to Skwentna in twenty-four hours and, sticking
with his schedule, stayed four hours feeding and resting his dogs
before he moved on. Victor Katongan, John Wood and Eep Ander-

son didn't even stay that long. They just checked in and out and perhaps caught a bite to eat. Anderson wanted to push through to be the first, if he could, into his home town of McGrath, about a third of the way to Nome. Those who arrived at Skwentna during the night tended to keep going, while daytime arrivals stayed awhile. The high temperatures still sent many to cover during the day and the mushers didn't want to waste the precious hours of cold weather the night offered.

Some took their mandatory twenty-four-hour layover and enjoyed the warm day at Skwentna while their dogs slept through what by Alaska standards was almost tropical weather. Race rules stipulate that once during the race a musher and team must stop for a full twenty-four hours of rest at a checkpoint. Where, was left to the drivers. Ron Aldrich, Bill Rose, Mel and Steve Adkins and Kelly Wages all stopped. Bud Smyth joined them and removed the cooker-popcorn machine from his sled. As is usually the burden for innovators, sometimes the innovation doesn't work, and Smyth's contraption had become too cumbersome, part of its weight coming perhaps from the kidding he'd taken about it.

Ken Chase also stopped for twenty-four hours, but his layover wasn't planned. His dogs were lagging, still showing the strain of the long fight before the race, and he felt he had to rest them. Huskies will fight long and hard, sometimes to the death, with two or three ganging up on one. Chase was lucky none of his dogs was killed during the fight. But the long battle had taken the energy from many of the team, including his seven-time leader, Piper.

"The dogs fought so long they were physically drained. What I should have done right there was take them to the vet and get some injections, but I didn't. I took them out and ran them, trying to test them to see if any were crippled. After the fight, I went to the vet to check and I could just sense it. Some dogs, you know. . . . I was walking them around and I could just sense it. Next day I had Tony Funk" — a race veterinarian — "come out and give my dogs shots 'cause I knew something was going on

"After they're drained like that, you've got to bring them back up and you just can't do it by pushing. I kept playing around hoping they'd pick up. I wasn't afraid to push them, but I was just afraid — they were so peaked, you know — that if they ever went out on me, that's where I'd be."

Sled dogs will reach a point of refusal, a physical and psychological level at which they'll go no farther. When they reach it they stop no matter where, and all a musher can do is rest them and feed them. It can happen in a village or it can happen in the middle of a barren stretch of trail, leaving the musher in a serious situation with no transportation out. Even one dog refusing to go can infect a whole team. When that one stops, the others sense he's getting away with something and they'll stop, too. That's where a trailwise leader like Piper proves his value. A good leader, who will go even when the others balk, can pull a whole team into action and keep the others going. Even with his own infirmities, Piper had kept the team moving, but Chase still had to ease the pace. He couldn't afford to push the dogs to that point of refusal. The fight and the hundred miles to Skwentna proved too much for one of his dogs and Chase left him there. Hoping to bring the dogs somewhere near their form before the fight, he rested the remainder of the team for twenty-four hours, then pushed on toward the mountains.

By the time Ken Chase left with Bud Smyth, all but one of the other mushers had gone. Chase's dogs hadn't yet come back all the way, but they would keep going now if he maintained that easy pace. For most of the rest of the teams and drivers, the miserable first mile of the Iditarod had just about ended.

Every time a musher hooks up a dog team, the first mile of running can be disconcerting. For that first mile, it seems as if every dog has to relieve himself one way or another, jump the gangline a few times, snarl and snap at his partner, wander to the edge of the trail to sniff a spot, tangle a tugline — anything at all a dog can find in his head to mess up a team. After about a mile of this the dogs tend to fall into place, bringing their minds to the job at hand, and everything smooths out, assuming the musher hasn't lost his temper with all the fooling around. In the extended 1,200-mile race, the first hundred or so miles become that miserable first one. The dogs have been used to their regular runs on training trails, but in the weeks before the race their schedule has been disrupted. They may have traveled thousands of miles in airplanes and trucks. They've been lying around in strange yards waiting for race day. Large crowds have gathered to wave and cheer them on their way. They've had to cross streets, face automobile traffic and thousands of people. All of it unsettles a mind used to the quiet trail. Once the teams reached Skwentna, though, feeling again the rigors of the trail, the dogs had pretty much settled down to the schedule of running and rest and feeding that would take them to Nome.

Also by Skwentna, the separation of the mushers and teams into groups according to their speed and schedules had become more pronounced. Some of the faster racers began pulling away from the others just on the relative strength of their dogs and their experience with the trail. Others had laid out their schedules before the race and were maintaining them. May's schedule kept him out front and Katongan ran right behind him. In a group not too far behind, Swenson, Peters and Riley, all previous winners, changed position, passed, camped, were passed by each other and by other teams including Lindner, Terry Adkins and Nayokpuk. While they weren't always together on the trail or in camp, they tended to maintain similar paces and often rested and camped near each other. Farther behind, other mushers fell into the informal groups they'd be traveling with until they reached Nome. They'd run about the same distances at relatively the same speeds, camp in the same areas, feed at the same places and rest about the same amount of time.

The trail out of Skwentna took the teams southwest for almost ten miles before the river turned northwest toward its source in the massive Alaska Range, the mountains that divide southcentral Alaska from the great Interior. The trail followed the river for about forty miles, sometimes on the bank, sometimes across frozen marshes and bottomland and sometimes on the snow covered ice, following the Skwentna upriver on a gentle rise that went from about a hundred feet above sea level at Skwentna to about eight hundred at the next checkpoint, Finger Lake. Usually each musher managed to find his own private difficulties with the trail, but just out of Skwentna, an obstacle jutted out of the snow and exacted a price from several who passed. The obstacle was a tree on a tight curve, and before all the sleds could pass, sixteen slammed into it and broke brush bows on its trunk.

Past the tree, the trail cut through the spruce forest and alder patches that lined the river until a short jog to the north led to Finger Lake and the comfortable log cabin home of Gene and June Leonard. Members of the Iditarod family since the race's beginnings, the Leonards always had run the checkpoint out of their log home high on the steep shore of the lake. They moved there after Gene, a former boxer, retired as a bar owner in upper New York State. Watching the race over the years had proved too much for Gene and with some borrowed dogs and help from friends he was running the race this year, leaving the chores of checker, cook and nursemaid for the fifty-five teams to June. Bags of food and supplies lined the trail on the lake but Gene wouldn't let anybody camp on the ice. "I have to drink that water," he said. Instead the mushers climbed the steep bank to bring their dogs into the deep snow around the cabin, cooking for the dogs, then stopping in to visit with June and each other and try the stew she kept simmering on the stove. The race finally had reached snow country; the Leonards sometimes measured depths up to two hundred inches around their cabin.

Few of the mushers stayed longer than a couple of hours at Finger Lake, although Emmitt Peters took his time while a veterinarian checked his injured leader's leg. The forty miles from Skwentna took most of the leading teams only about six hours, a run that demanded only a short snack break for the dogs, not a major rest stop. The mushers planned to camp at least once on the way up to Rainy Pass Lodge, then stay a little longer at the lodge to rest for the remainder of the climb into the pass and the harrowing journey down. Already there was the pressure of the competition. May was out ahead and while some racers predicted he'd wear his dogs down, nobody wanted to take a chance. As Lindner said at Finger Lake, "You go until you get over the pass. If anybody gets over and you get stopped in a storm, you're done."

About ten miles up the Skwentna River from Finger Lake, the trail turned up the Happy River Valley on its ascent into Rainy Pass. From the 1,000-foot elevation at the confluence of the Skwentna and Happy rivers, the trail rose to 3,000 feet in less than twenty miles to the divide in the Alaska Range. Ahead of the teams stood some of the tallest mountains in North America including the tallest, Mount McKinley, at 20,320 feet. The trail passed between lesser peaks to the southwest of McKinley, but those lower mountains still formed an imposing wall. The mountains nearest the trail rise above 5,500 feet and although the official elevations sound low, the blue-white peaks that confronted the mushers are as tall as any in the Rocky Mountain system. Geographers measure elevations from sea level and that measurement can be deceiving. The Alaska Range is based almost at sea level while mountains in other parts of the world may have bases as much as a mile high. Given that mile-high base, these Alaska mountains would be more in the neighborhood of 10,000 feet and a much greater challenge than is generally recognized.

From sea level in Anchorage the trail had risen only a thousand feet in almost two hundred miles. Now it would rise another two thousand in only about twenty miles as the mushers headed up into the mountains along the Happy River Gorge, a deep cleft between peaks growing progressively higher. The route crossed the gorge three times, sending teams up and down treacherous, steep, winding runs on chilling narrow trails. Some of the drivers feared the drops so much they wrapped chains around their sled runners or dragged heavy logs behind their sleds to slow the dogs. The ups and downs and curves and cutbacks presented the mushers with surprises at each bend in the trail, some natural and some man-made.

Rick Swenson, with his team running through the switchbacks at what he called a dead gallop, tried to control his dogs but rounded a tight curve and charged into Lee Gardino, stopped in the trail in a tangle of dogs. Swenson's dogs were going too fast, and before he could stop his team, "Whoomp, we're on them." Now two teams — twenty-eight dogs — needed untangling. "Had to help him out of there just so we could pass," Swenson said later.

Every musher has a story about Rainy Pass and a first-time racer probably hears most of them long before he ever reaches the divide. Most of the stories involve the descent, but the ascent proved the toughest for Del Allison, the businessman with, now, the twenty-dog team. "The worst part of Rainy Pass for me was the stretch between Finger Lake and Rainy Pass Lodge."

Allison left Finger Lake about nine in the evening with Ron Aldrich, following Ron Brinker by an hour or so. "We'd stopped to rest, but I didn't sleep much. I was excited, anticipating the pass. Everybody talks about how rough Rainy Pass is, how deep the ravines are, how steep the hills. There's areas you're going up where it's like a thirty-five- or forty-degree angle," Allison said.

"You're going along in the dark with the little headlamp on, but every time you really need it, the wire comes off the terminal post or something, and it goes out and you don't know if it's five hundred feet down or fifty feet up.

"So, we're going along and it is tough. You're grinding your body out and you're pushing the sled cause the damn sled has two hundred pounds of stuff and I weigh two-fifty and that's more than the dogs can haul up those hills.

"So anyway, we're going along and it's quiet up ahead and I hear this 'r-e-y-u-u-p, r-e-y-u-u-p' and I come up on Ron Brinker. Now Ron has a great sense of humor, always laughing, havin' a good time. So here he is and he's been working so hard he was sick and heavin' his guts out. I sort of felt the same way but I couldn't help saying, 'Ron, I just snacked my dogs an hour ago and I hate to see you go ahead and prepare a meal for them.'

"We went on past Ron and headed up the trail into real snow depths. On one switchback you're comin' through thick trees and there was a trail we crossed and there's dogs and a little pup tent covered up, almost, by blowing snow. I stop and step off the trail and go down to my waist in snow that might have been ten, twelve, fourteen feet deep and like quicksand. Here's a sled that says Eep Anderson. He's asleep in a little cabin there and there's this tent outside and my lead dogs crawled inside the tent. I had twenty dogs and half of them had crawled in the tent around this musher and he didn't even wake up. Here I am thirty or forty minutes fighting the dogs to get them back on the trail and this guy, it was John Barron, didn't even know. I finally got the dogs out on the trail. I wanted to catch the front end; Eep Anderson was here and I wanted to catch Swenson and the rest, but my dogs wanted to quit, they were tired. We were about half-way up the pass at the time.

"We probably ran about another forty-five minutes and then I'm comin' up at a peak area, then over and down. I'm always looking for this one switchback they tell me about where the trail's only three feet wide. So, I come down this trail and the dogs make a turn to the right and there's a lot of spruce trees there like a foot in diameter. I come down and the dogs make a turn and go right straight on the trail I'd just come down. The dogs had turned around and come right back at me. I said this is absolutely impossible. The snow's twelve feet deep; this can't be the end of the Iditarod Trail halfway up Rainy Pass. I stopped and put a snow hook in and I walk around to look. It turns out the turn to the left was so sharp it was impossible, so what they did was make a sweeping turn to the right and came back across the trail in sort of a figure eight.

"By this time it's about one in the morning and I come down off this to the Happy River and at the bottom there's two tents where Joe Redington and Susan Butcher are camped. Once you're on the river there's this hill; the trail goes up a mountain at maybe a forty-degree angle. My dog team got maybe twenty or thirty yards up — and the whole team laid down.

"I put the snow hook in so the sled wouldn't slip backward. There was no way it was going forward. I got off the sled and I went up. I had a hard time climbing up the damn hill, it was so steep. I petted everybody and I was talkin' to them because they had been working their buns off. I never had my whole team quit before. The only one who didn't quit was Sugar, and she's crazy anyway. Well, I walk up and I pet them all and I lay down with my leaders up there and I was pettin' them and strokin' them. I said okay, and I'm thinkin' we've just spent five hours on the trail and pretty soon I'm just thinking and we're laying there. And I fell asleep right there with my leaders of my dog team, all laying on a hillside at a forty-degree angle. I fell asleep like for maybe forty-five minutes right there in the snow and it's maybe five or ten below zero and I wake up and it's just like I'd slept for ten hours, and it was like I was late for a meeting or something. I came awake and here's the dogs and I realize all of a sudden where I am. I'm on the Iditarod Race. So I petted everybody and I walked back to the sled and I grabbed the handlebar and I said, 'Okay, guys,' and they came up. They just rose to the occasion. I can't ride the sled and I'm pushing and this goes on for probably half a mile like that. If there's an avalanche coming down there, you haven't got a chance. I wondered how in hell did a snow machine get up there. After that you hit kind of a little plateau with very winding trails and then there's Rainy Pass Lodge.

"I took my twenty-four at Rainy Pass. I was totally beat. I walked in there and the warm sun was absolutely beating through the plate glass windows and I laid down in the middle of the floor and went to sleep. They called me the Walrus."

Allison had made his run up Rainy Pass with half his sled brake broken, nothing except his feet to hold the dogs back on the downhill runs.

But, if the dogs want to take off, the brake can't help much anyway, as Joe May knew from his own adventure on the way to the lodge. Guides operating out of the lodge offered horseback hunts during the season, but throughout the winter the horses roamed freely for forage and returned to the lodge only when the caretaker put out their regular feed. Near the lodge, May's dogs saw the horses and gave chase, taking the musher on a wild ride through the dingweeds until the horses outdistanced the dogs and May could bring the team under control to return to the trail. About eight hours later John Wood's team took him on the same wild horse chase.

At the edge of Puntilla Lake, nestled into a high valley surrounded by jagged white mountain peaks, Rainy Pass Lodge offered comfort from the rigors of the trail. Each year Jules Mead and his wife, Leslie, who own Teeland's Moonshine Shop in Wasilla, sponsored a checkpoint and laid a proverbial groaning table. This year they'd set up shop at Rainy Pass Lodge, flown in supplies and prepared a feast for the mushers and race followers. A baron of beef stood out for the carving, while another roasted in the oven. There were steak, chile, stew, bacon and eggs, ham, soup, beer, soft drinks, coffee and snacks for everyone who entered. The feast the Meads lay out for the race always had been too much of a temptation for many, and the mushers usually find a way to spend more time than they can afford at the Meads' checkpoint.

It was into this comfort that Larry Thompson dropped the gear after our flight up from Anchorage. Inside, the scent of the food filled all the rooms of the lodge. Conversation was hushed in deference to the lumps lying on the floors and benches. One big yellow lump, in the middle of the floor of the front room, right in a ray of sun, rolled a bit, and there was Del Allison. On a couch under a window another exhausted musher slept, while several more rested in a downstairs storeroom. A woman sat in the front room sewing on the heavy wool pants Allison had ripped on a tree during the climb to the lodge.

Near a window veterinarian Tony Funk examined Gayle Nienhueser's arm, the one injured during the tumble in Mulcahy Park three days earlier. Judging by the movement under the skin, Funk believed the arm had been broken and Nienhueser, in obvious pain, wondered what he should do. To have his whole year's preparation ruined by a freak accident within minutes of the start would be a disappointment bordering on injustice. He finally decided to declare his twenty-four-hour layover at Rainy Pass and fly back to Anchorage with Larry Thompson to have the arm X-rayed and treated. Funk jury-rigged a splint with newspapers and Nienhueser boarded the plane for Anchorage. As it turned out, the arm wasn't broken, just had some ligaments torn, but he'd have to wear a cast for the rest of the race. The mishap compounded itself while he was gone. With the musher away and his team receiving only limited attention, some of the dogs jumped into a pitched battle and fought for some time before the people in the lodge heard the commotion and managed to separate the combatants. The fight left a couple of dogs with cuts serious enough to warrant stitching, and the team went into something of a depression similar to the one Ken Chase was attempting to bring his dogs through.

Outside of the lodge, several dog teams lay curled in the bright sunlight, resting for the remainder of the long uphill climb through the broad alpine valley to the top of the pass. More than a third of the teams already had passed through and were on their way down. Most mushers wanted to time their run down the pass so they'd hit it at daybreak and could make the whole run in daylight. In the yard to the east of the lodge, Ron Aldrich cut firewood with a chain saw while a revived Del Allison dipped water from a hole in the lake ice to give his dogs a drink. Lep Anderson knelt in the snow putting booties on his dogs to protect their feet on the climb, some of which was over rock exposed by the winds in the pass. Anderson had kept up with the leaders most of the way to the lodge, but finally the sickness had overtaken his dogs, too, and he'd had to rest them. He said he hadn't trained the dogs as much as he would have liked and the stress of the first part of the trail had worn them down some and made them susceptible to the virus. He was resting the team as much as he dared and would ease his way over the pass if he could.

Nearby Cliff Sisson fed his dogs and when one tried for a bite of another's meat, the offended dog jumped on the intruder. Sisson waded into the middle of the fight, eventually separating the two and, to punish the culprit, actually bit one of the dog's ears.

Rainy Pass Lodge stands on the east side of Puntilla Lake. On the original Iditarod Trail there was no roadhouse there and the trail traversed the western slope of the valley between Happy Creek Roadhouse, below the present lodge site, and Pass Creek Roadhouse to the north, a distance of about twenty-two miles. Researchers had yet to find the original site of the Pass Creek buildings, but the trail had to pass somewhere nearby, close to a large snowdrift that forms every year. That snowdrift serves as a natural monument to one of the tragedies of the trail — a place where a man lost his life in 1913.

C. C. Chittick, a miner from the mining town of Flat, had gone Outside that year to obtain financing to work his claim on Flat Creek. He was on his way back when he ran into trouble. In the evening of January 27, 1913, he pulled into Happy Creek Roadhouse. There he met a man named John Jacobsin, who had been waiting twelve days for a companion and a ride to Iditarod. The two joined forces and the next morning, in temperatures near thirty below with a strong wind blowing, they left Happy Creek with four dogs and a sled, headed for Pass Creek Roadhouse, then owned by a Mr. Anderson. With today's dog teams the trip could take three or four hours. Two men with only four dogs might make it in nine or ten. But Jacobsin and Chittick were never to complete the journey.

Five days after they left Happy Creek, the four dogs ran up to Anderson's roadhouse. They wore no harnesses, which meant they had been unhitched from the sled and had not broken loose. Anderson met the dogs and, sensing something amiss, encouraged them back down the trail. Three stayed with him while the fourth ran about three hundred yards ahead. At a point about a mile and a half from the roadhouse, Anderson found signs of activity, remnants of a makeshift camp, even a few spots of blood in the snow. Sheltering the campsite from the wind, a snowdrift rose next to the trail. The dog that had run ahead climbed the drift and sat on top for a time, then lay down. Anderson searched the site but found no evidence of what he had begun to assume was at least one missing man. He continued down the trail another four and a half miles until he came upon a sled. He began making ever-widening circles around the sled until he found Jacobsin's body about a hundred feet up the trail and fifty feet to the west. The man had frozen to death still wearing his parka. A second parka, later identified as Chittick's, lay at his feet.

The second parka led Anderson to assume a second man had left his parka with Jacobsin and gone ahead up the trail with the dogs loose in hopes of finding the roadhouse in the storm. The road-house keeper headed back toward his lodge to look for more signs of the missing prospector, and spent even more time examining the first campsite. But he found nothing new. He tried to take the four dogs back to the roadhouse with him but the lead dog turned back and perched atop the snowdrift where he stayed for several hours. Anderson had to return to the site and lead the dog away from the drift, pulling it all the way back to the lodge.

Eventually C. C. Chittick's brother, A. A. Chittick, reached the Pass Creek Roadhouse where, with a couple of friends, he organized a search. The brother offered a reward for anyone finding the body or at least providing some information about what had happened. But no one came forth. C. C. Chittick's body never was found, but old-timers on the trail assume he died under that snow-drift and animals scavenged the body in the spring when the snow melted.

There were many brushes with death in the days when miners and freighters used the Iditarod Trail but, despite the dangers, surprisingly few lost their lives. Even now, sixty-six years later, with all the air support and food drops and health care available during the race, a man is still alone on that trail, alone with the arctic elements that on a whim of the wind can turn a pleasant journey into a nightmarish battle for survival. In the Pass Creek area during the 1974 race, when the trail ran through Ptarmigan Pass, a group of mushers encountered a combination of wind and cold that sent the chill factor off the U.S. Weather Service's charts, which end at 130 degrees below zero. Fortunately, all those mushers escaped alive with relatively few cases of frostbite. But everybody involved with the race knew somewhere inside himself that some day, somehow, somebody would run into the combination of elements he couldn't survive.

Joe May, who's known for his philosophizing about the race, said, "Somebody's going to buy it in this race. It's just a matter of time. I'm surprised it hasn't happened already. You talk to any musher and every one of them has a story to tell." During a long interview he'd been animated, but as he touched on the subject of the dangers, his faced turned serious, his voice dropped almost to a whisper. "Some of them have come awfully close . . . awfully close. A couple in this race."

5. Rainy Pass Lodge to Farewell

JOE MAY'S FOURTEEN DOGS DRAGGED HIM OUT OF THE COMFORT OF Rainy Pass Lodge about three in the afternoon, just past forty-eight hours into the race. Behind him mushers were scattered all the way back to Skwentna. Ahead the trail rose for about eighteen miles through a gently sloping alpine valley from 2,000 feet at Puntilla Lake to 3,200 feet at the top of the pass, the divide between southcentral Alaska and the Interior. Wind had blown through the pass, sculpting terraces into the hillsides and in places leaving the trail bare. Lichens showed through the snow and rocks. May had been adhering to his schedule, still looking for the dirty weather that might separate him from the faster teams, but all he saw were clear skies, day and night, and fast trail. High in the pass his team gave him a taste of fast, though, as the dogs took him on a harrowing trip through a menagerie of Alaska wildlife.

On any stretch of trail, particularly with the added weight caused by an incline, the dogs can lose their interest. They slow down, maybe even fool around a little. As May described it, "You drive behind that team and they're ready to fall down and you say to yourself, 'Oh, my God, look at that.' They look like their heads are hanging and they're just plodding along. They haven't got

51

anything left in them. And if a ptarmigan flies up thirty feet down the trail they'll take off and almost jerk you off the sled. They turn on, look like a whole brand-new dog team. Actually it was flat boredom."

As May's team worked through the pass, the "ptarmigan" they saw was a small herd of Dall sheep. The dogs hadn't ever seen the white wild sheep of Alaska before and the sight was enough for the team to take May on the ride of his life.

"We were running about sixty feet behind them for a while. I had the brake buried and there's only about that much snow"—he indicated about an inch or two—"on rock cobble up there and I tore a groove right up the side of the mountain. Rocks were flying out the side and sparks were flying [from the metal brake] and fourteen dogs pulling that thing up the side of the hill and there was no way we were going to stop."

If the sheep had stayed in the trail May might have gained a bit on the faster teams, but instead they led him up the mountain on one side of the valley, then they turned and ran back, crossing the trail and heading up the mountain on the other side. Going up that second hillside, the musher finally began to regain control and was able to turn the team back to the trail. Now the boredom had ended and the dogs just wanted to run. They tore down the trail, too fast for May's taste, and there was no relief. Instead of falling back into a good pace after the excitement had worn down, the dogs came upon four moose in the trail and that set them off again. Only through the iron will of the musher did the team weave its way through the moose. This can be a dangerous encounter, as there have been several dogs killed—although not often in the race—by a moose demanding his part of the trail. At least twice in the history of the race it's been necessary to shoot moose to protect dog teams. After the moose, May's team again tore up the trail at too fast a pace. Then, when they should have been settling down, a flock of ptarmigan—the real thing, this time—took off down the trail and the dogs fired up once more for pursuit. By the time the team had exhausted the ptarmigan, they'd reached the top of the pass and May said he would just as soon have had them bored. "When we got done with the ptarmigan we were poised right at the top of the ice chute down into Rainy Pass, and the sun went down right on schedule and I'd never been through there before.

"I'm at the top of the ice chute and I've got these dogs hyper, about that far off the ground jumpin' and screamin' and I went down through there with fourteen dogs. What a trip."

Down through there was the drop into the Interior on a wind-blown, icy fall through hairpin turns, switchbacks, boulders the size of houses, and ravines lined by twenty-foot banks. The trail dropped a thousand feet in the first five and a half miles, and another three hundred in the next six.

To ease some of the sheer from the drops, the trail took a serpentine course, with so many tight curves that the drivers of the larger teams only saw flashes of their lead dogs now and again. One musher described his team as looking like a snake's back.

The trail just keeps getting steeper, and as Del Allison said later, "just falling away. I mean out of sight." Creeks cutting and receding over the centuries have left banks as high as fifteen and twenty feet. Said Allison, "I'm comin' off there with twenty dogs; the front of my dog team disappears and all of a sudden you come over that bank. I was probably coming down that mountain about twelve miles an hour, maybe fourteen and you're just working every stanchion of that sled and you're just rolling and you come off these areas and all of a sudden you're airborne and it's that first hundredth of a second that puts your heart in your mouth and then you see, well, it's only ten feet and it's not the end of the world. The guys who put the trail in with snow machines, I'm amazed we didn't find pieces of their machines along the trail."

The trail took several turns around boulders ten and twenty feet high, banging up sleds and tearing at the minds of mushers. At the creeks more problems developed. Chances are that creeks will freeze at a high-water mark in the fall. As they freeze, and the volume of water recedes with the contraction of the ice, a bridge of ice can be left over the dry bottom. The weight of the dog teams going over broke these unsupported bridges, leaving plates of ice to tangle the following teams and mushers and add to an already rough section of the race.

Through this most harrowing stretch of trail, May's screaming team took him on a wild ride down into the broad, hilly interior of Alaska. "They got cranked up and they tore out my brake on the run and stove up four dogs for me. They went crazy." May made the thirty-five-mile run from Rainy Pass Lodge to the Rohn River

checkpoint in about five and a half hours and stopped. Others
would take as long as ten or twelve hours. At Rohn, the front
runner took his twenty-four-hour mandatory layover and rested
his dogs, tending to those who'd aggravated muscles on the run
down the pass.

Victor Katongan followed May through the pass and stopped for
his twenty-four at Rohn also. The illness had worked into his
team, leaving the dogs dehydrated and needing rest. Behind came
Swenson, Peters, Riley, Nayokpuk and Terry Adkins, along with a
new name joining the familiar veterans.

Sonny Lindner, the young contractor from Delta, left Rainy Pass
Lodge in ninth position about midnight and ran up the pass at
night, alone. "You don't want to run through Rainy Pass chasing
somebody's can if you can help it," he explained. His only
company on the way up was a small herd of caribou the team had
to negotiate with a little. He made a run straight through to Rohn
with just a snack stop along the way, in about eight hours, passing
everyone but May and Katongan and arriving at the Rohn River
checkpoint third. But the sickness and the warm weather had hurt
his team and he had only ten left from the fifteen that started. Still,
no one discounted Lindner's chances, and in only his second race
he already had a reputation. During the race May assessed his
competitor: "Sonny's got a tough dog team and he's tough himself
and he's persistent. He absorbs things like a blotter. If he sees
something and if it's good it doesn't get away from him. He
doesn't have the dogs and equipment Peters and Swenson have.
He doesn't have the experience that Honea has and he doesn't
have the dogs Honea has. The difference is in what he's putting
into it on the back of the sled—he's really working."

The Alaska Range crossing brought Lindner closer to home. He
was the one whose dogs lived in minus-sixty-four-degree weather,
and once across the mountains the temperature dropped back to
his liking. "Now that I'm over the range and it's down to minus
thirty," Lindner said, "the dogs are eating again and running." He
stayed in Rohn River less than two hours, dropping one dog and
leaving ahead of everyone else.

Behind him the rest of the mushers made their runs through
Rainy Pass. Swenson careened through the boulders, almost
hitting two of them on a sharp left-hand turn. Swenson, who was

in his fourth race, said, "Just about smashed up on both of them, but we made it." Gary Hokkanen bounced off the two rocks but managed to keep the sled intact and kept on going.

Ernie Baumgartner, the electronics technician, descended the pass at night, and his leaders had trouble finding the trail. The dogs finally took him over one of the cliffs and they crashed, fortunately without injury. Richard Burmeister also crashed. He hit a bump and the jolt flipped him off the sled along one of the switchbacks. By the time he regained himself, he looked up to see the sled coming right back at him and ducked just in time to save his skull.

A day later, Allison stopped on the way up the pass to rest his dogs. There was a creek, Pass Creek, in the neighborhood of the original roadhouse, where there were open patches of water. Allison took advantage of the water to give his dogs a snack and a break. Into the scene drove Brinker, grinning: "I was waiting to see if I'd catch up with you."

Said Allison, "Here I am."

Brinker: "Hell, they said you'd never make it over here. This Rainy Pass is a piece of cake."

Allison: "You've got that right. This is a piece of cake. If it's like this the rest of the way over this pass, we've got it made."

Not too much farther on, their piece of cake lost its frosting as the two went over the edge into the ice chute and went roaring toward the Interior, Allison, without his brake, a feat somewhat akin to driving a Formula I racer on the Coney Island Comet without benefit of a steering wheel.

After one of those heart-stopping drop-offs into a creek bed, Allison's dogs jumped across a crevasse between two broken sheets of ice, but the sled didn't make it, sliding instead underneath a two-foot slab and stopping the whole team dead in its tracks. "My sled's so heavy I couldn't bounce it enough to go over the ice; the dogs went over the chunk of ice and my sled goes underneath and the gangline's caught in a crack. So here's my sled, driven under the ice and I've got twenty dogs on top and I'm wondering how I'm going to get my dog team out of there. I'm trying to pull them back and they want to go forward and I don't know what to do. You're almost at the point where you want to cut the thing and turn them loose and say I'll meet you at the

bottom of the hill because you know it's so steep you're gonna ride
the sled the whole way anyway, and the only reason you don't is
because there's four or five dogs in there that are probably mad at
them guys behind them and you may only have ten dogs when
you get there. But it's a creative process. You're working and they
relax, and they give you that one piece of breath and you drop the
ice hook in a crack.

"Finally I took my snow hook and tied it to the gangline and
disconnected the main towline from the sled. Now the snow
hook's holding twenty dogs and once I got the tension off the main
line I undid the shackle and pulled the sled backwards and got it
out from under the ice. Then I hooked the sled back into the gangline."

From there Allison and Brinker went on to the bottom of the
piece of cake and the icy river trails leading to the Rohn River
checkpoint.

For all the pitfalls of the Rainy Pass descent, the beauty of the
run through the Alaska Range wasn't lost on the mushers. Myron
Angstman, the lawyer with the setter in lead, made the run up the
pass at night after leaving the lodge at 2:00 A.M. The temperature
was twenty below on a clear night with no moon and so many
stars it almost looked as if there was more light than dark.
Angstman described a sky full of the bright greens and yellows of
northern lights so vivid he could see the dogs' shadows in the
snow. Allison too recalled the beauty of the steep blue-white
mountainsides, "going through the pass . . . looking up . . . the
mountains go forever up into the clouds." And Gary Hokkanen,
very serious about the race, in conversation later asked, "Did you
look up when you went through there? Prettiest place I've ever
been through, that canyon after you come out of the pass."

Once a musher had negotiated the rocks and holes of the ice
chute, "that canyon" Hokkanen talked about was the trail along
Pass Fork, a tributary to Dalzell Creek. The canyon was formed by
mountains on each side rising to 5,200 and 5,300 feet. Pass Fork
and then Dalzell Creek wound through the canyon until the trail
reached the Tatina River.

On the Tatina, the teams encountered another phenomenon of
Alaska winter: overflow. In late winter, as water begins to trickle
into the creek and river bottoms, thick river ice may still extend all

the way to the bottom, leaving nowhere for the water to flow except on top of the ice. The icy overflow freezes to dogs' feet, freezes to sled runners, soaks mushers' feet and hides holes in the ice that can swallow a dog or even a sled. Coupled with the overflow are patches of glare ice laid bare by winds. On the Tatina's ice there was little for a dog or sled to use for traction, and all the teams skittered and scratched their way toward the Rohn River checkpoint.

The overflow on the river was so bad that the trailblazers had had to move the trail off the river in places, and some of the mushers, even those used to the trail, had difficulty finding the checkpoint, particularly in the dark. For first-timers the problem wasn't so bad because they didn't know where it was anyway. Gayle Nienhueser, in the twilight, drove right on past the trail. Right behind him, Del Allison's team jumped up on the bank so fast he thought they might be chasing an animal. Allison looked down the river at Nienhueser, wondering if Nienhueser had the trail, then walked up to his leaders and saw other tracks going up the bank and into the woods. He returned to the river ice and hollered at Nienhueser, telling him he was off the trail, and then walked up to help the other musher turn his team. In the process of the turning, a male dog managed to catch a female in heat and soon enough they were entangled. There was nothing Nienhueser could do now but wait, so he and Allison sat on the sled and talked until the two dogs disengaged. Then Nienhueser followed Allison's team up onto the bank and into the woods. They had run only a few minutes before finding a long strip cleared out of thick trees an airstrip. Allison shone his headlamp and found a row of lumps on the edge of the clearing: bags of food set out for the mushers. Two trails led off into the woods, and back in the trees dogs were barking and howling. It was easy enough to figure out which of the trails led to the log roadhouse and checkpoint.

Bill Hall and Pat Hanley maintained the Rohn River checkpoint in a comfortable old cabin near another that may once have served as a roadhouse in the later years of the original trail. As testimony to the trials of the Rainy Pass stretch of trail, sled builder Paul Fleming had set up shop there. He had come to enjoy the race— but the pass always generated a little business and before he was done, Fleming had made major repairs on at least seven sleds.

Leaving the Rohn Roadhouse, the trail headed north on the South Fork of the Kuskokwim River, a shallow stream notorious for its overflow and glare ice. In some years the trail went a long way on the South Fork, but this year, after only a mile or so, it cut up into the brush to what mushers describe as a buffalo trail, through dense spruce forest. Bison, introduced to the area in the 1930s, still travel the trail, but probably of more interest to mushers is the fact that parts of the original Iditarod Trail are still visible here, mostly as a narrow cut for several miles through the trees. Modern-day explorers say you also can find original blazes in the trees from the 1910 survey, but the blazes now are about twenty feet off the ground.

The trail now passed along the base of a 5,800-foot mountain until it reached the Post River. If the race had continued through the woods mushers would have passed the remains of Pioneer Roadhouse and its dog barns, a remnant from the earliest years of the trail. Part of the original cabin, then known as Frenchy's, still stands, although a tree growing on the roof became so big that its weight collapsed one section. The race trail turned west up the Post River for a couple of miles until it crossed behind Tunis Mountain and bisected small Veleska Lake, then followed Tin Creek north a while to turn west again and head through scrub alder toward Farewell.

The glare ice and overflow on the South Fork and then on the Post River treated the mushers equally, exacting a price from the experienced, fast leaders as much as from the slower first-time adventurers in the rear.

As Lindner, in the lead, drove up the rivers he found his fast trail leaders not wanting to run on the ice and in the water; they kept jumping up on the bank and would just plop down and park. To keep them going, Lindner replaced the leaders with his favorite command leader, Barney, but Barney was a little slower than the others and the whole team had to slow down to Barney's pace. Behind Lindner, Swenson's dogs didn't like the ice, either. Half the fourteen dogs would run on the ice but the other seven kept wanting to haul up onto the bank where they could get a better footing without getting wet. "I think I've got pretty good lead dogs," Swenson said, "but when they get on that glare ice, they just don't listen like I want them to." On this stretch Swenson soaked, then froze, a pair of boots, but was able to change to new ones before any problems developed.

Darkness added more difficulty to the overflow. Howard Albert, the twenty-year-old Indian, didn't even see it coming. His dogs, running along the river, raced into the water, and his first knowledge of overflow was spray flying into his face. The flying water soaked his outer garments before he could stop. In this situation the mushers change quickly from mukluks to some kind of rubberized boots, either the vapor-barrier bunny boots or at least the shoe-pacs with rubber bottoms and leather tops.

Gary Hokkanen actually lost a dog under the ice when it fell through a hole the musher didn't see. Hokkanen stopped and extracted the dog but the dog now had a limp. Worse than the limp was the danger from exposure; when a dog gets wet in extremely cold temperatures, the water takes away the insulating capabilities of the thick undercoat. The dog must dry to warm up, which can be done with a fire or by going indoors. However, a dog, unlike a human, also can dry out on the run and Hokkanen kept going to Farewell.

A day behind the leaders, Cliff Sisson encountered the river with an unexpected dive, dropping onto the South Fork as he came out of Rohn. His sled smashed into an exposed stump and his brush bow snapped. Sisson stopped and examined the wreckage, then chopped out the stump, an act of sportsmanship that would help those following. He lost another hour repairing the brush bow, using a sapling from a nearby woods, then fed his dogs and headed on down the river.

Two days behind Sisson, Jerry LaVoie flipped his sled on the ice and lost his mittens and a nickle-plated .357 magnum revolver that was a favorite of his wife. The couple lived in a remote area of western Alaska in the upper reaches of the Anvik River, where a pistol is an important part of life because encounters with bears and moose are very real problems. They had bought this particular revolver because the fellow who owned it said LaVoie's wife could shoot it better than he could, so he sold it to her. The gun and mittens slipped out of the sled unnoticed and in the excitement of righting the sled, LaVoie missed them on the ice. A musher following brought them along later, just as another musher did earlier when he found May's mittens on the same stretch of river.

There were occurrences on the trail not easily explainable. Hallucinations become common as fatigue and poor diet, along with the stress of the race, work on the minds and bodies of the competitors. One of the mushers who was particularly sensitive to this sort of phenomenon was artist Jon Van Zyle, whose painted impressions of the trail, after he ran it in 1976, showed many realistic scenes but also explored the mental wanderings of the musher. He planned to paint another group after this race, and one of them would come from his experience as he worked his way up the Post River at night.

"A friend, a sort of mystic in Seattle, told me if I ever got into trouble during the race to say the words, 'White light surround us.' On the Post River, going at night, there was open water. Two dogs dropped through. I finally had to go up and grab the leaders and walk up there to the water to get them through. It was a scary experience and I said the words. A musher behind us told me he saw us on the river and there was a sort of glow around me and the dogs."

The piece Van Zyle painted from the Post River shows two mushers and teams at night, the ice an eerie dark blue, with even darker trees lining the bank. There's a strange light, like full-body haloes around the leading musher and his team — the Seattle mystic's white light.

Once off the Post River, the trail wound through thick spruce and then alder. In some places the trail looked the same for mile after mile, and at least one musher, Don Montgomery of Ohio, got turned around, and Allison and Brinker met him heading back toward the Rohn Roadhouse. No amount of argument could dissuade Montgomery from his course and he continued the wrong way, on a broken sled, to the previous checkpoint. In this stretch, too, the competition growing between Allison and Brinker, as among many other mushers in the race, reached a point of contention. Brinker finally pulled away from camp, a white grin breaking his four-day growth of thick black beard, and told Allison that was the last they'd see of each other until Nome. Allison, not ready to leave the camp quite yet, said, "It's a bet," adding a bit of extra competition to his own race.

For Joe May, the trail to Farewell was just too fast for the steady pace he wanted to maintain. Adding to the problem was the local buffalo herd. May's team chased one of the buffalo on the way into Farewell. "The dogs got cranked up. They went crazy. I didn't expect that kind of trail—hard and fast, and the dogs went bananas. Too fast, too fast."

For four days the mushers and teams passed through the Rohn River checkpoint on the way to Farewell, the trail's last outpost on the land of the white man's intrusion. The race had moved from the Anchorage area and the white man's influence into the rugged Interior, where the villages and streams and mountains bear names derived directly from Athabascan Indian words or from early Russian fur buyers who came up the rivers and left their names and religion behind. Today, the Indians, like the forest itself, have begun to regain what was taken from them, both names and things more tangible. Indicative of the reclamation is the battle to rename Mount McKinley, which was named by a prospector who liked the gold standard and the presidential candidate who favored it. *Denali*, the Athabascan word for *Great One*, is the name the Indians have proposed for the mountain. This was Indian country now, the second of the cultures the Iditarod Trail would pass through.

The Interior also meant colder temperatures, weather the mushers had been looking forward to. The low dropped to near minus thirty at night and seldom rose above plus ten during the day, under a cloudless sky in weather the flight service station at McGrath had taken to calling "severe clear." Almost every night brought northern lights and the moon reached first quarter and was moving toward a half.

The thirty-eight-mile trail from Rohn to Farewell took the leading mushers between six and ten hours; those following behind took as long as sixteen. My short hitch-hike hop in an airplane all the way from Rainy Pass Lodge to Farewell involved all of about forty-five minutes.

6. Farewell

THE AIR FORCE THAT SUPPORTED THE RACE DROPPED ITS TROOPS
on Farewell long before the mushers arrived. Larry Thompson
flew in first, carrying the gunny sacks filled with food and gear for
drivers and dogs, even bringing a sled for Eep Anderson. During
the day before the mushers arrived, the assortment of small airplanes dropped off race officials, veterinarians, writers, photographers, two commercial television crews and one from Armed
Forces Radio, along with friends of the mushers and adventurers
just following the race and helping out where they could. At times,
this crowd numbered upwards of fifty, all with one reason for
being there—the Iditarod Trail Sled Dog Race.

Farewell, three hundred miles from Anchorage, is an outpost of
the technological age in the hilly open space of Interior Alaska. It
serves as a flight service station within the McGrath complex,
supplying general aviation pilots with weather briefings and other
advisories including airport conditions. The facility also provides
navigation assistance to disoriented pilots and aids in search and
rescue operations. The permanent party at the station numbered
five, two couples and a single man. Harry and Patty Lacey, who
worked at Farewell, would serve as checkers for the race.

Three identical two-story residential houses line the south side of the only thing in town that could be called a street. On the north side stands a three-story building formerly used as offices and a bunkhouse. At one end of the street are three supply sheds and at the other end, where the mushers would pass, is a building with a laundry room and power plant and, in another building, mattresses where the mushers could sleep. Behind the three houses lies a giant airstrip, obviously built to handle aircraft larger than the force of Cessna 180s and Piper Supercubs that were now lining one side. At the end of the airstrip were tall radio and navigation towers, the only manmade objects that rose above the skyline.

The day sparkled bright and clear—and cold, the temperature rising above zero only in the height of the afternoon. The mushers regarded Farewell as one of the classy stops on the trail, and many planned to take their twenty-four-hour layovers there. Hot running water, clothes dryers, indoor cooking facilities and houses with warm beds made the place particularly tempting. Since one of the three houses was not in use, the Iditarod party moved into what would become the unofficial headquarters and soup kitchen for the next five days.

Before the mushers arrived, there was work to be done, and anyone standing around was prey to the chore assigners. The mushers' gunny sacks had been stored in a shed and had to be taken by pickup truck the length of the street to the laundry building. Along with everyone else I ended up horsing the heavy sacks into the truck and unloading them again at their destination. The burlap bags were arranged in a semicircle in alphabetical order so the weary racers could find the right bags as easily as possible. With that done, most of us gathered in the vacant house for the continuing conversation about race and dogs.

Holding forth from an easy chair near a window was Dick Mackey, who, until this year, had run every race since 1973. His win in the previous year, after an exciting sprint against Swenson down Nome's Front Street, was the first time victory was decided so close to the finish line. The story went that Mackey and Swenson, pushing each other, ran most of the way together. On the last day, Mackey began talking to Swenson, letting on how Swenson's dogs were faster, and his own dogs just couldn't beat Swenson when it came down to the last run. As the two teams came up off the sea ice into Nome, Mackey kept up his conversation about losing, but as they approached the snow-fenced chute, he sneaked a whip out of his sled, gave it a loud crack that gave his dogs the surge they needed to jump past Swenson's team, and Mackey's lead dogs crossed the finish line first. About half of Mackey's team crossed the line, then, exhausted from running the length of the street, Mackey collapsed on his sled while Swenson's whole team and sled crossed under the arch of the finish line. There was hesitation for only a moment. Did the lead dogs count or did the sled and musher have to cross first? Both mushers knew the rules, and Swenson quickly congratulated Mackey on winning the race, the first photo finish yet in the thousand-mile race. After six years of trying, Mackey had finally won—by a lead dog's nose—officially by one second. That one second made a $4,000 difference in prize money between Mackey and Swenson.

With his goal accomplished, Mackey had become president of the trail committee and worked at raising funds and generally directing the tremendous organization required by a race of this complexity. During the race he assumed the duties of umpire, but his talk along the trail wasn't about raising money or shipping goods or interpreting rules. His mind was on the trail and the dogs, and it was obvious he'd rather be racing.

Mackey and Shellie Vandiver, a musher who had also run the previous race, finishing twenty-ninth, talked in the front room of the house. Vandiver was working this year as health aide for the race and sometime cook as well. The two showed how divergent the attitudes toward the race could be, with Vandiver talking about the scenery and how she enjoyed all that she saw along the way, even kidding about how she saw more than she needed to because of the several times she lost the trail.

"I never see the scenery," Mackey said. "I'm concentrating on each dog. I'm watching the trail. I'm watching for overflow." Mackey had always been known as a hard charger in the Iditarod, and in every race had finished in the top ten. That someone would take time to look at the scenery didn't fit with his way of racing at all. "You know, I've driven this race six times," he said, "and this is the first time I've seen the back of the pack. Those guys are on a camping trip." Still, he did not totally disdain the campers. "Who's tough," he asked rhetorically, "the guy who spends two

weeks on the trail or the guy who spends four weeks on the trail?"
He recalled that in 1975 Steve Fee showshoed for two weeks to
make Nome because he wouldn't give up and no one broke trail
for him.

Even though he respected the toughness of the campers,
Mackey's interest was in the strategy of winning, and his way was
to push. "The dogs are tougher than the men. You can't drive a
dog to death; it'll quit first. And the man will probably quit before
the dog," he told Vandiver, who advocated milder treatment of the
dogs. Mackey, with a twinkle in his eye, told her, "You know, a
woman will never win this race. They'll never win because they
don't drive their dogs hard enough." Vandiver, who wouldn't
drive her dogs hard enough to win anyway, sat quietly; maybe she
believed him or maybe not, but she wasn't going to argue.

The silence didn't last long; there were too many subjects to
cover. Mackey switched to the early years of the race and thought
of the wives. "That first year," he told us, "no one knew what to
expect, and wives and sweethearts were crying at the starting line.
Now they don't worry so much."

He also remarked on how far the race had come in terms of
taking care of the dogs. People at first shipped bags of dry commercial feed and the care was minimal. By this, the seventh
running, foods had become almost exotic and there were none of
the familiar bags from store shelves. Care of dogs' health also had
improved tremendously.

The conversation carried late into the afternoon and as dusk
spread across the sky, mushers were expected momentarily. A
group of photographers walked out along the runway in minus-
ten-degree cold to catch a photo of the first team before the light
faded. To the southeast Mount McKinley rose, the dominant
feature in the country. A flock of fat white ptarmigans chuk-
chuked through the brush on the near side of the runway, and
then for no apparent reason the whole flock — perhaps a hundred
in all — burst into flight and the birds careened crazily across the
wide strip to more brush on the far side. Darkness came gradually,
almost like a shade being drawn from north to south. For a long
time, it seemed as if the shade stopped just above the western
horizon, leaving room for a thick red line between the dark sky
and the white ground. The beacons lit up and red bulbs on the

radio towers blinked into life, competing with the stars for holes in
the sky. The wait in the cold had been futile and the photographers trooped back to the buildings. Inside there was just about
time to take off heavy outer gear and settle into chairs when
someone shouted that a musher was coming. Up came the photographers, back into the parkas and mittens and hats, and they
headed out into the cold, rushing to the end of the street to peer
into the darkness. Far out toward the end of the runway they
could just make out a bobbing, bouncing, dim light, the headlamp
a musher was wearing to light his way among some moose
gathered on the airstrip.

Within minutes, the dog team trotted onto the street between
the houses and the bunkhouse. Sonny Lindner, his mustache
frosted thick with ice, answered checker Patty Lacey's questions,
then led his dogs down the street and into the shelter next to the
bunkhouse, out of the wind that had picked up since darkness.
Lindner didn't know how long he'd stay. If too many teams
showed up, he said, he'd move down the trail a ways and camp.
Too many teams made too much noise and kept his dogs from
resting well, and he'd rather let them sleep undisturbed even if it
meant he'd be a little less comfortable himself.

Once in the shelter of the building, the dogs knew what was
coming and even before Lindner stretched the gangline out and
sank his snow hook, the dogs had curled up in the snow for their
rest. With the dogs settled, Lindner went back down the street to
find his gunny sack of food. He brought the sack and his Coleman
stove into the laundry shack to begin the work of feeding the
team, first taking them some water. He fired up his stove and over
the flames put a five-gallon fuel can with the top cut out and
hinged. Into the can he dumped his frozen dog food with water,
leaving it to simmer.

Before Lindner's dog food was ready, Rick Swenson had pulled
into Farewell and behind him shortly came Peters, Riley, Honea,
Adkins, Nayokpuk, Garnie and Rick Mackey, Dick's son.
Swenson declared his twenty-four-hour layover — but he'd done
that elsewhere just to keep the competition guessing.

One after another they moved into the laundry room with
stoves and sacks and wet clothes, and went through a metamor-
phosis. Giants rode the sleds into the settlement and hauled the

gear into the laundry room, but in the warm room, as they shed parkys, down vests, arctic coveralls, bunny boots and big marten hats, the mushers shrank to the proportions of mere mortals, if not even shorter and thinner than the norm. Lindner was the first: his big parky went, then the blue gingham, marten-lined hat along with the sidearm he carried in a holster inside his parky. Finally the heavy brown Carheart coveralls, and Lindner was reduced to normal size.

Soon the once almost military-sterile laundry room reaked of rendered fat, Blazo fuel, Coleman stoves and cooking dog food. Mushers weary and dirty from the trail looked for space to cook. Clotheslines strung everywhere held what damp clothing couldn't be stuffed immediately into the two perpetually working dryers.

Most of the mushers looked tired, but there was a charge in the air. These were the front runners, and more than likely the winner of the race was in this first group to arrive at Farewell. These were the competitors intent on winning and tired or not, the race was all-consuming to them. Rick Swenson in particular kept up a constant banter as he prepared his dog food, wanting to know where all the other mushers were and when May would leave Rohn River at the end of his twenty-four-hour break. While Swenson talked, Emmitt Peters shook the snow off his parky and shook his head and sat down.

Peters had had a rough trip through the ice and overflow. His coat was soaked and he told anyone who'd listen, "This is the last. No more. I quit after this one. Don't know why I get in it." Even as he sat there, though, his dog food was cooking next to him in an army thermal-food container reworked a bit to function as a pressure cooker. This was an invention of army veteran Ron Brinker; Peters had seen Brinker's before the race and asked the other musher to make him one. The pressure cut the time it took to cook the dog food, speeding the whole process and giving the musher a little more time for sleep. There were many such innovations in the mushers' gear: for instance, most of the Coleman stoves had been engineered so that each of the two burners had its own pressurized fuel tank instead of one tank feeding both.

Despite his protestations, few in the room discounted Peters just because he said he was ready to quit. He was running his fifth race and he'd never finished lower than fifth. Not only had he won the race his first time out, but he had set the record. No matter what he said, he'd be out front somewhere when the racers approached Nome. Swenson's confident banter was meant to have an effect on competitors, and maybe Peters' comments were intended to lure people into thinking they didn't have to worry about him.

Swenson kept up his chatter as he fired the stove and put his cooker over the two burners. Into the pot he dumped fifteen pounds of lamb chops, right out of a box from the market. One of his sponsors was a Fairbanks meat market and the shop and butchers, reportedly, were turned over to Swenson for a whole weekend before the race just to prepare his food for the trail. While the lamb chops cooked, Swenson cut one-pound chunks of Philadelphia Brand cream cheese in half to give a half-pound piece to each of the dogs.

Several onlookers watched him and the expensive food. "It's a tough life when you're an Iditarod dog," he said and then walked out of the room to feed the chunks of cheese to his dogs, still fourteen strong and virtually untouched by the sickness of the trail.

The quality of the dog food in the laundry room wasn't always that high but, like knowledge about equipment and strategy, knowledge about feeding, as Mackey had pointed out, had grown with the race. In the first years, the mushers knew little of what to expect on a thousand-mile-plus sled dog trek, and many either used commercial dog food or the maintenance diet they had fed the dogs all year round. Some who had been sprint racers used feed formulas for sprinters, but it turned out that the lighter diet wouldn't stay with the dogs during the rigors of as long as three weeks' steady going on the Iditarod.

Not all mushers could afford the kind of feed Swenson gave his dogs but many tried to follow his theories. A major portion of most mushers' feed formulas is fat, as much as 40 or 50 percent of the mix. Not just any fat will do, though, and beef fat in particular had been found to be too heavy. Lamb fat is light and easily digestible and quickly turns to energy. Beaver meat also has highly soluble fat and the meat itself has one of the highest protein concentrations of any red meat. Trappers sell beaver carcasses for anywhere between twenty-five and thirty-five dollars to mushers during the race. Some mushers have experimented with chicken fat, also supposedly easily digestible. Because of complicated game laws, little game meat can be used legally, but Eskimos are allowed to hunt marine mammals and most of the Eskimo mushers put some seal meat in their formulas. May, who'd worked with a fish-processing company to develop dog food from byproducts, had been adding fish oil as part of his fat content, and the oil had a noticeable beneficial effect on the dogs' coats.

Red meat is the next largest part of most race mixes: horsemeat, beaver, lamb, beef, whatever the mushers can buy or scrounge. Fish also can be a major part of the diet, but experience has taught mushers that fish don't have fat and don't work so well in cold weather. Even salmon, which does have some fat, won't sustain the dogs in the cold. If a racer has the funds, he may send fish along with other foods to feed in warmer weather. Most mushers also add some kind of grain, meal or commercial feed to the mix for carbohydrates. Rice also may be a key ingredient. May, who was constantly studying the dogs and feed and all other aspects of the sport, said he'd seen a study that showed that dogs manufacture their own carbohydrates and don't need to be fed them. Mushers also add a small quantity of raw liver to the mix. Walter Kaso fried his liver first and said it cleared up the dogs' diarrhea. Some race mixes also include vitamin supplements and even electrolytes to speed digestion.

This year, almost every musher used a slightly different food formula, although most, with the notable exception of Swenson, swore by beaver meat. As the race progressed the concentrations of beaver in the food increased. The dogs would usually eat it, even at times when they refused other foods, but mushers had found once the dogs had been fed beaver they wouldn't easily go back to anything else.

Each dog received full meals of the cooked race mix, as much as two pounds a feeding at least twice a day, and sometimes more, particularly in bitterly cold weather. In addition to the regular meals, the mushers carried snacks they gave the dogs at rest stops between feedings. Again, everyone had his own ideas. Swenson said he gave the dogs chunks of beef heart. Joe Redington had a more complicated mix he called honey balls. Into the mix went hamburger, Saffola oil, powdered eggs, brewer's yeast, honey, wheat-germ oil, mineral salt and powdered vitamins. He mixed a big batch and then wadded the potion into one-pound balls to feed the dogs along the trail.

The quantities of food the mushers shipped and fed varied, mostly according to the amount of money the musher had available. Swenson said he had shipped 3,000 pounds of food out onto the trail, but that wouldn't all be eaten. With adequate funds, he could send various foods so if he ran into a situation where a dog wouldn't eat a particular mix, he had an alternative available. Should the weather turn unseasonably warm, for instance, the dogs might function better on fish than on a heavy fat and red meat diet, and Swenson would have that option available to him. Others couldn't spend so much money, and the amount of food shipped by mushers probably averaged between 1,500 to 2,000 pounds.

With all those ingredients going into the cookpots, and as many as a dozen pots going at any given time, it didn't take long for the air in the laundry room to get a little heavy. Between the heat and the smell, it was like hitting a wall for someone walking in from outdoors. As the mushers shrank and the foods cooked, the talk never strayed far from the race: who's where, how the dogs are, what happened on the rivers, some bluffing, some strategizing, some psyching the opposition, and the problem of the diarrhea that had plagued so many teams.

Almost every musher who came in grabbed veterinarian Phil Meyer immediately and told him about this or that dog, and Meyer was kept busy examining and injecting dogs with antibiotics and B vitamins. The sickness concerned everyone and had hit at least a dog or two in almost every team. Some of the stronger leaders hadn't been touched badly, however, and publicity about the sickness bothered Swenson. "They always write about the sick dogs," Swenson said. "Why don't they look at the good teams, the guys that know what they're doing?" Peters, who also had a healthy team, said the reason for the illness was that too many people gave the dogs their required rabies and distemper shots too close to race time, not leaving the dogs enough time to work off the shots. The shots should be given at least a month or two earlier, Peters stated.

Swenson, who had said he was running the best team he'd ever had, claimed to have had none of the illness. "All I know about dogs is if they're sick, leave them home," he said in the din of the laundry room." I don't know all that fancy stuff you guys know."

Whether or not Swenson and Peters had really figured out the best way to avoid the sickness, they were in any case bearing out the expectations of the bars in Anchorage — where no one was giving odds on either one of them.

Of the leaders, Jerry Riley had had the most trouble with the illness. There had been suggestions that he should scratch, but the word didn't fit into his vocabulary. He said that since he had hit the cold weather his dogs had picked up considerably. Still, when he came down the street and stopped, the dogs laid down while he was talking to the checker, and at least one didn't want to get up again.

Competition between Swenson and Riley was intense, bordering on bitter. Tricks, maybe, and strategies and previous races had led to a situation where the two barely tolerated each other. Swenson, in the laundry room while his food was cooking, did little to ease the situation, frequently punctuating his bantering with an antagonizing "Right, Jerry?" as he talked. Riley for his part sat quietly off to the side talking with Peters. He appeared to ignore Swenson's taunts and his concern in his conversation was the dogs and the race.

Once their dogs had eaten and curled up for sleep, the mushers took care of their own needs. Some ate out of the foil-wrapped packages that had been warming on top of the dog pots. Popular as a trail food for this kind of cooking was a small steak wrapped with a big chunk of butter. Several of the foil packages also contained pizza. In many of the checkpoints hospitality included stews and soups or meals in private homes. Here at Farewell Shellie Vandiver was trying to keep everyone fed. But even after hot meals, some of the mushers, despite the fatigue, had difficulty sleeping. Swenson, however, appeared tireless; even though he'd now decided to take his twenty-four-hour layover here and had nowhere to go, he still didn't sleep. After he ate he fell into conversation with Dick Mackey.

Mackey kidded him about the slow pace of the race so far.

"Course, if you were here running we'd be a lot farther down the trail," Swenson kidded back. "None of this sandbagging."

Swenson couldn't find the liver in his food bag and thought someone had stolen it, and he made no bones about who he thought it was. Mackey diplomatically let the subject drop and the conversation turned to strategy. Swenson, in only his fourth race, appeared to have figured out a master strategy for winning, or at least ending near the top. In his first year he finished tenth, then he won, then he finished second in the close race with Mackey and now again he was right there with the front runners. With about three hundred miles behind him he figured Peters was his strongest competition, although he worried, too, about May and Honea, whose teams he hadn't seen too much of. He let anyone know who'd listen that he intended to win this year.

"I know how to get Emmitt," he told Mackey.

"Get out in front of him and keep pushin'," Mackey said.

"Once he wears his dogs down, just once, they never come back," Swenson figured. He keyed his race to other mushers and his plan involved running with at least one other fast team, one reason at least being to ease the burden on his lead dogs. By following, his dogs didn't have the strain of finding the trail, or breaking through heavy snow.

As the mushers and teams filled the small outpost they began to crowd Lindner, and after just a five-hour rest and feeding, he hiked his team out into the darkness of the trail to camp out of the noise. May, finished with his layover at Rohn and with his team rested, pulled through during the night, arriving shortly after two in the morning, resting his dogs four hours and leaving at six. That put him some thirteen hours ahead of Swenson, who had to wait until seven that evening for the end of his mandatory stay. May left Farewell in second place, following Lindner by about six hours.

Throughout the night and next day, mushers and teams continued to arrive. At least ten took their layovers at Farewell because of the comforts of the station. Many more enjoyed the place a little too much after the rigors of the pass and the rivers, and lingered too long. The number of gunny sacks outside the laundry building gradually dwindled, but the laundry room stayed full of damp clothes, cook stoves, all manner of gear and even a dog or two that needed drying out. The dryers ran constantly.

For a while, young Rome Gilman, also taking his twenty-four, worked on his sled in the laundry room. He had an older, traditional sled and he'd now seen the speedy, light toboggans Swenson and some others were using, and he was attempting to fasten a piece of plastic to the bottom of his sled between the runners. He also tied down some of the stanchions that had loosened on the bumpy rides down Rainy Pass and on the ice of the rivers.

Musher after musher called for the services of Phil Meyer, and he was constantly administering to ailing dogs. Patty Friend complained her whole team had stopped eating and many of the dogs had the diarrhea. Meyer treated the dogs and Friend worried about a way to at least get the dogs to take some water or broth. Fearing dehydration, she had begun experimenting with a squeeze bottle, like a liquid-detergent bottle, that she could fill, then lay gently on a dog's tongue while squeezing a little liquid into the dog's mouth, allowing the dog to swallow naturally. The experiment held promise for resolving a growing dispute among the mushers about the use of tubes to force liquid into the dogs' stomachs.

A day after he treated Friend's dogs, Meyer faced a different, more difficult problem. Bud Smyth pulled into Farewell carrying, covered up in his sled, a dog that had died. Like many of the other mushers, Smyth had had his problems before the race. While he was training on the Big Lake Road near Wasilla, a car doing maybe seventy miles an hour had hit the front end of his team, dragging the dogs more than 150 yards down the road. Seven dogs were hit, although none killed. Smyth himself had chipped and sprained his ankle and dislocated his elbow. The dog he brought into Farewell was one of those hit by the car.

The dog had been treated for pneumonia at Rohn, and other dogs in the team also appeared to have pneumonia, leading Meyer at first to blame the disease for the dog's death. Race officials and publicists were particularly sensitive about the subject of dead dogs and whenever possible demanded that an autopsy be performed to determine the cause of death, with an eye toward reprimanding a musher who may have mistreated a dog. So at Farewell Meyer performed a necropsy on Smyth's dog. (Veterinarians are happy to point out that they use the proper term, *necropsy*, for the post-mortem examination of an animal rather than the more common but semantically incorrect *autopsy* used by physicians.) Meyer worked over the frozen dog, finding blood in the abdominal cavity. "When you see blood, you look for organs that bleed — spleen, liver, kidney," he said. On the liver he found a tear about three inches long. He talked with Smyth, who said the dog died while they were on river ice. Smyth said the team hadn't gone by any stumps or rocks the dogs could have hit, but he did recall a tangle and wondered if in the yanking around to straighten it out he could have injured the animal. Meyer said he didn't think the dog had been kicked because there were no bruises, but he didn't think the injury was related to the auto accident, either. He eventually had to cut his necropsy short when one of his own fingers began to freeze while he was cutting into the frozen dog. At any rate, he could find no reason to blame the musher, and Smyth, who had followed the rules by bringing the dog to the checkpoint, continued in the race.

Dogs have died along the trail since the beginnings of the Iditarod. In the early years as many as thirty would die during a single race, but as the knowledge of care of the dogs has grown, the number of deaths has declined accordingly. By the time of this race the rate had dropped to less than .875 percent, actually lower than could be expected in the general dog population. Of eight hundred dogs in the race, only five had died by the time everyone reached Nome.

The mushers kept Shellie Vandiver busy over the stove. Rick Swenson, who complained he'd lost eighteen pounds since Anchorage, sat down to a breakfast of steak, pizza and eggs. When his friend from back in Minnesota, Hokkanen, came into the kitchen, Vandiver offered to cook him some eggs. "I like them in a big pile and slimy," the tall, thin Hokkanen said almost apologetically. A short time later she put a plate in front of him that most people would have had to look away from. "I never heard of anybody wanting them slimy before," Vandiver said with a sideways grin, "but I made them slimy."

"Best eggs I ever ate," Hokkanen said as he dug into the pile on his plate.

Lee Gardino, who had had to drop his only lead dog earlier in the race but was still a strong contender along with Hokkanen for rookie-of-the-year honors, talked with Dick Mackey. With his lead dog out, Gardino wasn't making the progress he'd hoped for.

"There's got to be a lead dog in that team somewhere," Mackey told him.

"I've tried every one of them, and they just won't go," the dejected musher complained. "I've tried every dog in every combination but I can't get one who'll lead." Mackey reminded him he was doing well anyway and to keep moving the dogs around until one of them took over.

Joe Redington, Sr. and Susan Butcher arrived together shortly behind Gardino and unpacked to cook for their dogs while Gardino was talking with Mackey. Despite six years of experience with the race, Redington still drove one of the most fully packed sleds on the trail. Even he admitted that he carried too much. He and Nayokpuk were famous for their full sleds. Redington and Butcher kidded each other about Butcher's job as Redington's leader. As Redington quietly went about the chores of feeding the dogs, Butcher kept up a constant chatter. At one moment she was talking about food and water, at another, about a bit of trail, and at another she mentioned a dog named Dandy who'd developed a limp. She thought it was psychological. Redington, who had a slight hearing problem, asked, "What?" A bystander told him she had a dog with a psychological limp. Through a sort of half-grin he said, "Oh, no wonder I didn't hear her."

Ken Chase, still bringing his dogs back to health after their fight, walked into the kitchen. He'd bedded his dogs down, but would eat before they did. Asked why, he said a good Indian always lets the team rest a while before feeding because it relieves some of the stress and relaxes the dogs, letting them digest their food easily. Myron Angstman, trying the same thing, made the mistake of leaving his dogs in sight, and through the kitchen window could see his setter Nick almost begging. The guilt was too much, and Angstman gulped his food quickly to leave and feed his dogs.

One of the subjects that had entered almost every conversation at the table and in the laundry room was the threat of a storm two or three days ahead. Although the sky had been clear for several days with not a hint of clouds, word passed that a storm was brewing. Jamie Smith, a pilot out of McGrath, said there had been south winds during the day, and south was the wind direction for stormy weather in the McGrath area. Cynics traced the storm story back to Swenson, who just might have started it to keep people in check while he took his twenty-four-hour layover. But Chase, too, said a storm was coming "two or three days ahead." Asked how he knew, his eyes narrowed and he recalled his Indian upbringing and simply said, "I've lived in this country a long time."

By the time the race reached Farewell, the first and last mushers had stretched even farther apart and it took almost a full five days for all to pass through. At Farewell word passed up the trail that young Mark Couch, after five days on the trail, had scratched at Rainy Pass.

The leaders were pushing on to McGrath and the time came to leave. Out on the airstrip a small silver Cessna 170 landed and pilot Ed Gurtler, a straight-backed man in a dirty red baseball cap, walked into the kitchen. Dick Mackey, who lived near Gurtler in Wasilla, said, "Hello, Ed." A couple of mushers who had been to his Innoko River Lodge, said, "Hello, Ed."

But from his chair at the kitchen table, Chase recognized his fellow Indian and with a voice that said welcome, called, "Crazy Horse!"

7. Farewell to McGrath

SEVERE CLEAR NIGHTS MEANT NORTHERN LIGHTS, AND AS LINDNER HEADED out onto the trail under just a sliver of a moon, the aurora borealis lit his way. The action and noise in Farewell had become increasingly hectic with the arrival of more and more teams, and Lindner had stuck to his word, leaving barely five hours after he arrived. As the first driver out of Farewell, he was warned by the checkers that the trail went about a mile and then split. "Take the left fork," Harry Lacey told Lindner.

At midnight Lindner drove his team across Sheep Creek, the northern border of the station, and pulled up into the spruce forest. As he moved along the quiet trail in the limited light and the shadow of the trees, his lead dogs had no scent to follow, only the feel of the trail and what the driver could see. The dogs and driver missed the fork, and instead of moving to the northwest, the team began a gradual curve toward the northeast that, if they followed it long enough, would turn them south around Farewell Mountain and take them back toward the South Fork and Rohn River. To Lindner the trail, which was marked, looked broken and used. He and the team went for more than two hours in the wrong direction.

As the night progressed, the trail curved more and more away from where Lindner thought he should be going, and he began to wonder whether he had missed the fork he was supposed to take. The realization took some time. He had seen no fork, and he was on a used, marked trail that was heading somewhat north. But as the curve became more pronounced toward the east, Lindner finally guessed he was on the wrong trail. He turned the team around and headed back the way he had come. In time he found the spot where the trail forked and he turned up the correct trail, but there he stopped. Instead of continuing on, leaving the false trail for others to follow, Lindner went to work cutting trees and saplings and tearing down markers until he had blocked out the wrong trail, so the teams following him couldn't make the same mistake.

For his sportsmanship, Lindner lost precious hours to those behind him. The approximately forty-five miles from Farewell to the Indian village of Nikolai took him more than fourteen hours. May, who followed Lindner out of Farewell six hours behind, made the same distance in less than ten, and that had to include at least one rest stop for the dogs.

But neither of those mushers arrived first into the next check-point, a village on the Kuskokwim River. May had said his team wasn't fast, but it was strong, better in deep snow and sloggy going. His team, however, was faster than he wanted people to know. The trail to Nikolai was fast, at least for the front runners, and Peters too showed how fast his team was, injured Digger and all. Still complaining about the race, Emmitt Peters left Swenson on his mandatory layover at Farewell and, an hour behind May, Peters crossed to Nikolai in six hours and twenty minutes, an incredible average speed of seven and a half miles an hour — average because he too had to stop and at least give the dogs a snack. He passed May and then Lindner along the way, beating them both into Nikolai by about an hour. He had to make as many miles as he could while Swenson and the others were taking their twenty-fours so they would just about catch up by the time he finished his in McGrath. Except for the first year, when he took his layover in his home town of Ruby, Peters had taken his rest in McGrath, much of it in McGuire's Tavern.

The trail from Farewell paralleled the South Fork of the Kuskokwim River about eight miles to the east of the river, and went north by northwest. Trailblazers avoided the river when they could because it's shallow and as a result is notorious for overflow. Instead, they marked the trail through spruce forest out of Farewell until they reached the area now known as the Burn.

The Burn used to be spruce forest and tundra veined by creeks. But in 1977 all that changed when the largest wildfire ever recorded in Alaska burned across 361,000 acres, leaving standing only charred tree trunks and a few spindly sticks. Three hundred thirty persons fought the fire for the months of August and September but they could only contain it a little until it burned itself out. The firefighting effort cost $2.5 million in materials, fuels, equipment and salaries.

Where trees once protected the trail, there was now nothing left to break the winds that came howling across the Interior plains as the mushers began to cross the Burn. In some years, a lack of snowfall combined with wind left the trail bare, making the crossing all the more harrowing because of what gravel, tree trunks and bare ground can do to sleds and runners. This year there was snow, making the crossing a little better, but during the day, after the leaders started across, the wind began picking up, perhaps the first indication of the storm everyone had been predicting. Still, the sky remained clear, and into this cloudless sky Ed Gurtler made the first of my several hops with him in the silver and green Cessna 170.

Everyone who knows him says Gurtler is one of the best pilots in the Interior, where he's been flying for twenty years, and the name Crazy Horse slipped from my memory on the takeoff from Farewell. We flew out over the Burn. On the trail below, weaving through the spindly regrowth, a musher waved from his sled. Behind him, across a wide expanse of snow, Mount McKinley rose in the Alaska Range. With a sly grin, Crazy Horse asked, "You want a picture of that?" With the sun and dog mushers and Mount McKinley in the background, the answer could only be, "Sure."

Quicker than protective reaction, the little airplane went into a diving turn to the left and ended up screaming earthward toward the musher who by this time must have been ready to drop flat on the ground. Only through grit-teeth determination could I keep the musher and the mountain in the camera viewfinder. Very soon enough became too much. The shutter was released, the camera dropped, and I found myself clutching an overhead bar that evidently had been put there by the manufacturer for just such occasions.

Gurtler — Crazy Horse — pulled the plane out of its dive, smiled and asked, "Want another one?"

I mumbled something about being a writer, not a photographer, and he turned the airplane north again toward Nikolai.

Over the river village we flew smack into a wall — thirty-five-knot winds, the first of the winds that would whip the trail for the next week and a half. The gust slapped the airplane around, sending twitches of fear into a passenger unused to flying in small craft.

Below, the mushers pushed toward Nikolai into a wind that sent snow driving across the open space, obliterating the trail and tearing at the hot-pink surveyors' tape that marked the way. In the open area there was little enough to hang the tape from, and what tape was there eventually disappeared into the wind, leaving little for the teams to follow. The drivers had to trust their leaders' senses of smell and touch to stay on the trail.

In this lonely, open stretch of trail the first fear crept into the mind of Gary Hokkanen. Fear wasn't one of the subjects discussed much among the mushers or with writers. But on a thousand miles across the wilds of Alaska, there had to be fear — on the terrifying run down Rainy Pass, in the water and overflow, in the intense cold, the missed trails, the drop-offs and climbs, the teams that got away, and the chance encounters with wild animals. Moving through the Burn, Hokkanen saw big black humps out in the fields and for a time didn't know what he was seeing. Gradually he came to realize he was looking at resting bison, and the fear began to work on him. "There's not even a blade of grass to hide behind out there," he said later. "It scared me. What if one of them wanted the trail?" Fortunately the bison were more interested in staying down out of the wind than challenging Hokkanen for the trail, and he passed without incident.

After the Burn, the trail went across tundra and river bottom, and through some unfrozen creeks and across the ice on others until it dropped over the bank onto the Kuskokwim River shortly before it flowed by Nikolai. The teams had to maneuver a tricky turn: the trail going into Nikolai was the same one the teams would use to go back out toward McGrath. It's not too difficult to miss the turn and go on to McGrath, missing Nikolai altogether, an omission that would disqualify a musher. Fortunately the residents of the village had put signs out to guide the mushers. One read, "Nikolai, one mile." That sign was ten miles from the village.

As the teams approached Nikolai, the first visible sign of settlement, three crosses on the peak of the Russian Orthodox Church, guarded the village skyline. The church, like the names of many of the villagers, was a vestige of the days when Russian fur traders came up the Kuskokwim in the early 1800s. Most of the buildings and homes of the village were log, including the new community center which served as the race checkpoint. The church was of frame construction, though, and the village boasted a large modern prefabricated school. During the race, the schoolchildren adopted mushers and followed their progress, catching autographs if they could when the mushers came through. Some even interviewed their favorites and wrote stories about them.

The residents of Nikolai, few more than a hundred strong, greeted the mushers warmly. Village chief Ignatti Petruska orchestrated the scene as checker for the race. As race marshal Pat Hurren described events:

"The chief comes out and directs everything. If a musher asks for water, nine people materialize with water. A snow machine escorts the mushers into town and the whole village escorts them out. Villagers take food out of the bags, stir it while it's cooking and help feed the dogs. They feed the musher and watch every spoonful as it goes from plate to mouth. These are poor people, maybe the poorest on the trail, but they put out the most."

Hospitality like that offered at Nikolai had posed a problem for race rule-makers, who originally wanted the mushers to be entirely self-sufficient. Because of the generosity shown in the villages, the rules were changed to allow mushers to accept help at checkpoints, taking away the fear of being disqualified for accepting help from a friendly villager. The rules were still strict about accepting help between checkpoints, but at the villages most help was acceptable. However, there were still interpretations. Such an interpretation in the previous year's race may have cost Emmitt Peters the victory. Peters supposedly accepted warm water and, after it was reported, race officials held him up at Solomon, just thirty-two miles from Nome. They held Peters for an hour even though nothing in the rules called for such action. Peters followed Mackey and Swenson across the finish line only thirty-six minutes behind them, almost half an hour less than the hour he'd been held up. The whole race might have turned out differently.

But last year was forgotten; there was a new race to run and Peters blazed into Nikolai just past four days into the race, stayed three hours to rest and feed his dogs and then left for McGrath. Lindner stayed only four hours and left two hours behind Peters, but May stopped for twelve. Behind them teams were stretched out for more than 150 miles and would push through Nikolai for the next four and a half days.

Among them, two days behind the leaders, Ron Brinker beat Del Allison to the village, still intending to stay ahead until Nome. Brinker arrived several hours before Allison but he was still there caring for his dogs when he spied Allison coming up the river toward the village. At 250 pounds in a giant red parky, Allison wasn't too difficult to recognize behind his sled. In the twilight Brinker checked out quickly, then sneaked his team behind a couple of houses on the edge of town where Allison wouldn't see him. As soon as he knew Allison was situated and the sky had turned dark, Brinker and his team slinked down onto the river and turned off toward McGrath — a close one, but Brinker wasn't ready to lose the bet quite yet.

He needn't have worried. Just the size of Allison's twenty-dog team was enough to hold him up. Twenty dogs made a lot of work. For one thing, with the trail chewed up and then frozen again, the going had been tough on the dogs' feet and most of the mushers had been using booties. It took Allison two hours and forty-five minutes just to put booties on the eighty feet on his team, long enough to give Brinker a good head start.

The booties, developed over the years of dog mushing, had been made mandatory for the Iditarod and served several purposes. They prevented snow from balling up between the pads on a dog's feet and also kept the pads from freezing. On hard, icy trails they prevented cuts and, in cases where a dog did cut a pad, a bootie could protect the wound while it healed. The booties were generally made from a heavy material such as mattress ticking cut in U shapes and sewn together in a sort of pocket. These were fastened with Velcro or tape just tight enough to stay on but not cut circulation. Several mushers had experimented with different styles and material to find booties that would wear better and stay on the dogs' feet longer. May had developed a bootie that had a little tuck just above the joint of the foot and leg and was fastened with a wide Velcro band to a square stitched to the canvas. In a test run, he bootied all the twelve dogs he was driving and went forty miles, during which the dogs threw only two of the booties. Herbie Nayokpuk, the Eskimo from Shishmaref, made his booties from moosehide and sealskin, using a drawstring to hold them to the dogs' legs. One musher said the booties looked like high-class gold pokes. The importance of booties was reflected in the requirement that a musher carry eight booties for each dog when his team left each checkpoint.

Booties figured into an effort in 1974 that showed how much Alaskans watched the race and wanted to be involved. That year the trail was particularly hard and icy, and many mushers ran through booties quicker than they'd expected. A call for help went out and the Anchorage *Daily News* printed an article about the shortage, complete with instructions on how to make booties. Over one weekend, and at their own expense, Anchorage's Iditarod fans produced more than 7,000 booties and brought them to the paper's office for shipment out to the trail. Two sets even came embroidered for Mary Shields' lead dogs Cabbage and Lightning.

Many of the mushers put booties on their dogs' feet before they went out onto the punchy, icy forty-five-mile trail from Nikolai to McGrath.

McGrath was one of the larger settlements along the trail and more people meant more confusion for the mushers. Trappers' trails and snow machine tracks crisscrossed the race trail everywhere, leaving the mushers a confusing maze to find their way through. The wind blew away many of the trail markers, and flying snow filled in tracks that could have been followed. To make matters worse, the trail all looked the same. At this point the race generally followed the Kuskokwim River; however, the river, like many slow-moving plains rivers in Alaska, kept winding back on itself as if someone had started making an S and just kept going, looping back and forth ad infinitum. To follow the river through all its curves would double the distance, so instead the mushers continuously passed through spruce forest, dropped down to cross the river, then climbed into spruce forest again all the way to McGrath.

Several teams lost the trail, including Peters, who was the first to arrive in McGrath. Peters made the trip in just more than six hours, his fastest time ever from Nikolai. And he made the fast time despite losing the trail. For the last several miles into McGrath Peters followed the river, taking a long path he was sure of rather than chance losing his way by following one of the trails wandering through the brush. Behind him several more mushers lost their way and also took the river, including Ernie Baumgartner, who lived in McGrath and had trained his dogs on the very same trails.

Peters' race across the trail from Farewell brought him into McGrath for his twenty-four-hour layover with plenty of time to rest and still keep a good time spread between himself and some of the other racers. He was the only musher to make McGrath on the fourth day of the race. May and Lindner caught up the next morning, May dropping two dogs before leaving. Passing Peters at McGrath, May now regained the lead. Swenson reached McGrath eighteen hours after Peters.

For four more days teams followed the trail from Nikolai to McGrath in blowing and drifting snow that John Wood called sugary. "Everyone's saying the trails are hard and fast. They're soft and slow," he complained after a particularly difficult trail.

Bud Smyth, driving his ten dogs toward McGrath, watched the team intently. Some of them had been hit by a car, one had died, and the team had been affected by the sickness. Smyth was running well behind the leaders, and on that lonesome stretch of trail one of the thoughts that insinuated its way into his mind was giving up, calling it quits for the year. "I just decided to scratch. I let them slow down to their own speed." The dogs fell into a slow trot of maybe three or four miles an hour and Smyth assumed he was done for the year. Then his leader, Bimbo, stopped and lifted his leg on a tree. The act of total disdain for the race proved too much for the competitor in the musher. Later in McGrath he described his reaction. "When that happened I got mad at them. I blew up. Gees, I got mad. I got mad and tuned them up right there." In a deep baritone voice hoarse from shouting, he said, "We came in at a lope." And that was the end of the quitting talk as well.

A few hours behind Smyth, Brinker, having successfully avoided Allison, drove his team through the spruce, down onto the river, up into the spruce and on and on. For the endless hours on the sled, mushers must entertain a thousand thoughts between Anchorage and Nome and many of them lead to improvements in care and feeding.

Brinker, who'd already invented a pressure cooker, said later, "You know, when you're on the sled you think of everything. Like booties. Why wouldn't children's socks, like for a five-year-old, work? You could sew pads on them."

The thoughts rolled on as Brinker made his way in the dark through the confusing trails and river crossings. At times he nodded off, at least into deep drowsiness if not total sleep. This happened often, and drivers even tied themselves to the sleds rather than risk falling asleep and falling off. Between the sleep and the time he spent thinking or daydreaming, Brinker lost track now and again. At one point he woke up and looked around and everything looked as if he'd been there before. "I looked up and it all looked the same. We kept crossing the river and up into the woods. Every time I came down on the river it looked the same. I finally decided my leader had turned around on me, but I stopped and looked at what way the other dog tracks were going and sure enough he was going the right way. That Rabbit. Four times I had a conversation with him about going the right way and every time he was right. Three times we went my way and ended up on dead ends." Brinker laughed through the growing darkness that beard and wind were making of his face.

By the time the campers Dick Mackey had talked about came up off the river into Nikolai, the leaders were already approaching the gold-rush town of Iditarod, the halfway mark. In the group bringing up the rear was Harry Harris, so sick with stomach flu he spent half his time bent over the drive bow, while Richard Burmeister, a little ahead of him, had such a bad throat by the time he reached McGrath that he couldn't talk. There was little medical help available on the trail, unless one was running with the two doctors who happened to be in the race, and there was only a public health nurse at best in most of the villages, and because of their remoteness, the public health clinics were reluctant to pass out medicines since there was no guarantee as to when they'd see more. Still, help was available, because instructions for care could be sent along the ham radio network that monitored the race. While the campers were in Nikolai, a medical problem arose farther up the trail in Iditarod — one that would require the services of Dr. Jim Lanier as well as the ham radio operators at Nikolai and Iditarod.

Four days after the leaders, Lanier and the others crossed the forty-five miles to McGrath, the last mushers on the windy, confusing Kuskokwim River.

8. McGrath

In McGrath we have Christmas, New Year's and Iditarod," commented Erin Gerrin, who with Bill Penland maintained the twenty-four-hour watch to check the teams through the Kuskokwim River town. For the days the race passed through, the town took on an air of festivity, much of it emanating from McGuire's Tavern, one of two bars in town and thus one of the only two between Anchorage and Nome.

Founded in the early part of the century approximately at the head of navigation on the Kuskokwim River, the town serves as the trading hub for the central Kuskokwim country. Originally the town stood on the north side of the river, where it had grown up around Clough's Roadhouse at the confluence of the Takotna and Kuskokwim. But, as Alaska rivers will, the Takotna one year cut off one of its serpentine bends, altered its course and opened into the Kuskokwim more than a mile downstream, leaving the village isolated on a slough that eventually silted in and left the community high and dry. Over the years residents moved across the river and built the present town, leaving behind the cabins that had been homes and businesses. Rotting among the other remains are the hulks of three river boats, the *Quickstep*, the *Tana* and the upper structure of the sternwheeler *Lavelle Young*, left there when the hull was turned into a river barge. The remains of the boats were discovered in the late 1970s and the pilot house from the *Lavelle Young* was lifted out by helicopter and taken to Fairbanks because in 1903 it had carried Captain E.T. Barnette en route to his founding of that city.

Willow and alder have all but covered what's left of the old town and the new town is an odd mixture of Alaska bush village, bustling rural town and glass-and-metal technology. Log houses stand next to frame ones. Government blueprint homes line a couple of streets and one dark-green building looks like a false-fronted row of store fronts right out of a western movie. Rising above the town, giant communication towers wink red at incoming aircraft. From the modern glass-and-blue-metal Federal Aviation Administration building weather reports and pilot advisories keep airplanes in the air over the western interior. Long an air hub, McGrath was the site of the first air mail delivery in Alaska when pioneer aviator Carl Ben Eielson flew a bag of mail there from Fairbanks on February 21, 1924, marking the beginning of the end of the usefulness of dog teams. The importance of air travel to the town is evident: the main taxiway and alternate runway also serve as McGrath's main street.

The other main street, running north and south, winds in from the bush past the BLM firefighting headquarters, through a residential district, and past the school until it cuts between the FAA building and Bobby Magnuson's Fly by Nite Airline, a major air charter service in the area. Down this street the mushers came to check in with Erin Gerrin or Bill Penland, who operated out of a small room in the FAA building. Writers, photographers, mothers and wives paraded in and out of the room constantly, helping themselves to coffee, picking up what information they could, checking in and checking out, the mushers finding the families they were to stay with and generally running Erin Gerrin slightly wild.

Into the excitement of McGrath pilot Crazy Horse delivered me, bringing his small airplane down smoothly despite the winds blowing across the runway. As if it knew the way by heart, the airplane taxied along the runway, down the main street and almost up to the door of McGuire's Tavern. Inside, cries of welcome came through the dense cigarette smoke and over-flowing crowd, and the name Ed Gurtler disappeared for the rest of the trip. This was his country and everyone who knew him moved to welcome Crazy Horse. Babe and Goog Anderson, brothers of Eep, who was a day behind the leaders in the race, welcomed the pilot and bought a round of beer. Emmitt Peters, who had blazed into McGrath, stood between the Andersons nursing a glass of Seven and Seven. Several swizzle sticks from previous drinks lay in a pile on the bar and the three men talked about the race with Crazy Horse, but not for long. From the back of the room a few solid plunks from a guitar drew the pilot's attention and Crazy Horse headed for a large round table hidden in the smoke. There, Puddin' Anderson, Eep's wife, talked with a man as she and he passed a guitar back and forth, testing, plunk-ing, trying a chord or two. The man was Crazy Horse's brother Frank and they greeted each other warmly. Frank had come to McGrath from the Innoko country where he'd been trapping, to sell beaver carcasses to the mushers. He said so far he'd sold eleven beavers for twenty dollars each. Then, realizing he was speaking for the record, he said, "Write down thirty dollars."

From the corner of the bar Peters overheard the conversation about beaver and joined the group with hellos to Crazy Horse and Frank. He had another Seven and Seven in hand and as he finished one, the Anderson brothers would send over another. Cleaned up and relaxed, Emmitt Peters was enjoying his twenty-four-hour break, which was scheduled to end at 10:30 that evening. He planned to leave shortly after that. A short, thin Indian, his raven black hair slicked back, he peered at people through yellow-tinted glasses and approached them with a half-nervous grin. But he talked confidently, telling Frank to contact his sponsors if he wanted to sell beaver. He also sounded confident about the race. "I got here faster than ever — six hours from Nikolai." He looked at my notebook and said, "You tell them the competition is better than last year, but not good enough for Emmitt." Maybe his team was running better, maybe the injured Digger had improved, maybe he simply felt better or maybe the Seven and Sevens were doing their job, but the complaints of Farewell were gone. Still, he talked about this being his last year.

"I want to get established, settle back and sell my breed. I've got forty dogs and my mother and my dad and my sister are all mad at me," he said, referring to the time and money that the race was costing and the care that the rest of his dogs needed while he was away. "They're glad to see me up front, though."

He turned away to autograph someone's Iditarod Trail Annual, a sort of program for the race published by Dorothy Page — the Mother of the Iditarod — of Wasilla, a key person during the formative years of the race.

Peters returned to the conversation to say his dogs couldn't have been better. "I train hard early. Fifty miles a day for three days, then thirty miles a day for two days, then a day of rest. Two weeks before the race I slow up, let them play. I take them four miles out, four miles back. That lets the cuts heal and the muscles heal and grow. Then on the race, they come up to a peak and by McGrath they can't get any better." Between sips on his drink he took a whiff of antihistamine from an inhaler.

"Still got Digger in lead. He doesn't run as well as the others but as long as he gees and haws, he's fine."

Digger had been with Peters as long as he'd been running the race. During the first couple of years the dog ran in tandem lead with another of Peters' famous leaders, Nugget. Nugget led the team Carl Huntington had won the race with in 1974 and the next year, back in Peters' team for his first Iditarod, she led him to victory as he set a record that was to stand for five years. Sadly, the year after she won the race for Peters, Nugget slipped her harness while they were training near Anchorage. Two days later she was found dead by the side of a road, the victim of a passing automobile.

At a shout from Goog Anderson, Peters returned to the bar where there was yet another Seven and Seven ready for him. By this time he was talking about leaving around midnight and as he pulled on the unending supply of drinks, the hour was set back farther and farther. Goog and Babe kept him going as he talked, signed annuals and generally enjoyed his time off from the race.

Babe and Goog weren't too happy with brother Eep's progress in the race. Babe, who had run the race himself a couple of times and done well, said, "Don't talk about Eep. We're mad at Eep." Their brother, whose team had been sick, was a full day behind the leaders. The brothers hadn't given up, though. They figured with a storm coming, a whole new race could begin right there in McGrath and Eep could catch up and still be right in the middle of the leaders.

Not everything in town was happening in the tavern. Joe May, still relentless in his schedule, came into town shortly after ten in the morning of the fifth day of the race. While Peters passed his time at the bar, May fed and rested his dogs according to schedule for a little more than four hours. Then, after two in the afternoon, leaving two of his original fourteen dogs behind, May crossed the airfield and went over the bank onto the frozen Kuskokwim, back in first place, out front and chasing the only team in front of him, the imaginary, ephemeral Number One, out into the gold country that gave the race its name.

All day word rippled through McGuire's as mushers came into McGrath. Lee Gardino, despite the loss of his leader and the troubles he was having keeping the team going without one, was the first rookie to arrive. Others followed, and each brought a wave through McGuire's. "Joe and Susan." "Joe Garnie." "Joe May's leaving."

At the round table Crazy Horse picked up a guitar. He plunked a string, then another, then struck a chord and before long was playing and singing a nasal country and western tune with Puddin' and Frank joining him. As people gathered around to listen and drink beer, ham radio operator Herb Rosenthal, in a corner behind the players, attempted to maintain contact with the trail over the noisy interference around him.

Because McGrath provided the only stores, bars and restaurants along the way, plus invitations to private homes, many mushers elected to spend their twenty-four-hour layovers there; Joe Redington, Susan Butcher, Jerry Riley, Terry Adkins, Sonny Lindner, Gary Hokkanen and Lee Gardino all joined Peters for a day. Others rested briefly.

Swenson, who already had stopped for his twenty-four hours at Farewell, instead of following May out of town, stayed, watching Peters, apparently keying his race to the team he figured to be his strongest competition. That didn't mean he was watching only Peters, though. A few others had him worried, too, and he kept tabs on all of them. The watching led to a humorous early-morning confusion.

After the rule infraction called against Peters the previous year, Swenson watched his own act closely. His wife, Kathy, joined him in McGrath, but he wouldn't let her near the dogs for fear someone would consider her some kind of outside help. He was particularly worried about Riley calling him on something. That didn't keep Kathy from watching the other mushers, though, and letting Swenson know as others prepared to leave. Several had Swenson's interest, and one he wasn't sure of was Terry Adkins, the air force veterinarian from Wyoming. About 5 A.M., Adkins got out of bed, went outside and rummaged through his sled bag. Word filtered through the houses: "Terry's up." This wakened Don Honea, who began working on his own sled and giving his dogs some water. That in turn brought Swenson to his feet and just about the time he was awake and moving, Adkins, who started it all, smiled at everyone and went back to bed, leaving two wide-awake mushers to decide what to do. Honea, who was farther along in his preparation, finally went. Swenson waited, apparently figuring as long as Peters was in sight, he was all right.

Peters, for his part, was sound asleep upstairs in the FAA building after having been rescued from McGuire's. Neither Swenson nor Riley had stopped in at the tavern, and while some of the others did drop by, it was only for a beer or two. The Andersons kept Peters in tow throughout the afternoon as he pushed back his time of departure. By the middle of the afternoon, he was talking about leaving at midnight rather than 10:30, and as the winter sun began to set the hour was pushed to 2 A.M. Tales of Peters' adventures in McGuire's spread through the town and by 6:30 Shellie Vandiver had had enough of it.

With a friend along for support, she confronted Peters and the Andersons, who denied anything but having a good time. "We love Emmitt," Goog told her.

"If you love Emmitt, why do this to him," she asked.

Then, with a little help, she and her friend ushered him out of the tavern and over to the FAA building, where they bundled him into a sleeping bag and he slept until morning.

Peters' leaving didn't stop the party, just slowed it for a moment. The revelry went long into the night with the Gurtlers and Puddin' Anderson providing the music. Revelers had come by plane from Anchorage and as far away as Nome to join the McGrath regulars and watch the race pass through. Peters wasn't the only musher to stay too long at the bar. A couple of others did, too, and one tried to go back on the trail while he was still in no condition for it. Twice, onlookers had to chase his team as his dogs went the wrong way down the runway, heading back toward Anchorage. On the second try the helpers turned the team in the proper direction and the dogs hauled the musher down onto the river.

Peters slept his party off and at 7:40 in the morning of the sixth day into the race was finally ready to leave, about ten hours after he could have. The time lost didn't bother him, though, nor did it bother Swenson, who saw him preparing and signed out right in front of him, at 7:38. By the time they left, Joe May already was in Ophir, thirty-six miles ahead, and preparing to leave for the long stretch to Iditarod.

Over two days, the leaders passed into and out of McGrath and as they left the slower mushers took their places. Each had his own story of the trail, his own joys and difficulties, some humorous, some of danger, but mostly of trials and hard work. For Mel Adkins, the truck driver from Willow, the difficulty he ran into in McGrath spanned a century. As Adkins was preparing to leave, a television crew from the British Broadcasting Corporation tested his patience with its own more modern problems. The crew wanted night shots of a musher leaving McGrath, but the cameramen were used to scenes they could manipulate. First, Adkins, in the glare of spotlights, had to say goodbye three times to the family he'd stayed with before the shot was acceptable. Then he was told to bring the resting dog team to its feet while a cameraman tried to get the right picture. No good. "Can you get them to lie down again?" That can't exactly be done on command, but let a racing husky alone for a while and invariably he'll lie down. Soon all the dogs took advantage of not moving and curled up again.

At a cue from the director, Adkins called them up for the second time and the motion was good enough for the cameras. With the dogs standing, the director told the musher to drive the team about a hundred feet ahead and then stop at a spotlighted circle on the runway. Adkins agreed and chucked the team ahead, stopping with the sled in the circle of light. But one of the cameramen wasn't satisfied with the footage.

"Can you back them up and try again?"

Adkins looked at the team in helplessness. You don't just tell ten dogs to back up when they're all straining to go forward. Dogs don't go backwards. The musher stood there a moment, frustration in his expression, then, deciding, with a quiet *hike* he disappeared out of the circle of light, moved like a shadow across the runway and dropped down onto the river and the quiet security of the trail, far out of civilization's camera angles and lights. He left behind a slightly befuddled BBC crew standing in the glow of its own lights on the runway.

As Adkins traveled down the frozen Kuskokwim out of McGrath, young Rome Gilman and Bud Smyth pulled into town in the dark within an hour of each other. While their dogs slept in the street outside, the two fell into chairs in the checker's room of the FAA building. Gilman, a little over eighteen years old and the youngest ever to run the race, hadn't been living up to his promise to win. The pen he was carrying to endorse the check in Nome had long been forgotten. But he was already planning for the next year, explaining, "I know just how I'm going to train. Those guys told me we were training just the same, but they weren't."

Smyth, tired and hoarse from tuning up his team after they almost quit on him, listened to Gilman's complaints. He was looking at someone more than twenty years his junior, young enough to be his son, and finally the complaints were too much. He regarded Gilman for another moment, then said, "I wish I was eighteen. If I was eighteen, I'd put those dogs on my back and run all the way to Nome. Got a good pair of lungs, but my throat's a little sore. I feel a hundred years old, maybe a hundred and four."

Young or old, both showed the effects of the trail, and their conversation gradually dropped off until they were leaning back against the wall, asleep where they sat.

In the bright sunlight of the twenty-second consecutive severe clear day recorded at McGrath, with the temperature around zero, Bethel lawyer Myron Angstman fed his dogs outside the FAA building. Nick, the combination English-Irish setter who looked mostly Irish, cavorted around the rest of the team, which was still in harness. Sled dogs seldom get the chance to run free. Though trained, once they're loose, they have a habit of forgetting where they belong and will head out for adventure. One of Del Allison's wheel dogs, Andy, had had an overnight foray in McGrath and came back too tired to run for a day. Nick's was a different case.

"Nick's doing fine," Angstman said. "Have to use a little setter psychology on him. He sleeps in the sled or inside whenever I do. I let him run loose a lot. He's physically tough enough, but the stress has really bothered him. He was really down the second day but he's picked up since. He's eating well, drinking well. He won't drink outside, though."

Nick for his part ran around the team, playful. He jumped and nipped, took a bite of his food and didn't wander far, behaving much like a pet around his master while the man worked. The dog looked as if he was enjoying the whole thing, like a dog out in the park to chase a Frisbee or jumping at the back door to go out for a walk. Angstman said Nick belonged in the team. It wasn't just a joke to take a setter to Nome; he expected the dog to pull his weight, do his job over the long haul.

While Nick cavorted, across town another dog was part of a more serious drama, one that had been unfolding since the race the year before. Dehydration had always been a serious problem for the dogs on the trail — for mushers too, for that matter. But where a man would take water when he needed it, sometimes, although a dog would need moisture desperately, he'd refuse to drink. Mushers had tried all manner of methods to get hesitant dogs to drink, flavoring water with meat juices, mixing extra water into food, and whatever else they could think of, but even then there were times when dogs just wouldn't drink. During the previous year's race a few drivers had adopted an idea from veterinarians who treat larger animals and experimented with intubation, running a tube down a dog's throat to get water into the stomach. The practice immediately became controversial, with some mushers adamantly in favor and others, along with many of the race vets, just as adamantly against it. Still others were apprehensive, watching to see how it worked and how the controversy would be resolved. Race rule-makers decided to allow tubing, but only at checkpoints with a vet in attendance.

Dick Mackey had been a proponent of tubing, defending it as a justifiable way to keep the dogs healthy, and he'd done it the previous year when he won the race. When the team his son Rick was driving got sick, some of the dogs refused to take water and in

McGrath it was decided to give them liquid through the tube.

With race veterinarian Tony Funk and the television crew from the BBC watching, the tube was inserted down one dog's throat, but to the horror of everyone watching, the tube went down the wrong pipe. Funk reported later the dog was unhurt because he realized the mistake before any water was pumped into the dog's lungs, but it was only because the vet was able to work quickly. To be fair, there had not been any injury, and just getting water into a dehydrated dog had to be of help, no matter how it was done. Fortunately the minds of other mushers already were at work on the problems of the trail, and the tubing controversy would be resolved before the race was over.

As Brinker thought about booties and others thought about watering reluctant dogs, another trail-inspired idea was paying off for Walter Kaso, the easy-going bush resident who'd come to Alaska from Brooklyn. Kaso's team was one of the few that managed to escape most of the illness problems of the trail. Mackey had once told him that if he fried the liver he fed his dogs instead of giving it to them raw, they probably wouldn't develop diarrhea. The experiment worked during training, so Kaso fried all the liver he had sent out along the trail, and most of his dogs never did get sick. At McGrath, Kaso still had all sixteen of the big, rangy sled dogs that had started the race. Few others could match that, even with only a third of the race gone; among the leaders, Swenson still had all fourteen of his dogs, but May had dropped two and most of the others had dropped at least one. Riley, who dropped four in McGrath, now was left with eight.

Crazy Horse, a little under the weather from the jam session at McGuire's, wouldn't allow himself to fly for twenty-four hours after he'd been drinking, which gave him the opportunity to watch the parade through the checkpoint for another day. The mushers in the parade somewhat resembled a small community moving across the face of Alaska and as a community were subject to all a community's attributes. For one, rumors ran rampant, growing in the imagination of people alone on the trail. One of the rumors that bothered the mushers had it that Isaac Okleasik still had many of his dogs running on the neckline. That meant he had come as far as McGrath barely working some of his dogs. The neckline connects a dog's collar to the gangline and serves only to keep the dog pointed straight ahead. If a musher wants to rest a dog, he'll take him off the tugline so the dog can just run along with the team and not have to pull. The fact that Isaac hadn't needed the tuglines led some mushers to fear he might later be able to hook all the dogs up and just pull away from the other teams. Herbie Nayokpuk, however, like Isaac, an Eskimo from the northwest coast who'd been running near him much of the time, said Okleasik hooked the dogs up once he was out of sight of checkpoints and took them off again before entering the next one, just to worry people.

In the morning the ongoing party at McGuire's wound down to its lowest ebb, but by midafternoon the place began filling again with the Anderson brothers holding down their corner of the L-shaped bar and Puddin' plunking her guitar at the round table. At times the crowd kept three bartenders hustling. In the back of the bar, his equipment spread over the pool table, Rome Gilman worked on his sled.

Eep Anderson had made it into town to join his family and made his preparations to leave while in the bar. He had brought his sled indoors for packing and even at two in the morning, his young daughter Squeaky and niece Anita followed along to help.

Eep was all seriousness. His brothers watched but they weren't feeding him drinks. As he moved in and out of the bar, the two girls followed, trying to help and feeling important.

Said Squeaky, "Dad, your ax is very dull. Look at this."

Eep looked, shrugged, and went back about his work.

Anita: "Take this?" She held up a bundle of cloth that looked down-filled.

Eep: "Nah."

Anita: "You'll freeze to death."

A man at the bar leaned into the scene and said to Anita, "You're tired, you ought to get home to bed."

Anita: "Yeah, but I got to see my uncle off."

The observer muttered some sort of retort.

And Anita responded, "Yeah, but he's not your uncle." Turning back to her work she held up a handful of dog harnesses. "Fourteen dogs, Uncle Eep?"

"Eleven," Anderson said and Anita went about sorting out the right harnesses for the team.

By the time Anderson headed off into the growing light of dawn, his family felt a little happier about his chances. The dogs looked better, jumping and wagging their tails after a good fourteen hours of rest. As it turned out, the day was Puddin' and Eep's fifteenth wedding anniversary and just before he left, they popped the cork on a bottle of champagne for a goodbye toast. Then they kissed, and he was gone, following the rest of the teams over the bank and down onto the river for the short trip to Takotna, where he had trained.

Not everyone made it out of town so easily. Susan Butcher, delayed by Joe Redington, had to drive her team around the block a couple of times as if looking for a parking place. Since she and Redington were pacing each other, she had to wait for him to leave. He had changed sleds at McGrath, replacing the one he broke at Knik. With all the gear he carried, it took Redington some time to pack the new sled and in the meantime Butcher, all ready to go, had to drive her anxious team through the streets of McGrath until Redington was ready. Once his sled was packed, he called his dogs up and the two teams headed for the river, and the now well-worn trail.

Behind them, still in McGrath, Karl Clauson, the other eighteen-year-old still left in the race, was readying his gear. Taking advantage of the McGrath Post Office, Clauson shipped his dirty laundry back home to Mom in Wasilla. Unfortunately he didn't check the laundry bag and along with the clothes, he shipped his packet of stamped, postmarked cachets, the envelopes that were part of the mandatory gear he had to have to clear each checkpoint. The cachets were part of the commemorative aspect of the race, recalling the early mail deliveries by dog team, and after being marked again in Nome would be sold to benefit the race. But Clauson managed to ship his home, and the checker failed to notice as the musher left McGrath. Farther along the line another checker would, though, and the mistake would cost Clauson at least a day.

Back at the FAA checkpoint room in the early morning hours, Brinker slid into one of the steel-gray government chairs. He'd just been through the trail on the snaky part of the river and had had arguments with his lead dog. He was tired, but he was still ahead of Allison and, despite the fatigue, from his position near the rear of the pack he still could look at the leaders through the binoculars of humor.

"I'll bet Swenson is resting three of four hours outside the checkpoints so he can come in smokin'," Brinker said, his dark four-day growth of beard looking like anyone else's ten-day. "Emmitt will make his move at Grayling. He might have got drunk at McGuire's but once he's on the runners he's as serious as a heart attack."

As he talked, Brinker came more alert, leaning forward, his hands on the knees of his bulky army-issue arctic gear. "Guess I'll go harness up my troops, see if we can't close the gap on the big guys." With that the former soldier headed out the door into the darkness.

Behind Brinker still more mushers were to arrive in McGrath. It took almost a full five days for everyone to pass through. Harry Harris waited in town a day for his fellow Fairbanks musher, Kelly Wages, but once Wages reached the checkpoint he decided to scratch, the second to drop out of the race. Then the last of the teams cleared McGrath, although it took Don Montgomery three tries because his dogs enjoyed the comforts of the town. Each time Montgomery headed down to the river, the lead dogs turned around and headed back for McGrath.

By now all the drivers had taken their twenty-four-hour layovers and as they headed into the middle third of the race there would be fewer changes in position as the faster teams separated themselves from the rest until the race moved along in bunches of teams. May continued his chase out front after the elusive Number One and behind him Peters, Swenson, Riley, Lindner and Honea followed, themselves chased by Albert, Terry Adkins, Baumgartner, Redington, Butcher and Mackey.

9. McGrath to Ophir

AFTER SPENDING ABOUT SIX HOURS IN MCGRATH AND IGNORING THE COM-
forts it offered, Joe May dropped two dogs and drove the remaining twelve across the McGrath runway, down the riverbank onto
the Kuskokwim and headed for the confluence with the Takotna,
on his way into the gold country where strikes and stampedes in
the early 1900s led to the blazing of the original Iditarod Trail.

May followed a trail first used by prospector Thomas Ganes
who, with other potential gold miners, crossed the Kuskokwim
River into the upper Innoko Drainage and struck gold at Ganes
Creek in 1906. For that winter and the next summer as many as
eight or nine hundred miners managed to make their way to
Ganes Creek. As prospectors overflowed the available claims they
spread out, and strikes were made on nearby streams: Yankee
Creek, Fourth of July Creek, Cripple Creek and Ophir Creek. But
the push for gold was relentless and the men moved farther and
farther from the original strike. Among them were William Dikeman and his partner John Beaton, who floated back down the
Innoko River to the river known then as the Haiditarod and up the
Haiditarod until they made their own strike, the first in the Iditarod District, in 1908.

With the first influx of prospectors into the upper Innoko country, a winter trail was cut from Kaltag, which lies to the northwest on the Yukon River, down across the marshy Innoko Lowlands, through the village of Tolstoi, and on to Ophir and Takotna. The trail was used to bring mail and supplies to settlements along the creeks and on into Takotna in 1906, '07 and '08. After the Iditarod discovery, miners and freighters cut a loop that began at Takotna, ran through to the mining communities of Flat and Iditarod, and returned by way of Ophir. In 1910, when Goodwin and Brooks surveyed the trail from Nome and Seward, they included the Iditarod loop rather than the trail through Tolstoi because Iditarod looked as if it would become the population center for the district.

Since the first strikes in 1906, miners have worked the Ophir District almost continuously, if not actively mining, at least main taining the claims. When the United States cut the price of gold loose in the late 1970s, the price rose enough to make mining profitable again and miners once more came into the district in large numbers, and long inactive claims were working again.

The race trail first followed the Takotna River from McGrath to Takotna, crossing and recrossing another winding river and following low hills and scrub brush for about seventeen miles. May's team took just about three hours, then he stopped for the nine-hour rest his schedule demanded before pushing on to Ophir, another nineteen miles down the trail.

Takotna had grown up with the mining district and by 1910 was a riverboat landing and supply point for the claims and settlements on the creeks, supporting several roadhouses and freighting businesses. The town has survived, supported largely by an Air Force station, but still serving as a supply center. A population of fewer than fifty lives and works in the collection of maybe a dozen buildings situated around an air strip along the river. Around the town, mining roads and Cat trails — named for the bulldozers that made them — cut through the country in several directions. A wagon road built between 1919 and 1923, now maintained by the state, leads on to the northwest from Takotna toward Ophir.

This road overlaid the original Iditarod Trail to Ophir, and the race trail followed it, giving the mushers relatively easy going along the nineteen miles to the next checkpoint. Even with the easy trail, however, some of the teams apparently lost their way;

anyone following the race by air could see tracks in large loops off the trail where dogs and drivers took unscheduled detours. Those loops and the time spent on wrong trails were costly to many of the teams. No matter how diligent the trailblazers were, natural elements constantly conspired to tear down trail markers. Few mushers could say they made it all the way to Nome without losing the trail at least once or twice. Although those experienced with the trail lost the way occasionally, lost time was particularly telling on the new mushers. Gary Hokkanen felt that he had a fast team, but he kept getting lost. "Knowing the trail helps," he said. "I kept catching the leaders, then getting lost. They'd pass and I'd never even see them."

As May pushed on toward Ophir, the rest of the mushers began funneling out of McGrath, not wanting to let him get any farther ahead, particularly with a storm threatening — a storm that could put a large separation between them. The situation was the kind May had been hoping for. "My race was planned. The thing that could do it for me was dirty weather," May stated afterward. "If I got nasty weather and a heavy trail I could be competitive with those faster teams. My dogs are slower but they're awful tough and they're consistent. I was watching the weather real close. The dogs were tough enough. With some dirty weather between us, I could have pulled the plug and got a hundred miles ahead — they never would have saw me until Nome."

But Swenson, Honea, Peters, Lindner and Riley saw the storm coming too, and knew what May's team was capable of. They weren't going to let May get that far ahead if they could help it, and they set a fast pace as they chased him toward Ophir. Riley, running with only eight dogs, took less than three hours on the trail to Takotna, and the others ran just as fast. And as they raced along the trail past the historic gold creeks, the storm clouds gathered closer around the leaders. On the day after they left McGrath, the weather service was reporting hundred-knot winds at Ophir, winds that were pushing the storm clouds closer.

The high winds cost a day of flying and by the time Crazy Horse and I were headed toward Ophir, most of the teams had passed. The airstrip at Ophir was three miles from the checkpoint, so Crazy Horse simply landed on the river, dropping me right where I wanted to be. He wanted to return immediately to McGrath and prepared to take off again, but the river was too narrow to allow the airplane to turn around to rise into the wind. To turn the plane, a man had to hold onto a rope attached to the wing, dig his heels into the snow and act as a pivot while the pilot revved the engine and the airplane spun on the pivot. The trick worked, though it took a good healthy pull on the arms, but once turned Crazy Horse took off easily.

Many of the buildings from Ophir's gold rush are still standing. The gold strike at Ophir Creek came two years after the one on Ganes Creek, but the location proved the more strategic commerce and communication point and Ophir grew into a larger community, the population center of the Innoko Mining District and a main stopping point on the Iditarod Trail. At least two roadhouses were operated in Ophir into the 1920s and the post office remained open until 1957. On and off since that time people have lived there, but the population at the time of the race had dwindled to one, and many of the original buildings have been scavenged for construction materials or were destroyed by a fire in 1978.

The cabin that served as the checkpoint was owned by Dick and Audra Forsgren, who used it as a getaway place from their home in McGrath. The cabin was a stout, square-logged bastion, built in 1936 by a Norwegian miner named John Myklebust, who obviously knew how to build. The cabin had survived to the present with no major repair work needed. The Forsgrens, like many along the trail, had been involved with Iditarod since the race began. Dick had served several terms on the race's board of directors and the two had maintained the checkpoint at Ophir since Year One. This year, Audra welcomed everybody with a smile and a warm bowl of rib-sticking soup. But, despite the warmth of the welcome, there was a gloom in the Myklebust cabin.

Lee Gardino, the leading rookie musher into McGrath, had come into Ophir not ten hours behind the leaders, but two days later he was still there. He sat on a couch by the window, his face down in his hands and his brother sitting next to him nervously trying to make the musher somehow feel better.

Gardino had a smile at his mouth, but not in his eyes. He was just sitting there, waiting until Bobby Magnuson could fly in and take him and his team back to McGrath, where they could catch a flight home. For Gardino and his dogs, the race was over.

He had brought the team as far as Ophir mostly by his own will, without the help of a lead dog. But finally even his own determination couldn't carry the team. When they left Ophir, Gardino said, the dogs were healthy, even playful, but they wouldn't move down the trail. They'd go maybe one or two hundred yards, then just jump off to the side and lie down or roll around in the snow.

"It's in their minds," the dejected Gardino explained. "They're healthy and happy, but they don't want to run. They won't go without a leader to pull them along — keep them strung out and going." Gardino had managed to drive the team just ten miles out of Ophir, sometimes a couple hundred yards at a time, but after those ten frustrating miles, he turned around and went back to scratch. The twenty-mile round trip with the reluctant dogs took Gardino twenty hours. Then he sat another day in Ophir waiting to be taken out.

As he sat there in John Myklebust's cabin, those unsmiling eyes reflected all the money, time, hopes, disappointment and embarrassment at having to quit. No matter how tough or capable he was, he was not going to Nome because one dog, his leader, broke down and had to be dropped.

The drone of an airplane overhead relieved some of the discomfort, at least giving Gardino something to do as he began gathering his gear to meet Magnuson for the flight out. But before they could go, Magnuson had to check out another victim of the race.

Out on the Innoko River runway at one of those serpentine curves was a small plane nose down in the snow on the bank, its tail assembly high in the air and one wing buried. The crash was the result of a takeoff with too much power, too much wind and not enough runway before the curve. Fortunately no one had been hurt and the owner had asked Magnuson, if he could, to fly the plane out. The wing was bent and a ski damaged along with parts of the tail, but the pilot figured Magnuson could do it. And sometime after the race, Magnuson went in, jury-rigged some repairs, got the plane airborne, and managed, in spite of the damage, to fly it all the way to Anchorage.

While Magnuson was looking at the wreckage, Gardino and his brother moved Lee's gear down to the airplane and soon the musher and his dogs flew off toward McGrath.

The moving of Gardino's equipment from the cabin floor uncovered a dark irregular stain in the gold-colored rug. Audra, catching someone's gaze toward the stain, explained. Several drivers had slept on the floor the previous night when the bulk of the teams went through, among them young Karl Clauson. During the night, according to Audra, he kept several others awake with his restlessness and eventually his screams. Audra related that he'd yelled several times, "Oh, no, not again!" In between those shouts, he'd mumbled something about Bigfoot. And while he slept and wrestled with his dreams, he'd developed a nosebleed. By morning the blood from his nose covered an irregular circle five inches in diameter, darkening the faded rug. She said he'd appeared unfazed, though, and went out with the rest to harness dogs and hit the trail for the next stop, Iditarod.

During the day and overnight on the ninth day of the race, as the leaders were running toward the Yukon River, several mushers toward the rear of the race stopped at Ophir: artist Jon Van Zyle; Gayle Nienhueser, who injured his arm at the start, Terry McMullin, a trapper from Eagle who had to drive his dogs 150 miles just to get to a road so he could drive to Anchorage for the race; Brinker, and Allison. Brinker, though, was still maintaining his lead in the bet with Allison and left about five and a half hours before Allison got there.

Also arriving were two mushers off on a different adventure. Dennis Kogl and Laurie Larson had just driven a dog team from Mount McKinley National Park to McGrath. There had been no groomed trail for them and they had taken forty days to slog through deep snow for three hundred miles through the park and the Alaska Range. But that was just the beginning of their adventure. Now they were on their way to Prudhoe Bay, following the Iditarod Trail as far as Nome, where they planned to head north along the coast of the Chukchi Sea and across the arctic to the oilfield. They hoped to make the trip before spring brought the ice breakup, after which they couldn't cross rivers.

Their outfit was quite different from the ones the racers had. Their team of big eighty- and ninety-pound freighting dogs pulled two sleds tied together, one behind the other. Instead of riding the runners and driving from the rear of a sled, Kogl and Larson had tied shortened skis into the gangline in front of the first sled, behind the wheel dogs. The driver slipped into the skis and then held on to the gee pole, a length of birch that extended forward from the sled and gave the musher leverage to steer the heavy load. In effect, the driver was skiing behind the dogs and steering at the same time. In the early days, when the principal reason for dog teams was to haul freight, the gee pole was standard equipment, so named because it was on the right side of the sled. As the main purpose for dog teams changed from freighting to racing, the gee pole became an unneeded appendage, since the lighter racing sleds could be steered just as easily from the rear and were faster without the pole. Still it served well for the kind of trip Kogl and Larson were attempting.

Their dogs looked to be in excellent shape and brought admiring comments from the mushers. So far they hadn't had any problems with any of the dogs and Kogl felt that was due at least in part to the more relaxed pace. When Brinker told him his dogs looked so good they ought to have been in the race, Kogl told him, "That's why they look good—they're *not* in the race."

Even though they weren't part of the competition, Kogl and Larson were welcomed to a bowl of Audra Forsgren's soup at the table in the Myklebust cabin. While conversation around the table never strayed far from the race, at the few times it did the subject was usually the Alaska lands debate. Congress at the time was considering the disposition of federal lands in Alaska and, to prevent any development from intruding into wilderness lands, the Carter administration had named several new national monuments in Alaska to protect the areas temporarily. The action had brought immediate and loud reaction from Alaskans, the loudest being against the declarations. Most Alaskans were affected.

McMullin, for one. McMullin ran a trapline out of Eagle, in northeast Alaska, a village that had become a hotbed of resistance to the monuments. Although most of his trapline lay outside the Yukon-Charlie National Monument, McMullin did have some small line cabins along his trapline inside the area and had planned to build a home inside what were now the boundaries.

Kogl, who operated a dog team tour business in Mount McKinley National Park, had a cabin inside the new Denali National Monument, an addition to the park. He too was worried about losing his place.

A radio played in the cabin most of the time and at every newscast people stopped talking to listen to another update on the lands debate in Congress. In between the newscasts the station, KYAK Big Country Radio in Anchorage, played, about every third song, a twangy country tune called "The Old Iditarod Trail." After a while the song became so tedious that even the mushers who liked country music winced when they heard the introductory chords.

Even something as close to home as the lands debate couldn't keep minds off the race for long. And even for these drivers, so far out of contention that they had no chance for a top spot, the race was consuming, and their experiences on the trail filled the conversation.

Brinker and Van Zyle fell into a discussion about sleeping on the sled, and Brinker related his experience of falling asleep while he was heading into McGrath. Van Zyle said he worried about it enough that he had actually tied himself to his sled so he wouldn't fall off if he was dozing.

Brinker harnessed his troops and left Ophir, and a few hours later Allison joined the crew at the table. The topic of conversation remained the same; only the speakers changed.

McMullin looked at the others and said, "Somebody ought to record the conversations guys have with their dogs."

To that Nienhueser nodded his head and agreed, "I caught myself a couple of times talking to them. If one ever answers, I'd quit."

"Oh, I've got one who talks back," Allison said, "I talk and she barks and yowls, just talkin' to me."

But Van Zyle offered the clincher, saying his dogs even talked with each other: "My leader last night came back to talk with my wheelers. Just, 'Hi, how are you? Beautiful night.' Then he turned right back to the trail and went on."

Allison recalled his team picking up and chasing through the biggest flock of ptarmigan he'd ever seen. He said there must have been three hundred birds in one group he saw flying across the trail between McGrath and Takotna.

The mention of McGrath brought up a few tales about the town and taverns and the toll they had taken on some of the mushers. Audra, on hearing of Emmitt Peters' exploits in McGuire's, said he was still looking a little rocky at the time he came through Ophir.

One of the other mushers mentioned finding a team belonging to one of the Eskimos anchored in the trail to Takotna. A mile or so farther he encountered the musher himself, asleep in the middle of the trail. When awakened, the musher asked where his team was and then trudged back down the trail toward the dogs and sled.

A rumor was following the race that another Eskimo, Herbie Nayokpuk, one of the most popular racers, had sick dogs that wouldn't eat, and he was looking for a place to scratch.

Nienhueser was still nursing his injured arm, wearing the removable splint when he could, but taking it off when it got in the way as he worked with the dogs. He was still nursing dogs too, after their fight in Rainy Pass. A couple had cuts and gashes and one had a big gouge out of his paw, but Nienhueser said the dogs for the most part were coming back well.

Though the day had sunshine in it, clouds were forming on the horizon and the winds were gusting. Kogl and Larson offered me a ride all the way to Iditarod but time pressed and it didn't look as if I could afford the loss of two or three days.

Crazy Horse had landed but said he'd rather pick me up at the airstrip up the trail a ways, so Dennis and Laurie said at least ride with them that far.

Off we went, Dennis on the skis up front, Laurie on the rear sled and me in the middle, standing on the runners of the front sled. Standing on the runners brought a rush to the senses: the gentle rasping shush of the runners, the slight rush of wind in the face, the visual joy of watching the dogs pull as they plodded ahead, and a feeling that the whole operation was alive as the twists in the trail moved through the sled's bending wood into my feet and up my legs.

We passed several old buildings, fading and falling remnants of the hectic mining that once took place here. For a moment we were Harry Revelle and his men hauling the mail from Seward to Iditarod over this same trail in 1914. All too soon we came to the airstrip and after stopping for only a moment, Dennis and Laurie went on and disappeared into the alder at the end of the strip, following their adventure into the mountains.

The heavy whine of an airplane engine ended any reverie and soon we took off toward Iditarod.

Behind us we left the comfort of the Myklebust cabin and Audra Forsgren's thick soup. Ahead clouds gathered.

Through the rumor mill on the trail word came that the storm had hit, piling up snow, blowing the trail away, and that Joe May had stopped.

10. Ophir to Iditarod

OUT OF OPHIR ONTO THE NINETY-MILE TRAIL TO IDITAROD, FIVE DAYS INTO the race, Joe May, as he had most of the way, was leading everyone. He left Ophir in the morning, and beginning in the early afternoon the racers right behind him passed through, stopping only a few minutes. First Honea. Then Swenson, Peters, Katongan, Riley and Lindner, checking in, checking out and following May out into the Beaver Mountains.

The trail out of Ophir followed flat ground through thinning stands of spruce, gradually climbing into the Beavers, a range of the Kuskokwim Mountains. A nicely cut trail went through some birch stands and up terraced slopes, but as it rose into the low mountains the trees thinned, exposing the dogs and mushers to the increasing winds that began howling unobstructed off rounded and bare mountaintops — mountaintops that in gentler weather looked like bald heads with rings of hair beginning at the temples.

But this wasn't gentle weather. Fierce winds blew snow off the mountains and into the faces of the dogs and mushers, and flung away the hot-pink surveyor's tape marking the way. In minutes, the snow filled in and obliterated what trail there was and whatever tracks might have been left. The dirty weather May had wanted was closing in around the race — the kind of weather he thought his dogs could slog through while faster teams had to stop. But when the weather hit, not everything went the way May had hoped, and when his team ran into the storm, instead of slogging through it, the dogs took sick and the whole works ground to a halt.

In the Beaver Mountains, in a storm, with the trail sickness finally overtaking his team, May broke his schedule — the schedule that had kept him in front much of the way so far. And there in the Beaver Mountains May caught up with Number One.

Throughout the race May had been chasing the shadow of the legendary Leonhard Seppala, following the ghostly runner tracks of the man to whom the race was dedicated. Now, alone, Joe May had a talk with Leonhard Seppala.

"I caught Seppala. We had a long conversation. Different things happen to different people out there. Some people aren't sensitive to those sorts of things and maybe it wouldn't bother them," May recalled, "but if you're susceptible to that sort of thing it can be a little spooky.

"I had to camp out there in the Beavers. There was nobody within thirty miles. It's really desolate, the wind was blowing, the dogs were sick — I had eleven out of twelve dogs sick. I went down into a gully and I cut some spruce boughs. I bedded the dogs on the boughs and dug a snow cave for myself. There was some dead wood and I got a nice big fire going.

"It was eerie. It got real eerie. The wind was moaning up on the summits. I put up a tarp for the wind and I laid out there that night. If it was ever going to get you, it was going to then. First you're alone, then after a while you don't think you *are* alone. Yeah, it's spooky, real spooky. The dogs felt the same way I did. When it's spooky that way, the dogs are the same way. They're very quiet, very quiet.

"I talked with Seppala and he kept asking, 'What are you doing, you fool?' He had the inside track, he knew the outcome. All he tells me is to go faster."

On that night as he talked with Seppala in his gully camp with his dogs lying quiet on their spruce boughs, May had to come to a decision. With eleven dogs sick, he was going to have to break the schedule that had kept him out front. "After you spend that much time with the dogs, when the dogs are sick, you're sick. When they got sick I pampered them and fed them every couple of hours. The sickest dogs ate steak, I ate dried food. When the dogs got sick I cut my daily mileage in half and ran that way for five days."

Thirty miles behind him, the storm had brought everyone else to a halt, too, and the racers behind May waited, watching for someone who would go first and break trail. Many of the mushers took shelter in a cabin built on a site where once had stood the only roadhouse between Iditarod and Ophir. In 1916 when a mail route was established along the northern section of the Iditarod loop, Fritz Walter built the roadhouse about thirty-three miles from Ophir. The roadhouse burned down in 1924, but in 1931 the Alaska Road Commission built a shelter cabin on the site of Fritz's Roadhouse and the remains of that cabin, though leaky, provided shelter to the mushers as they waited out the Beaver Mountain storm. Group after group of teams passed through, using the cabin for what little shelter it offered from the winds.

May nursed his dogs until a break in the storm. Then he broke camp and headed at a slow pace toward Iditarod.

Behind him his followers broke camp, too, and the chase began all over again. Somebody stood up and went, and the rest followed the trailbreaker. They followed May into Iditarod, Honea arriving first, but the chase had a different tone by then with May cutting his speed in half. He wasn't going to stay out front any more.

Even with the race moving again and teams passing along the trail regularly, there was little for others to follow. The incessant winds filled the runner tracks with snow almost as soon as they were made, so no team made the difficult crossing on a completely passable trail. Ron Aldrich, who left Ophir just hours behind the group behind May, reported that the trail simply was gone. Winds were hitting forty miles an hour as he drove through the Beavers. "I couldn't see anything. I had to trust my leaders to stay on the trail by feel and scent." Aldrich's dogs actually held the trail well and he traveled the ninety miles faster than the first few teams did. May, after having to stop, crossed from Ophir in about twenty-eight hours. Swenson and Peters took more than twenty-seven, but Aldrich made it in about twenty-six.

Others behind them took longer, even one who had a little help. Allison was a day and a half behind Aldrich and although bothered by winds he had a bright sunny day for the first part of the trip. He was almost a day behind Brinker, but still trying to catch him and win their bet. As he passed out of the woods into the open part of the Beavers, Allison got unexpected assistance. He still had nineteen dogs in the team, a number that under some conditions could get out of control. As Allison enjoyed the sunny scenery, his dogs spotted a small herd of caribou. Allison's quiet jaunt through the mountains quickly became a harrowing rip through the pucker brush. The dogs chased the six caribou for about three-fourths of a mile, away from the trail. Then the caribou stopped. The dogs stopped. With Allison screaming and trying to regain control, the two groups of animals stood cautiously and stared at each other. Then the caribou started, jumped and took off back toward the trail, the dogs in hot pursuit. The dogs chased the deer across the trail again, with Allison just barely holding on. Then the caribou helped. They turned back to the trail and, once on the solid footing, headed for Iditarod as fast as they could go. They ran about a mile and a half down the trail in the right direction, straight toward the next checkpoint, taking the dogs right along with them.

"I let them go and they flat flew — twenty-five miles an hour. I was working hard just to keep stuff from bouncing out of the sled," Allison said. The run helped close the gap on Brinker. Though he'd left Ophir almost twenty-four hours behind his personal opponent, Allison reached Iditarod only an hour after Brinker left.

John Wood of Chugiak crossed the same trail at night, like Aldrich having to trust his lead dogs to feel and smell their way along what he could sense in the dark was a smooth trail. At times he turned on his headlamp to show the way, but with the team going well, he turned it off again to save the battery. With everything going smoothly Wood even dozed a little. But the dozing wasn't to last long as Wood was jolted awake by the sled bouncing and bumping and nearly shaking him off. He brought the team to a halt, wondering what had happened. He turned on the light and went up to find his leaders sitting down, looking at him expectantly. They were off the trail. Wood hauled the dogs back on.

Back on the trail and moving in the right direction, Wood went through the whole process again, turning off his headlamp, again beginning to doze. As soon as Wood nodded, he was jolted awake when the team took off once more, as if the dogs could tell when the musher wasn't paying attention. Again he brought the team to a stop, walked up and found his leaders looking at him with the same expectation. "My leader just decided he wanted to camp," Wood stated later. At times like that, even if he wants to stop, too, the musher can't. Once the lead dog decides he can get away with it, he'll try to camp every few minutes. Lee Gardino, without the vital leader to pull the rest of the dogs along, had to withdraw from the race. Wood, as tired as he was, simply had to stay awake and keep the dogs moving, just so they'd know who was boss.

For four days dog teams and drivers crossed the Beaver Mountains, and no one escaped the damaging wind and blowing snow. Just as the front runners had holed up in the shelter of the broken-down cabin at Fritz's Roadhouse, so did the last group. Gene Leonard, Ron Gould, Jim Lanier, Harry Harris and Don Montgomery all hid out from the storm inside the aging cabin. Snow blew in through the walls, the roof barely sheltered them at all, and the floor was gone, but in the storm the place was a palace, albeit a leaky one. The mushers took to calling the shack the Lettuce Crate.

Afterward, Montgomery, a successful insurance executive from Ohio, remembered the place so fondly that in 1981 he donated money to buy building materials to repair it. In the winter of that year, Swenson and Lindner went in to the cabin and rebuilt it while they cut trail and trained their dogs. The cabin became a checkpoint known as Don's Cabin during the 1981 race and Don Montgomery served as checker.

Crossing the Beaver Mountains proved no less challenging by airplane than by dog sled. Crazy Horse flew the plane easily from Ophir to Iditarod despite the heavy winds. We were well behind the leaders and decided to skip Iditarod in order to catch up, so we followed a well-marked track we thought was the trail but turned out to be an abandoned tramway. Returning to Iditarod, we got directions and found the trail, only to discover it had blown over. After a good deal of flying back and forth to locate runner tracks, mushers or pink tape, we watched the sky close in around us.

At first it became more difficult to make out details on the ground, particularly in the snow where shadows were disappearing. Soon all that was visible were the dark shapes of trees sticking up toward the airplane. The scene was turning rapidly into a whiteout or, in the dying afternoon, a grayout, the feared phenomenon of the north when sunlight is diffused by haze and falling snow, and everything loses its definition, presenting a field of all white or gray.

Locating the trail from the air soon became impossible and as dusk fell we realized we weren't going to make it to the next checkpoint. With all our crisscrossing of the trail we didn't know exactly where we were. Crazy Horse handed over a chart. "With all that boating you do, do you know how to navigate?" I nodded and looked on the chart to see how high the nearby mountains were. I didn't want us flying into a field of white that turned out to be solid ground. The highest mountain was 1,200 feet. Crazy Horse immediately brought the plane up a couple of hundred feet. In the haze no landmark could be seen to locate our position. Then Crazy Horse did what he called an old Indian trick — though I remembered it from Boy Scout manuals. Bringing the airplane down almost to treetop level, he flew along a downhill stream, following it until he found a larger stream, and then he followed that one. As we were studying the ground for landmarks, I got the distinct feeling we also were looking for an emergency place to land. Following streams, we came to a river that had to be the Iditarod. Fortunately, the chart had the river's bends drawn correctly and we followed the river until, out of the falling, thickening snow, the buildings of Iditarod appeared. There was no fancy flying now, no time for extra checks. It was getting too dark and the snow was too heavy. Crazy Horse took one look at the wind direction and brought the airplane down onto the slough, bouncing along on the skis until he came to a stop next to another plane already parked.

"We're going to be stuck here for a while," Crazy Horse said as he looked at the sky and then around at the old buildings. "You know, the first time I came here I was just a little guy, me and my brother peeking out of the covers on a dog sled."

There was still something to be said for using dogs to travel in this country.

11. Iditarod: The Present

CRAZY HORSE STOOD ON THE ICE OF THE IDITAROD RIVER SLOUGH AND looked over at the old buildings of the historic gold-rush town. The most imposing was the facade of the Northern Commercial Company, the Hudson's Bay Company of Alaska, two and a half stories high and leaning into the wind. Only the tops of the other buildings showed over the high bank.

"The first time I came here," Crazy Horse repeated, "I was five or six years old." His father had run supply boats up the river and later his brother worked on the boats, while young Crazy Horse worked in the mines at Ophir.

High on the other bank of the slough, a small cabin released smoke into the haze of the growing evening. To the right of the cabin, past an old warehouse on pilings, several white canvas wall tents had been pitched, their stovepipes also sending up smoke to drift into the air. The tents were for students from the Iditarod School District, mostly Indian children, learning from a white schoolteacher how to survive in the wilderness. An Indian man walked out from the tents and met Crazy Horse, and the two renewed an old friendship.

Over at the cabin Jim Flemings was greeting the mushers and working on a stew on a wood-burning stove. Outside, his two teen-age boys worked on their 1940s-vintage snow machine.

Flemings' wife Kathy sat aside in their living room, suffering quietly from the pain of burns she had received a couple of days earlier. The Flemingses weren't rich by any means; they lived on what Jim made trapping and working as an assistant big-game hunting guide. Knowing this, the folks in McGrath had shipped them food to make the stew for the mushers, along with a pressure cooker to make it in. Kathy had been working over the stove while the stew was cooking when the lid blew off the cooker. The lid hit her face, blackening both eyes, and scalding liquid had poured down her chest and arms, causing severe burns. Fortunately, radio communications had been established and the ham radio operator at Iditarod was able to contact Jim Lanier, the pathologist who was running the race, back at Nikolai. Lanier prescribed emergency treatment, and race veterinarian Phil Meyer helped treat Kathy. Later a radio patch through Talkeetna brought more advice and treatment. The wounds had been cared for, but Kathy, in pain, was waiting for a trip out; a pilot at McGrath was to come in and take her back to McGrath for a commercial flight to an Anchorage hospital. So to Jim fell the chore of cooking for all the mushers while taking care of their young daughter Bump and an infant Kathy had been nursing. The pilot also was to bring formula for the baby.

Shortly before dark an airplane ducked out of the mist and landed on the slough, and Medfra Jack Smith came up the path, but he wouldn't be able to take Kathy out immediately, considering the way the weather was coming down, so he was there for the night. Flemings offered bowls of stew and then stood against the sink-board, smoking, watching and listening to the collection of people in his cabin.

A tall, thin man, his clothes seemed to hang from him as if on wire hangers rather than on shoulders and hips. But inside of that thin, fortyish body was the strength that could survive in a rugged land. Of the many people who live in the Alaska bush, Flemings and his family come as close as any to living the independent life. When Fort Yukon, in the upper reaches of the Yukon River, became too big for them, Jim and Kathy and the two boys packed all their belongings into a river boat and began an odyssey all the way down the Yukon and up the Innoko and Iditarod to this place, a trip of maybe a thousand miles, in search of a more remote place to live. Iditarod wasn't the end of the odyssey, either; Flemings was building a home for them farther away yet, in the Beaver Mountains.

The conversation continued where the one in Ophir had ended; foremost in the minds of Flemings, Medfra Jack and Crazy Horse were the most recent machinations by the federal government concerning land in Alaska. Less than 1 percent of the state's 586,412 square miles was privately owned. When the territory became a state, the new state government was promised 103 million acres, but the selection process had bogged down. Then, with the passage of the Alaska Native Claims Settlement Act, the state selections had to be reconciled with forty million acres promised to Alaska's Natives. Within the claims act was a section calling for designation of the remainder of federal lands according to use. When President Jimmy Carter designated fifty-six million acres in the state as national parks and monuments, sport hunting and fishing and several other activities including trapping were effectively prohibited. The restrictions were those Terry McMullin and Dennis Kogl had complained about at Ophir. Medfra Jack's guiding territory fell within a monument as did the area where Flemings worked for another guide. Dick Peterson, who was running the race, had lost some of his guiding area, too. The men who were tied to the land debated the lands issue, a concern that bound some of them together even more than the race did.

Outside, veterinarian Phil Meyer was whittling by the tent the school group had let him use. He hadn't expected to stay long at Iditarod and had brought only his black instrument case and a sleeping bag. For three days he'd been eating food left by the mushers with utensils he carved from wood rescued from the fire stack.

The leaders had passed through the ghost town two days earlier, most of them arriving between ten and midnight on the seventh day of the race. May, Honea, Peters, Swenson, Riley, Lindner, Redington and Butcher had all spent the night on the slough and enjoyed the hospitality of the Flemingses, pushing back into the mountains in the morning.

Behind them came the others for five more days. On the third evening of the race passing through town, Bill Rose and John Barron sat over bowls of stew at the Flemingses' kitchen table.

Barron told Rose about a dog who'd eaten a bootie. "It just disappeared. He puked it up a day or two later, but he didn't eat for a while."

Now halfway to Nome, they talked about the joys and trials of the trail, how the trip had been and what they might have missed.

"I'd damn well rather be out here away from Anchorage," said Barron, who lived in a bush cabin on the Yentna River.

"You're out of your rabbitin' mind," said Rose, who looked a little like a ruddy Orson Welles. In a trail-weary voice he said, "I want to be near my honey. I'm tired. I want Mama."

While they talked, Ron Brinker and Cliff Sisson hunted through the food bags on the slough ice looking for their sacks. Then they started their stoves and filled their cookers to prepare the dog food. The temperature dipped to ten below zero as their headlamps lighted their work areas. Everything took longer in the cold. For most people working in warm places in Iditarod that evening, chores went relatively smoothly, but out in the cold on the river ice everything slowed down and equipment became less than cooperative. Stoves that flamed up instantly on a summer campout took priming and warming to work in the cold. Gloves and mittens had to come on and off, fingers stiffened and became uncooperative, hats fell into the soup, snaps and zippers froze and turned unworkable in those stiffened fingers, and big chunks of frozen dog food had to be cut apart, sometimes with an ax. The dogs, tired and stiff from the run, resisted or at best tolerated being moved as the drivers examined their feet, removed booties, checked their health and looked over harnesses for chewing and wear. The race wasn't a matter of saying "hike" and riding the runners to Nome. Everything in the family of dog and musher took time and care to keep moving, and in the cold took all the longer. An inexperienced man frustrated by the cold, reluctant gear could lose patience easily, but for the people in the race each chore had become part of a way of life, and each frozen snap was accepted as just another minor irritant to be overcome.

While Brinker and Sisson got through their problems on the ice, a group gathered around a bonfire in front of Phil Meyer's tent.

Flemings joined them. He touched a match to a store-bought Pall Mall, one of a carton of cigarettes a film crewman left for him after he saw Flemings rolling a cigarette. Flemings drew on his smoke and then said all the activity in the house gave him a headache, and he was glad to be outdoors and away from it. He talked softly through thin lips.

Nodding over toward the buildings of Iditarod, which had disappeared into the darkness, he said, "Some people were here looking at the buildings. Didn't even ask who they belong to. They want to make Iditarod a historic place."

Flemings questioned the value of that. Iditarod was five hundred miles from the nearest road that could bring a tourist. The buildings were falling down; many had been stripped for firewood. The place had more practical uses, particularly as his home. Recently at another historic mining town in Alaska, miners who held claims there had bulldozed the buildings to the ground because they were afraid they'd lose their mining interests if the place became a national historic site. But for Flemings it was the solitude and the way of life of Iditarod that really mattered.

Someone suggested money could be found to restore or stabilize the old buildings, preserve them for the future and maybe even find some practical uses for them.

"That's change," Flemings said.

"Is change so bad?" Meyer asked. "Not all change is bad."

"Change is bad," the trapper said. "When things change, things go wrong."

And Flemings saw change coming. For a man who developed a headache with five people in the house, change would only mean more people in the house, more headaches.

The conversation gradually drifted into the lands discussion again and the group slowly disbanded to find places to sleep.

The next day dawned hazy, and snow began falling at first light. In the cabin Meyer and Flemings talked about caring for dogs. Behind the cabin Flemings had six big freighting huskies, the transportation for his trapline and for picking up mail and supplies in Flat. Living isolated and far away from the luxury of veterinarians' clinics, Flemings and his two boys listened to every word the vet could offer.

Meyer was heating instruments on the wood stove to perform a minor operation on one of Cliff Sisson's dogs.

They talked about health and feed and care, and Meyer asked Flemings if his dogs needed worming. He had some medicine. Flemings said he didn't use worming medicine. "Use green moosehide with the hair still on it. Cleans them right out. Don Montgomery said we should use some pills. I tried them and didn't get a worm out of them, not even out of the puppies. Green moosehide."

"That should work," Meyer said as he thought it over while he put his instruments into a pan of disinfectant to sterilize them.

When it was heated he took the pan outside, with Flemings and the two boys right behind, the father telling the youngsters they should watch and learn all they could.

The operating theater for Meyer was the frozen slough of the Iditarod River. The dog had a cut under the eye from a fight with a teammate, and Meyer took two stitches, closing the wound. After about five minutes of calming the dog, stitching and cutting thread, he stood up. "Operation completed," he said. "It's fortunate it's a warm day and we could do it outside." The temperature was five degrees above zero and snow had fallen the whole time.

Despite the snow, the sky was clearing and Crazy Horse and Medfra Jack Smith were looking toward their airplanes. Starting the cold engines could be a problem without sources of heat. Almost every automobile in Alaska has an engine-block heater that connects to the car's cooling system, circulating and heating the coolant and keeping the engine warm enough to start. Most airplane engines also have some sort of heater but all of them run on electricity. Iditarod was maybe only a hundred miles from an electrical outlet and those airplane engines looked real cold.

Medfra Jack heated a can of motor oil on the Flemingses' stove and then poured it into a gasoline-powered electrical generator, which he fired up and plugged into his airplane.

Crazy Horse watched him but the offer to use the generator when Smith was done brought a look of disdain. The Indian pilot favored his own tried-and-true method developed over years of flying the Interior.

He took a large flexible hose, like one of those used for exhaust from clothes dryers, from the rear of the airplane cabin. Then he rummaged through the gear in the airplane until he pulled out a little one-burner army-issue stove, the kind used to heat C-rations. He fired up the stove on the third try and placed one end of the hose over it. The other end went under the blanket he'd wrapped around the engine. Twice he changed the position of the outlet, once to the other side of the engine and once to the cabin, and his airplane was warm enough to start even before Medfra Jack's electrically heated one.

While the engine warmed I used the time to wander across the slough and look at what was left of old Iditarod. The Northern Commercial store and warehouse stood high on the bank, leaning but still sound enough to walk through. Long shelves and display counters that had held canned goods and clothing were empty, but ledgers listing sales and credit accounts still lined the walls in what must have been the bookkeeper's office. The ledgers for the spring, when the men were just setting out with their grubstakes, all were listed on the debit side and the ones for the fall, when the miners came in from the summer's work on the creeks, showed payments on the credit side. Upstairs there was a bunkhouse and even private rooms, some with the mattresses still on the beds.

Snow filled what must once have been the streets past a couple of supply stores, a telegraph office and a concrete bank vault that stood alone, the building that had surrounded it having been stripped for firewood.

Papers scattered on the floor of the vault told of miners depositing gold dust in ounces, cashing checks, borrowing a summer's grubstake, withdrawing and depositing money. Weathered ledger pages recorded the transferrals by the men and women who had made this place home during the gold rush. The papers already had been sifted through, and no familiar names remained; still, the thought that the romantic and not-so-romantic figures of Alaska's gold rushes had touched these slips of paper dated 1911, 1912 and 1913 brought the frontier very close. The Miners and Merchants Bank vault wasn't a museum with everything displayed neatly in glass cases. This was where the accountant had worked, where he'd filed the very papers that now littered the floor. The people who worked in the bank had left these records behind when there was no more gold, as they moved on to the next in a dwindling series of stampedes. This was the floor where boots, maybe even with a little of that precious dust on them, had trod the boards as the miners came to change their gold into money.

Some of those boots had followed a path that led about a quarter of a mile south to an aging, collapsing building that Jim Flemings had said was Tootsie's place, which he thought might have been the first massage parlor in Alaska. More likely, though, the place was a boarding house. Inside, small rooms held metal-framed beds still supporting rusting bedsprings. A large kitchen was dominated by a rusty woodstove that must have cooked countless meals. A water tank big enough to be a boiler was connected by pipes to several of the rooms including one that held a gigantic metal bathtub, probably a steam room or bathroom for the dirty men who would sit down, clean again, at the dinner table. The wooden frames, the narrow staircase, the roof, the fleur-de-lis wallpaper were all crumbling as the earth and the wild reclaimed their own after man had used up what had been needed. In a sense, the earth had also reclaimed the miners, the men who had gone farther, up more distant creeks, still looking for the bonanzas of their dreams until their breed had all but vanished. Few were left, but they were still part of Alaska, represented now by men and women who would attempt to drive dog teams a thousand miles just for the joy of it — for the sense of accomplishment and perhaps for tradition — taking a chance to win some prize money while living the great Alaska adventure.

The sounds of airplane engines starting up crashed into the mood of Tootsie's place.

Back on the slough Brinker called out, "Hello, where have you been?" A glance toward the disintegrating building told the story.

"Did you sleep over there?"

"Well, I always thought a writer should spend at least one night in one of those places."

"You coulda picked one that had somebody in it," he laughed.

The noise of the airplane engines blotted out any more conversation as they warmed up in the shadow of the NC Company's pier.

Years ago, paddle wheelers had nestled against the pier, bringing up their steam as they prepared for the return trip after carrying in the men and women who would mine the creeks, build those now collapsing buildings and make a settlement that would thrive for less than five years before the dirt began to thin out.

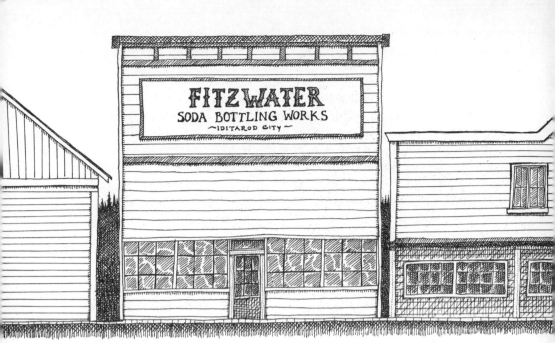

12. Iditarod: The Past

IN 1910, WHILE THE REST OF THE COUNTRY MOVED TO INDUSTRIAL CITIES, the town of Iditarod grew up on the last frontier to serve the last great gold rush in Alaska. It anglicized its name from the Ingalik Indian word *haiditarod*, meaning *distant*, or *distant place*.

Word of the strike made by William Dikeman and John Beaton on Otter Creek on Christmas Day of 1908 traveled slowly, and it wasn't until 1910 that the stampede began. A few miners came over from the Innoko District during the winter of 1909 and '10 but the real rush began the following spring, when as many as three thousand miners pushed into the Iditarod District.

Iditarod became the center of the mining district because it sat at the head of navigation on the Iditarod River. In years of high water the paddle-wheeled boats could make their way all the way up to the slough and the pier in front of the Northern Commercial Company. In other years they stopped at the settlement of Dikeman, named for the prospector, where shallow-bottomed gasoline launches lightered the cargo and passengers the remaining twenty-five miles. The boats of summer brought all the mail and freight and much of the winter's supply of food. The rest of the year the townspeople depended mostly on sled dog freighters to bring mail and supplies, and on reindeer herders for meat.

Considering the gold rush atmosphere, Iditarod was a quiet town. There were few rowdies and even fewer crimes. Deputy Marshal Donovan had to content himself mostly with caring for the occasional overimbiber at one of the town's saloons, and even there he had help. Alice MacDonald, known as Mrs. Mac, owned the MacDonald Hotel which allowed no bar, no music, no gambling and no women. Mrs. Mac didn't tolerate sinning and, so the story went, she could break up a fight between two drunks faster than anyone in town. She also served as nurse and doctor to the injured miners and even after two doctors set up practices in town, the miners came to her to stitch them up.

The town was so quiet, in fact, that Deputy Donovan sent for his wife and children, who were living Outside. The quiet was probably due to the fact that the stampeders who went into the Iditarod had worked other creeks, were veterans of other gold rushes. Hard work and the northern climate had weeded out the weaklings, grifters and slackers, who preferred Dawson, Fairbanks and Nome, where the living was easier. The miners who came into the Iditarod came knowing what needed doing and went about it seriously, with little attention to the frivolities. Also calming the place was the fact that, like the deputy, many of the claim operators and miners had their families with them, either brought up from the Big Outside or married and raised right there in Alaska.

Through the summer of 1910 Iditarod asserted itself as supplier, hosteler, and government and recreation center for those working the creeks, overwhelming the town of Dikeman, which for a time sought to compete. During the time when there was a question as to whether Dikeman or Iditarod would survive, George M. Arbuckle, editor of the *Iditarod Pioneer*, defended his city with chauvinistic fervor, losing no chance to belittle Iditarod's competitor down the river. On one such occasion he took the town of Dikeman to task over its difficulties with water supplies. Someone had been shipping potable water from Iditarod to Dikeman at a cost of two dollars a barrel, leading Arbuckle to chide: "Dikeman professes to be a real live and coming town and yet it can't even furnish an acceptable chaser unless it buys the goods from Iditarod City."

Iditarod prevailed and by October 1910 the *Pioneer* carried advertisements for three hotels, six cafés, eight saloons, a barber, two doctors, two dentists, five clothiers, six general stores, six lawyers, a drugstore, a bath house, an undertaker, two banks, a sheet-music and musical-instrument store, two tobacconists and a sweet shop, along with all the freighters, suppliers, and warehouses. A year later a man with the improbable name of Everest Fitzwater even opened a soda-bottling works.

One business in town didn't advertise in the papers. Along the back edges of the settlement, lining a quiet street, was a row of low one- and two-room cottages, each with a name over the door: Fanny, Annie, Nancy. Cribs, they were called, and the paper, on the few occasions it found the area worthy of note, politely referred to it as the restricted district. Quiet by gold rush standards though Iditarod was, it had its share of sinners. The finer elements of town tolerated or at least ignored the Row, but more than one matron of the town's higher society was known to have sloshed across a muddy street in her finery rather than pass one of the girls on the board sidewalk. Iditarod tolerated the restricted district for more than a year, probably recognizing the need of comfort for the lonely men on the creeks, but in the fall of 1911 one of the girls, Japanese Mary, was found dead in her bed, strangled with a shoelace. The crime never was solved, but the town's elders closed the Row for good and shipped the girls elsewhere.

Other women besides the girls of the Row followed the gold rushes through the Yukon and Alaska. They too were veterans of previous stampedes, but they survived with their reputations intact. Among them were the "hello girls" — the telephone operators. By late 1910 Iditarod had a telephone system, and Cora Smith, who had worked the first switchboard in Dawson some years before, had taken a job as operator. With her she brought her sister Lillian, who had worked the phone system in Fairbanks. Lillian later married one of the steamboat men and moved to Anchorage. When her husband, Henry Watson, became a secretary under territorial Governor George Parks, a bachelor, Lillian served as official greeter in the absence of a territorial first lady.

Through the summer of 1910, as the town grew out of its tents and into frame buildings, the miners at Flat Creek and Discovery Otter worked toward a payday no one had predicted. Early estimates had said the pay wouldn't reach $200,000. But no one could really know until cleanup, at the end of the summer, when miners sifted through the dirt they'd worked all season and recovered whatever gold there was.

Doc Madding, who employed eighty-five men at his claims along Flat Creek, reported a cleanup of $10,000, but everyone figured that was low and that he didn't want to reveal the truth. George Riley, the biggest operator on Otter Creek, west of Flat, said he had a cleanup of about $16,000, but again the veterans knew that no one was going to brag. Despite the quiet in the Iditarod, many mine owners employed armed guards to watch the sluice boxes during cleanup. By October 1, the Miners and Merchants Bank had sent $400,000 of gold Outside and the American Bank, just a few weeks in business, had sent $200,000. The Iditarod was proving to be a much larger producer than anyone had expected. The final estimate of gold taken out during that first full year of operation went over a million dollars.

In its peak year of production, 1912, the Iditarod District yielded $3 million in gold. Over the years, $14 million was brought out, which made the district the third largest gold producer in Alaska.

Almost as soon as they moved in, the people of the town began clamoring for a better trail to the coastal supply cities. In winter, mail and supplies had to travel up the Richardson Trail from Valdez to Fairbanks, then down the Yukon River and overland from Nulato. Alaska Roads Commissioner Wilds P. Richardson visited Iditarod in the summer of 1910 and promised a trail to be cut to Seward through Knik to the head of the railroad at Kern Creek. That fall, Walter Goodwin started out with a survey party from Nome and Anton Elde, coming from the other direction to meet him, worked from Kern Creek. They surveyed and brushed out a trail connecting near Rainy Pass, but even before they could finish, gold miners were cutting routes to the sea. Doc Madding and Harry Johnson, whose brother John "Iron Man" Johnson was a dog freighter and racer in Nome, went out in November of 1910 and made Seward in a little more than fifteen days by dog team.

With the gold in from the creeks, those miners who could afford it, once they saw the termination dust — the first snow on the mountain tops — went Outside for the winter. Those who could not remained to spend the winter living on their meager summer earnings. All the winter supplies and food had to be in before freezeup, of course, and in 1910 the *Pioneer* reported only eighty head of beef in town at the close of navigation — and those already consigned to restaurants. The newspaper predicted the town would run out of meat by February. However, two herds of reindeer were driven from Unalakleet during the winter, and the citizens of Iditarod were saved. Shortages of varying impact were a way of life on the frontier. Two years later the storekeepers and saloon owners ran out of beer and cigars, but fortunately the whiskey supply held out throughout the winter.

Winter distractions were important, and aside from the Row girls, the saloons and the basketball games at the Arctic Brotherhood Hall, there were few. The long days of cold and darkness, fed by a lack of funds, loneliness, a great distance from loved ones and whatever else the mind could conjure up, brought many a lonely man to the brink of insanity. Much of the deputy marshal's time was taken with collecting the shell of a man who'd lost his mind to the deprivations of the arctic winter.

One such man was Niels Jensen, a foreman for Doc Madding at Flat Creek. Folks around Flat said he'd been working too hard and took to giving impossible orders to the men working the sluices in the fall of 1910. When Madding replaced him, the *Pioneer* called it "the last blow to unseat his reason." Fearing a violent situation, Doc Holmes, the deputy marshal in Flat, went up to Jensen's cabin to see him. Unwilling to risk a battle or an escape, Holmes told Jensen that Madding wanted to see him over in Iditarod. Jensen thought this over and then took off running, covering the entire eight miles so fast that two men had difficulty keeping up with him. Once he reached the marshal's office in Iditarod he realized he'd been tricked and he put up a fight. Three men subdued the foreman and took him inside, where he was charged with being mentally unbalanced. During his short incarceration he became more violent and even managed to escape. Recaptured, he stood trial before a six-man jury that found him hopelessly insane. The people of the town, as reflected in the newspaper, were sympathetic, hoping he would come out of it, but he was destined to make the trip so many took to the Mount Tabor Sanitarium in Oregon.

The following February, Deputy Harry Sheppard led a caravan of five big dog teams taking six insane persons over the trail to Fairbanks, all to be sent to the sanitarium. Later, two men from town visited a friend at Mount Tabor and found the conditions deplorable. Some of the biggest type ever used in the town's newspapers related to the poor conditions that former residents found themselves in when sent for recovery at the institution.

Not all the victims were fortunate enough even to escape to Mount Tabor. Just as many took their own lives.

That first fall a man named Frank Hammond tried to kill himself with a shotgun at one of the roadhouses. When the shotgun failed, Hammond tried to slit his throat. Three men wrestled with him to stop the attempt. During the scuffle an employee of the roadhouse grabbed one of Hammond's gold pokes and poured the dust into his pocket. The three men grabbed the thief and dumped him upside-down to recover the dust, but in the meantime Hammond bled to death. On another occasion Otto Windhorst, a veteran of previous gold rushes at Dawson and Nabesna, found himself broke in Iditarod. He was known to have always kept a bank account of a couple thousand dollars, but a winter trip to San Francisco had eaten well into that account and in the spring of 1911 he returned to Iditarod broke. He worked a while on a tramway that was under construction between Iditarod and Flat but started complaining to people that he was getting a bad deal. On July 1, 1911, Otto Windhorst waded into a shallow part of the Iditarod River and slashed his throat so deeply with a razor that he almost cut his head off.

In addition to the reports of insanities and suicides, almost every issue of the Iditarod papers carried a column of letters from Outside asking if anybody knew the whereabouts of this or that man who was known to be in Alaska. How many of those missing fathers, brothers, husbands and sons ended up the way of Jensen, Hammond and Windhorst is anybody's guess. The depressions are no less today. Alaska still has the highest rate of suicide in the nation.

The tramway that led to Windhorst's demise caused headaches for a lot of people. A quick transportation link was needed between Flat, where most of the gold was, and Iditarod, where it could be shipped out and supplies brought in. Travelers walked, skied, or drove dog or mule teams between the two towns, and one H. H. Ross even drove a Model T Ford back and forth. But there were always problems. In late spring of 1911 — breakup

time, when everything turns to mud — Alex Toben was driving his
team of horses up from Flat when one of them slipped and fell on
the other. Before Toben could raise the horses, the one on the bottom had drowned in the mud.

In November of 1910 Ross and Earl Slippern announced their
plans to build a tramway connecting Iditarod and Flat. They estimated the cost at $40,000. By April the idea had been taken up by
the Mutchler brothers, who began construction, hoping to have it
ready by the opening of navigation. But by July they only had two
and a half miles of track laid and sold out to the Iditarod Traction
Company, owned by the Wilson brothers. The ITC expected to lay
the rest of the square log rails to Flat and be operating by mid-Au-
gust. The Wilsons already had sixteen mules, the flowers of Mis-
souri, in town to haul the cars along the tram. Almost on schedule, they drove in a golden spike on August 23, 1911 and the rails
began carrying people and freight over the eight miles between the
two towns. The trip took three and a half hours, and freight cost
two cents a pound to Flat and, if hauled in to Discovery Otter by
wagon, three cents a pound.

A month after the opening, the district entertained one of its
more spectacular crimes. Two masked highwaymen held up the
tramway — on horseback, no less. The bandits, who witnesses
described as very nervous, escaped with $35,000 in dust from the
Bonanza Association on Flat Creek and $182 in cash collected
from the passengers. The robbers rode off across the tundra while
the tram continued on to the Summit Roadhouse, where authori-
ties in Flat and Iditarod were informed. Posses formed quickly and
rode to the scene of the crime. The lawmen followed the tracks of
the tramwaymen and found one poke of gold within a hundred
yards of the tracks. A searcher found another about a mile up Cot-
tonwood Creek and a third lay about a half-mile farther in a draw
that opened into Otter Creek.

The two outlaws disappeared, though, and the posse eventually
quit the chase. In small towns like Iditarod and Flat, however, the
townspeople didn't take too long to decide on suspects. Two men
in Flat without visible means of support eventually drew attention
and could go nowhere without being watched. The two men,
Louie Gorman and Angus Bronson, stayed around Flat for a while,
but the community's eyes and ears became too much and they

said they were going to try their luck at Georgetown, a small settlement about fifty miles to the southeast. News of importance traveled quickly even among the scattered Iditarod settlements, and
when the two failed to appear in Georgetown, that was evidence
enough for the deputy marshal to form another posse and take off
after them. The posse, gone eight days, returned with Bronson and
Gorman, who had been traced to Takotna. Gorman was held in
Iditarod and Bronson in Flat, while the lawmen gathered as much
evidence as they could. Almost a year later a jury found Gorman
guilty of the holdup, but Bronson's trial ended in a hung jury and
he was set free with a warning to disappear from the country. So
ended the careers of Iditarod's only two recorded highwaymen or
tramwaymen, whichever.

In another celebrated case a prostitute nicknamed the Black
Bear, reportedly because of tufts of hair on various parts of her
body, in cahoots with a roadhouse keeper who kept the whisky
flowing, managed to lift the pokes of two miners who were giving
her a lift Outside. When the theft was discovered farther up the
trail, the two miners immediately turned on the Black Bear. She
denied guilt, but as the case unfolded, the keeper of the roadhouse
eventually confessed and turned state's evidence against his
cohort. Convicted, he served a prison sentence, but the jury failed
to agree on the Black Bear's guilt and she was freed.

Every area in the country had to have its shoot-out, if only to live
up to future generations' concepts of the frontier, and the Iditarod
District was no exception. The biggest shoot-out in the district happened in Flat on an early September day in 1912, but it bore little
resemblance to, say, the gunfight at the OK Corral. A hawk chased
a flock of ptarmigan onto the town's main street. Seeing a tasty
potential dinner, town residents came through their doors blasting
away with any kind of firearm they could get their hands on. By
the time the carnage was over almost everybody had at least one
plump bird for dinner; the druggist had bagged one, the grocer
two, and even a dog managed to grab one. Fortunately all the humans escaped without wounds and lived for the evening meal of
roast ptarmigan.

Although most of the people in the Iditarod had been in other
gold camps and seen them fade, they still worked to establish a
permanent settlement. By 1910 citizen committees had formed to

improve conditions. One of the first raised $1,000 to improve navigation on the river so steamers could come all the way up from Dikeman no matter what the water conditions.

In 1911, after a fire razed an entire block on the north side of Front Street, the residents voted 209 to 56 to incorporate, the only town in the territory so far to do so. The first order of business for the new government was to form a fire department. The town already had two chemical hand trucks, one kept at Manuel's Saloon in the north end and the other at Suter's General Store to the south. In early June of 1911 the town council voted to buy two steam pumps, 1,000 feet of four-inch main and 2,500 feet of fire hose. A contract was drawn with the Cascade Laundry to provide steam for the pumps and a firebell was affixed atop the Northern Commercial building, the tallest structure in town.

The tragedy the town's citizens hoped to avoid happened before the new equipment could be shipped up the river. George Wallace noticed the gasoline lamps in his Board of Trade Saloon were flickering one night, and as he was checking the problem one of them exploded, filling the room with flame. The fire spread quickly to Harry Bridge's pool hall in the back of the saloon, and he lost five pool tables and a piano. Behind the building, as they wrestled to save their horses and wagons, the fire engulfed the feed, freight and tent stable belonging to Pat Keys and Phil Mayhan.

Soon flames were coming out of windows all along Willow Street and before they could be stopped they destroyed the Miners Home Hotel, with its saloon, restaurant and tonsorial parlor, along with $6,000 of beer stored in the basement. Next door, another victim was the Ophir House Hotel, owned by Carrie Stoner who earlier had been burned out of a roadhouse at Little Delta. Harry Boaz's general store at the corner of First and Willow burned down along with the Moose Café and Lodging House owned by Jimmy Nikskimoto, who also ran a free employment bureau out of his establishment. Several other businesses were damaged including Fitzwater's soda-bottling works. The fire eventually burned itself out but left a large section of downtown Iditarod in smoldering ruins.

Nevertheless, now that it had a government and a fire department, the town began to take on all the aspects of a settled community. Isadore Goldstein was advertising a complete line of ladies' and gents' furnishings. The Iditarod Undertaking Parlor announced that it specialized in embalming bodies for shipment Outside.

The first baby, a girl, was born in Iditarod in November 1910 to Mr. and Mrs. John Bagoy. The next summer Iditarod had its first wedding, when Arthur Field married Jessie Somarindyck the day after she arrived on a boat from the Outside, a mail-order bride. The ceremony was performed by the U.S. Commissioner E. M. Stanton, son of President Lincoln's secretary of war.

While he took every opportunity to promote the town's growth, not all businesses received cheers from the *Pioneer*'s Arbuckle. One enterprising businessman was hauling ice into town and charging $9 a hundredweight for it. Arbuckle thought this price outrageous, writing: "Think of a man getting a skinful of 5¢ beers on a New York roof garden, only to be compelled to hand out about 11 bucks the next day to take the swelling out of his head. . . . Ice selling for $9 a hundredweight in the heart of Alaska — could any soft-footed pilgrim from the far off shores of the Great Lakes believe it?"

Arbuckle's competitor in the newspaper business was Major J. F. A. Strong, but he had bigger things in mind. Strong ran the weekly Iditarod *Nugget* for a while but moved on to Juneau, where he founded the Juneau *Empire*, which survives to the present. He also served a term as territorial governor.

Iditarod sent a representative to the first Territorial Legislature in 1913. Harry Roden had to travel by dog sled to Ruby, on foot to Fairbanks, by stagecoach to Valdez and finally by steamship to Juneau. The trip took thirty days and he was paid fifteen cents a mile plus $900 for the sixty-day session. Years later at the age of ninety, as the last surviving member of the first territorial meeting, Roden addressed the opening session of the 1964 Alaska Legislature. In his comments he noted, "That year we passed an appropriation bill of $65,000 to run the territory for two years. . . . We didn't have the money then, either."

Iditarod had a full schedule of social events to make the frontier life more comfortable. In addition to the basketball games at the Arctic Brotherhood Hall there were weekly dances, although a shortage of women apparently made the dances less than sensational. The brotherhood even offered eligible women in Flat free passes on the tramway and free admission to the dances if they'd attend.

Through it all the town depended on dog teams for its winter transportation, freight, mail, entertainment and even religion, and the teams brought in many of Alaska's famous people.

Archdeacon Hudson Stuck of the Episcopal Church, who criss-crossed the state to carry the word of God, visited Iditarod several times to hold services. Stuck, whose book *10,000 Miles by Dogsled* detailed his travels in Alaska, in 1913 was part of the first success-ful climb on Mount McKinley. A companion of his on that climb, Harry Karstens, hauled freight into Iditarod early in his career, bringing on his first journey six hundred pounds of freight from the steamer *Minnesota* after the boat was locked in the ice of the Shageluk Slough of the Innoko River. Karstens later became the director of Mount McKinley National Park and Karstens Ridge on the mountain was named for him.

The Reverend S. Hall Young brought Presbyterian services to Iditarod and Father Rossi, a Jesuit, often came down by dog team from Nulato to say Mass.

Iron Man Johnson, winner of the 1910 All-Alaska Sweepstakes Sled Dog Race in Nome, hauled freight into Iditarod, brought mail from Nome, and visited his brother Harry at his claim on Flat Creek. Another famous musher, Frank Tondreau, known along the Yukon River as the Malemute Kid, also brought supplies into the district with dog teams.

But the dog team residents anticipated most belonged to Bob Griffis, who held the mail contract from 1910 until 1914. Griffis brought the mail from Fairbanks through Nulato and Kaltag, up the Innoko River to Diskaket, then to Iditarod and Flat. In his first year he contracted for two hundred pounds per trip, but that was raised to four hundred pounds per week in 1911. Despite Good-win and Eide punching the trail through to Kern Creek in 1910 and 1911, Griffis held the Yukon River route for three more years, over the protests of the citizens of Iditarod, who wanted their mail faster. Griffis also performed freighting chores and headed the large Wells Fargo gold train that went out in 1912.

The trails weren't always easy ones. In late April of 1912 Griffis left Kaltag with eight days' worth of provisions and one hundred pounds of mail. That time of year is one of the most difficult for moving about in Alaska because many of the streams have begun to break up. When Griffis reached the Mud River, fifty miles north of Iditarod, he found it totally without ice. In order to cross he built a raft and piled dogs, sled, mail and provisions aboard. Once he was free from shore and floating, the dogs all moved to one side and the raft tipped, dumping everything into the river. Griffis lost his whole outfit, saving only the mail. Two trappers found him on shore, weak, wet and almost helpless in temperatures that had dipped below freezing. They helped him to Diskaket, about eight or nine miles away, where he eventually recovered.

Griffis hauled the mail over the northern route through the spring of 1914, but the next winter Harry Revelle of Seward landed the winter mail contract and the mail now began coming from Seward. Revelle's contract called for hauling 350 pounds of mail four times a month. He accomplished this by using relays of dog teams stationed at roadhouses along the Iditarod Trail.

With so many dog teams around it was inevitable that sooner or later someone would start a race. The first monied race took place in Iditarod on January 1, 1911 and ran about twenty miles in a circular route through Flat and back to Iditarod. Claude Shea, a freighter from the Nome area, won, making the course through deep snow and a storm in two hours and twenty-eight minutes. Second was Dan Campbell, who drove the Northern Commercial team of bird dogs and malemutes. The teams then consisted of only four or five dogs, compared to today's fourteen or sixteen. Top sprint mushers today make twenty-five miles on a fast trail in about an hour and forty minutes.

The town saw several more races that winter and the next, including some grudge races. F. Coke Hill, a young lawyer, had been a prime promoter of dog racing in Iditarod and ran a team himself. He finished second in one of the December races in 1911, but apparently there was some bad blood between him and another racer because Ben Bromberg, who was driving the NC team, challenged him. Bromberg deposited $100 with the *Pioneer* and so did Hill. They didn't get to race until the second Iditarod Sweepstakes — January 1, 1912. The judge for that race was none other than George M. Arbuckle, editor of the paper. Hill won the sweepstakes and Bromberg came in third, losing his $100. Hill, perhaps flush with victory, said he saw no reason why Iditarod couldn't put together a first-class dog team for Nome's All-Alaska Sweepstakes, the biggest race in the territory. Hill, while in Nome the year before, had finished second in the 1911 Sweepstakes. Fox Maule Ramsey, a Nome businessman who sponsored teams in that race, even wrote to Hill suggesting the town find a team, estimating the cost at $500. There were some attempts, but Iditarod apparently never did field a team in the sweepstakes.

Interest in the All-Alaska was high, though, and when the telegraph system extended its wires to Iditarod, one of the first subscribers was the Budweiser Saloon. Inside the Budweiser artist John Strelic had hung his paintings of dog teams and the local countryside, and among the paintings was a blackboard. The saloonkeeper had contracted for 1,500 words on the race and, thanks to the telegraph, they were all printed carefully on the blackboard while patrons kept up with the progress of the mushers from Nome to Candle and back. Scotty Allen won the race that year, beating teams fielded by Ramsey.

Eventually one musher came to dominate Iditarod's local racing scene. In the winter of 1912 and 1913, Joe Jean won several races including the January 1 Sweepstakes, a handicap race in February and another on St. Patrick's Day. By this time Coke Hill, who had gotten racing started in Iditarod, had moved on to a new stampede at Ruby on the Yukon River. Hill, now U.S. Government Commissioner in Ruby, had taken his interest in sled dog racing with him. He organized a sweepstakes in Ruby and invited Iditarod to send a musher. Joe Jean was the obvious choice.

Jean had the pick of the dogs in the Iditarod, and along with them he took to Ruby $1,500 people had asked him to bet on himself. The race was scheduled for April 27, and Jean allowed himself seven days to drive the team to the starting line. Weather slowed him down and he didn't make it on time, but Hill and the rest of Ruby's citizens agreed to postpone the race a week so the Iditarod musher could compete. They shouldn't have waited. Jean won the fifty-eight-mile race to Long City and back and took home all the betting money from the accommodating citizens of Ruby.

The next season Jean again raced at Iditarod but another musher, Store Sternberg, beat him in the first race, setting a record with a team belonging to Nels Glantz, who owned the Grand

Hotel in Flat. On January 14, 1914 the first Iditarod ladies' race took place, and Sternberg let a Mrs. Swanson run his team. Mrs. Swanson won the $300 race on a Wednesday. The next Monday, after the team and sled had sat idle, Sternberg hitched the dogs to haul some water. Everything went fine until the dogs tried to pull the sled heavily laden with water barrels. At the first lurch the sled completely gave way and fell to pieces. Examining the wreckage, Sternberg discovered that someone had sawed partway through all the stanchions on the sled except the ones closest to where Mrs. Swanson had stood. That someone had really meant to keep Mrs. Swanson from winning the women's race. Of the act, the *Pioneer* sniffed, "It's difficult to conceive of anyone in the community being guilty of such a dastardly act."

A man famous for his ability with dogs had perhaps the most profound effect on the Iditarod District. The death of a Japanese prospector in the lower Kuskokwim drew the interest of Jujuiro Wada, who went to investigate what he felt were mysterious circumstances. His search led him to the Iditarod. (The paper referred to him as "Wada the Jap," which was not unusual. Prejudicial references were common; Chinese were regularly called Chinks in print and a particularly bitter term, *siwash*, referred to the offspring of Indian and white parents.) Wada attempted to learn if his countryman had been murdered but in the process he also did some prospecting, eventually finding some decent pay along Bear Creek near Iditarod.

He filed claims immediately and began seeking financing for a major operation on the creek. Wada made two trips Outside over the winter of 1912 to southern Louisiana to visit E. A. McIllhenny, a Tabasco sauce heir who had once done ornithological research in the arctic and eventually purchased some of the Bear Creek claims. But it was a trip to New York where Wada talked with the Guggenheim Syndicate that his influence began to show.

Wada made his trips to Seward by dog team and was known as a fast musher, but even so he'd sometimes leave the teams at roadhouses and snowshoe alone when the snow was too deep for the dogs. On his trips he always took time to write back to the newspaper with information about the condition of the trail and about people from the district he met along the way. Appreciating the information and perhaps coming to recognize Wada as a man of influence, the *Pioneer* dropped the "Jap" and began referring to him as Mr. Wada.

After his long trip from Alaska, Wada had to sit in a waiting room outside the Guggenheim offices in New York. Out of politeness someone offered him a ham or egg sandwich, but Wada told them "No, I didn't come all the way from Alaska for an egg sandwich. It's a square meal or nothing."

Prior to Wada's visit, the Guggenheim Syndicate, operating as the Yukon Gold Company, had purchased and operated many of the high-paying claims in Canada's Yukon Territory and had already begun working its way into Alaska, bringing the efficiencies of large-scale operation, and crowding out the individual prospectors. Representatives of Yukon Gold already had looked over claims in the Flat Creek area and in the summer of 1911 had employed a hundred men to sink test holes along the creek. The representatives claimed they came as operators, not speculators, and planned to work on a big scale, offering employment to large numbers of miners, but they ran into resistance. By the end of July 1911, the Guggenheim representative, a Mr. Copeland, left for Fairbanks, saying the asking prices for claims along Flat Creek were too high for the ground's value.

Cleanup that year was reported at $3,061,695, and apparently the high stakes and Wada's visit renewed the interest of the syndicate. In 1912 the Guggies returned and began to buy everything available. By May of 1912 they had purchased most of the claims on Flat Creek, although there was at least one notable holdout — Mrs. Fred Carter, who had purchased interests in two claims owned by tramway worker Jim Mutchler. The Guggies offered her $1,500 for her interests, but she refused, holding out for $3,000. They never did come to terms and two of the richer claims on the creek, the Jumbo and the Prospector, remained in her control.

That didn't deter the syndicate, however, and when the packet boat *Susie* arrived in June she carried 575 tons of Guggenheim mining equipment from Dawson. Included in the shipment was the huge Hunker Creek dredge, and the Yukon Gold Company began mining in earnest along the Iditarod's gold creeks.

With the coming of the Guggenheim machinery, the old-timers began packing up and leaving. The newspapers carried news of strikes in other parts of Alaska — Ruby, Aniak and the Kuskokwim — and the *Pioneer* was actually paying for reports on strikes in Mexico and Bolivia. Still on the rise, Iditarod already was looking at its decline.

From late 1912 through 1914, while the Guggenheim dredges were working, the Iditarod began a gradual fade. By 1920 the population had dwindled to about fifty persons and the next census found only eight. In 1940 one person claimed the town as home. The post office, opened in 1910, closed in 1929, and Flat, with maybe a hundred residents, became the population center of the district as the airplane began to replace other methods of transportation.

The heyday of Iditarod had taken its toll on the surrounding landscape. As residents cut through the forest to construct their buildings and fuel their fires, they denuded the land for miles around. Even today few trees stand more than three or four feet tall within sight of the town.

Apparently no one lived in Iditarod for several years until the Flemings family arrived in the early 1970s. But now, as Flemings stood in front of his cabin looking at the abandoned, leaning buildings of the old town, he saw change coming. The race came through every two years and there were those people looking at the town as a historical site. Those weather-tested eyes saw change approaching. Flemings sold his cabin and, in a letter inviting me to visit a few months later, wrote that his new address was a "three or four day walk from Flat."

But vast Alaska, with its population of less than half a million, has the way of a small community. What goes around comes around, they say, and when the Flemings family left, they sold their land and cabin to a man who combined two traditions: he had mined in the area at places like Red Devil and Julienne Creek, carrying on the old tradition begun by William Dikeman in 1908, and he joined the new tradition begun in 1973 with the first Iditarod Trail Sled Dog Race.

The man was Dick Wilmarth, who won that first race, and when the mushers passed through in 1981, Wilmarth sat in that same cabin, welcoming the racers with coffee and doughnuts and a big smile, talking dogs and gold mining in conversations that spanned more than half a century.

13. Iditarod to Anvik

IN THE SHADOW OF THE TOWN THAT GAVE THE RACE ITS NAME, JOE MAY, for the first time since he'd taken his twenty-four-hour layover back at Rohn River, watched another team run out of a checkpoint ahead of him. Past the remains of the Northern Commercial Company, first Emmitt Peters and then Sonny Lindner drove their dogs back down the slough and down the river toward the low mountain where the trail would turn west toward the Yukon. May watched as he fed and rested his sick dogs.

May had caught Seppala, but the pack of racers had caught him. He was absorbed into the front-running group as if they could not tolerate the nonconformist who had to run alone ahead of them.

Most of the leading racers stayed a whole evening and night at Iditarod through much of the storm, leaving in mid- to late morning on the eighth day of the race. The front end of the race had now separated into distinct groups; there was some overlap, but the bunch with May, Lindner, Peters, Swenson, Honea and Riley stayed out front. Right behind them came another group that included Terry Adkins, Redington, Butcher, Mackey, Albert and Baumgartner. Other groups ran together as well, ending with Lanier, Gould, Harris, Montgomery and Leonard at the rear.

140

Occasionally the two leading groups would be together, those in the second bunch catching the first at the checkpoints. But even though two mushers might be in the same place at the same time, one was preparing to leave while the other had to feed and rest his dogs as he watched the mushers he'd caught head back out onto the trail, still touchable but maybe eight hours ahead.

The leaders pushed on toward Shageluk, Anvik and the Yukon River. The first group of drivers made the sixty-five-mile crossing to Shageluk in less than twelve hours. Skies cleared as the race moved across the rolling mountains but the wind never abated, screaming in gusts as high as sixty-five miles an hour off the balding mountain tops, ripping into dogs and mushers. Jon Van Zyle said he actually saw a sled and driver blown over by the winds.

After following the Iditarod downstream for a couple of miles, the trail turned west to cross a series of smaller and smaller hills as it took the mushers and dogs toward the broad valley of the Yukon and Innoko rivers. On the way the dogs and drivers passed small frozen lakes; two rivers, the little Yetna and the big Yetna; and gradually flattening terrain that terminated in a cliff where the land dropped abruptly into the river valley. The teams negotiated the drop of more than two hundred feet to Shageluk Lake, crossed the lake, went down a slough and came into the Innoko River village of Shageluk. Don Honea of Ruby, the village corporation president with the Clark Gable mustache, arrived in Shageluk first, making the run in just more than eleven hours. But nobody was letting anyone else get very far ahead. All of the first group arrived within an hour. The rest of the field was spread out four days behind.

A day later, after spending more time lost, Gary Hokkanen found his way into Shageluk but, as he was finally approaching the village, noticed the hulk of an old snow machine rusting by the side of the trail. Just as he was near enough to make it out, he saw a fox sitting on the seat. The fox saw Hokkanen at the same instant and both man and animal jumped at the surprise. "We both must have jumped five feet," he said later. Fortunately, the dogs paid only passing attention to the fox — fortunately for a couple of reasons. For one, Hokkanen didn't have to chase the fox through the thick alder that lined the slough. But there was another danger. A couple of years earlier some dogs in one of the teams had been bitten during the race by a rabid fox and the musher had had to drop the dogs. They'd been innoculated and didn't develop rabies, but the danger always exists.

Two days behind Hokkanen and three days behind the leaders, Ron Brinker followed his lead dog Rabbit across the mountains. He'd left Iditarod at two in the afternoon but, unlike the leaders, took his time on the trail, spending twenty-four hours on the way to Shageluk. Part of that time was spent overnight in a camp he made up in the hills. He camped alone, cooking dog food while the dogs rested. Later, after the dogs had eaten and settled in for the night, Brinker sat by his fire staring into the flames and thinking. He heard another musher off in the distance. At first the other man was so far away Brinker couldn't make out the exact words, but the tone of voice was easy to figure out. Somebody's dogs weren't doing exactly what they were supposed to be doing, and the driver was yelling to get them back on the trail or do whatever it was he wanted them to do.

"He kept getting closer and I kept hearing this and finally I could make out the words," Brinker recalled. "That's when I realized there must have been a dozen guys in the race had the same name for a lead dog I did. All I could hear out there in the dark was, 'You son of a bitch!'"

As Brinker laughed at his joke there by his fire, the other team and driver came closer and closer until the dogs ran into his circle of light. The sled and then the driver followed and the laughing stopped. Brinker had to look into the big, smiling face of Del Allison and realize he'd lost the bet. Allison had caught him and they were still almost five hundred miles from Nome. They shared the camp that night and went on to Shageluk together in the morning, arriving just eleven minutes apart.

The village of Shageluk, population about 170, is nestled into a bend of the Innoko River on the eastern side of the broad valley that holds the Innoko and the Yukon rivers. Contrasting with the older log homes of the village are a new school and a new bath house/laundry that also provides safe running water. The Iditarod Trail brought the mushers through the middle of town, where they rested their teams near the school. On the western edge of Shageluk, a fifty-foot bank dropped down to the Innoko where the dogs again picked up the trail to Anvik, across about twenty-eight miles of frozen bottom land, marsh and the Yukon.

Crazy Horse, whose father had worked the boats hauling supplies on the Yukon, Innoko and Iditarod, and who had worked the boats himself, said that some years, when the flooding is particularly bad, a boat can actually cross here from the Yukon to the Innoko, dodging treetops along the way, as far as forty miles over what normally would be land.

Up and down the Innoko and along some of the streams that feed it are clusters of small, aging buildings, most of them with stick racks next to them. These are the fish camps of the residents of Shageluk, the summer homes where people go to catch salmon as the fish fight their way upstream to spawn. Fish that isn't sold ends up drying on the racks for the winter supply of food. Here the race trail had been cut through deep snow, past some of the fish camps and out into the swampy land between the rivers.

Through the sparse trees and hummocky muskeg, the trail wound toward Anvik, then fell away into a broad expanse of white that was more than a mile wide and stretched north and south to the horizon. This was the Yukon River, the Mississippi of Alaska, the winter and summer lifeline to the Interior.

In the telling, the trail seems to have covered a large area, but in fact the area is large only psychologically. To put things in perspective, the Iditarod Trail on a map of Alaska compares with a pencil line across a sheet of 8½-by-11-inch paper. But if the large size of the trail is psychological, the large size of the Yukon River is physical, and the Yukon's space is real indeed as it flows more than 1,800 miles out of Canada's Yukon Territory and bisects Alaska until it reaches the Bering Sea. In places the river is three miles wide and in others, only a foot or two deep, flowing slowly on the course that first takes it directly west, then turns to the south around a range of mountains until it can turn west again and flow across a massive delta into the sea.

In both winter and summer the river serves as highway and supply line for the villages along its banks. From breakup to freezeup boats towing barges work the river, hauling food, fuel and supplies to the people who live and work in the valley. The great stream brings salmon, too, some of which swim all the way to Dawson, some 1,200 miles from the ocean. In the days of the great gold stampedes, paddle wheelers brought miners and shopkeepers and trappers in and took their gold and misfortunes out. In winter the river ice becomes a highway for snow machines and dog drivers and a landing strip for aircraft. For centuries the winter highway has linked the villages along its banks. For early prospectors, it was the route from Dawson to the new gold rush at Nome, even serving for one of those miners as a bicycle trail all the way from Dawson to Nulato. The Yukon River was most of the trail as the relay of mushers in 1925 raced with the diphtheria serum from Nenana to Nome. Even now the river serves as a winter highway, particularly with the cost of air travel so high. And, for a length of the Iditarod Trail Sled Dog Race, it became part of the race track as the mushers began to look north along 140 miles of river trail that would end at Kaltag.

The leaders crossed the land between the rivers quickly. After resting from around midnight until nine in the morning on the ninth day of the race, Jerry Riley drove the trail to Anvik in six hours and arrived ahead of the others. His team was drooping, though. He left Shageluk with eight dogs and when he hit Anvik he had one riding in the sled. He dropped that dog at Anvik.

The front runners ran on broken trail, but some of the mushers following found the trail from Shageluk to the river difficult going. The long open valley provided little protection from the winds, and drifts had piled up, obliterating the trail. Patty Friend, the Bureau of Land Management carpenter and former instructor in the National Outdoor Leadership School, tried to fight her way through the snow in the dark without her headlamp. She and Eep Anderson spent three and a half hours going nowhere, plodding back and forth through deep drifts, trying to locate the trail and taking valuable time and energy from themselves and their dogs. Her trip took more than eight hours while others made it in less than six.

Bob Chlupach of Eagle River also fought the drifts between Shageluk and the river, taking several of the wrong options in the confusing maze of trails. He had been gaining on that second bunch of leaders but by the time he struggled into Anvik, that group was rested and already heading upriver toward the next stop at Grayling.

Even with team after team passing through it, the trail filled in again. For John Wood, one more battle with the trail and deep snow almost ended his race. He broke trail through deep drifts all the way across the flats and river to Anvik. Since the beginning, Wood had been complaining that the trail was well broken for the first mushers who went through, but nobody went back and broke trail for those coming behind. So the thirty or so mushers stretched behind the leaders had to break their own trail much of the way." I could sit down and tell you all the places it's been bad, but it's all but a hundred miles," Wood would recall afterward.

After another tough section of trail, Wood was just about ready to give up. At Anvik he wanted to call his wife back in Chugiak and discuss with her the possibility of scratching. Wood felt that it was only fair, after all the help she had given in preparation for the race, that they talk it over before he quit. At the Anvik Community Center, the checkpoint, Wood asked how he could find a telephone. Most of the bush villages in Alaska have only one phone, which is connected to the outside world by satellite. Operators are paid to monitor the phone and take messages. One of the people in the checkpoint gave Wood directions to the telephone building, which was most of the way across the village, about a mile. The musher had just come 620 miles across the face of Alaska, much of it working hard, fighting wind and snowdrifts, and the last leg of that trip had been particularly demoralizing. One more mile of walking, across the village of Anvik, looked like too much and Wood, instead of making his call, faded into sleep on the floor of the community center. Despite the noise around him he slept through the night and in the morning he awakened rested. He checked his dogs and they, too, had rested well. They came up lively and when Wood looked them over, he decided to go on. He had made a decision to drive a dog team some four hundred miles farther rather than walk a mile to make a phone call.

Not everybody made it past the Anvik Community Hall the way John Wood did. The people of Anvik had laid out a feast in the hall, with pots and bowls and plates of food, much of it wild game — moose and caribou and salmon. In and out of the bustle of the new log building, Rudy Demoski checked teams through and talked with anyone who was willing. The race excited Demoski, and he wanted to be part of it. He had run the Iditarod three times and come in fourth in 1974. He planned to run again and was constantly bartering, talking, thinking money and preparing his race. Dog racing in his family goes a long way back. There was a Demoski racing dogs upriver at Nulato in 1910 in the heyday of the Iditarod gold rush.

At one point Demoski ran back into the community center excitedly, saying to anyone who'd listen, "I just made a deal with Isaac for his whole team — next year." If it was true, the combination of Okleasik dogs with Demoski's could produce a top team. Isaac Okleasik of Teller was known as one of the most knowledgeable dog men in the state. Although he never won the Iditarod, he did win the state centennial running in 1967, and other mushers constantly visited him to buy dogs or just talk and learn.

But Okleasik's race had ended for this year. He slumped on a long bench, a cold strangling him so badly that every time he tried to talk all that came from his throat were gurgles. The cold was the result, more than likely, of falling asleep in the trail back near McGrath. He had to scratch at Anvik and was waiting for an airplane to take him to Bethel and the nearest hospital, about 140 air miles to the south. When the race pilot finally got him to the hospital, he was diagnosed as having pneumonia.

Herbie Nayokpuk, long a favorite in the race both for his fast teams and his friendly manner, also reached Anvik with problems. His dogs had gotten sick and he too began talking about quitting. He didn't think he could drive the team much farther but planned to keep going a while to see if they'd pick up. If they didn't, he'd just go until he found a place with an airstrip large enough to land a plane that could haul out his whole team and all his gear.

For Ken Chase, the turning point at Anvik was different. Chase came home; he was the village corporation president and his family was a major force in the village. All the way along the trail he had been nursing his dogs, bringing them back from the fight that had drained them so badly back in Anchorage. He had been running the venerable lead dog Piper in swing for much of the way to ease the strain on his most reliable dog. Piper had led Chase's team in every Iditarod, man and dog being the only ones to have competed in all of the seven races. But now in Anvik, the dogs nestled right into their home lot and when it came time to leave, they balked. But Piper was rested and recovered by that time, and when it looked as if Chase was going on, Piper decided he was going, too, and he literally pulled the rest of the team out of the dog lot through town and out onto the trail. As his team was recuperating, Chase had been gaining steadily in the race. From close to last position at Skwentna, he had come back to where he left Anvik in twenty-third place. Still, he was almost two days behind the leaders.

For some, the hospitality of the Anvik Community Center was welcome, but for the leaders there was no rest. Each of the drivers in the front-running group stayed at Anvik between three and a half and six hours. Lindner went out first after just three and a half. May was second after four, but his time in Anvik, though short, was well spent.

May was still nursing the dogs that had what he referred to as the plague. Several of his dogs were sick and although determined, he was still breaking his schedule to cut his mileage in half. The dogs were coming back but not all of them had recovered and May, like Nayokpuk, was thinking of cashing it in for the year. As he looked over the recovering dogs, though, he decided he could go on. "The dogs were healthy enough to start with that they were able to overcome it. Some of them relapsed as much as twice but they were basically healthy," he said. In Anvik a race veterinarian asked him if he had any dogs who weren't drinking or eating.

"Yeah, I got a couple," May said.

"I'll put some water in them," the vet said.

May, who had been outspoken against tubing, said, "No. I'll drop the dogs first. I'm an ethical freak or something. No. No. No."

The vet said he wasn't going to tube the dogs and over May's protest brought out a gallon jug filled with warm water. A short plastic spout came out of the cap.

He told May to take the dog by the muzzle and open his mouth. The vet said he'd just lay that spout on the dog's tongue and the dog would swallow. May said no, that it wouldn't work, but when the vet poured, the dog just laid there and gulped the water down. Explained May later, "It's a natural function for a dog to swallow when he's got water on his tongue. I was really happy." That was just enough to get May stimulated. There were a lot more miles on the runners for thinking before Nome.

Of the leading group, May and Lindner seemed to pay less attention to what the others were doing, running on their own schedules rather than keying their time to other drivers, and they left Anvik for Grayling — eighteen miles upriver — within fifteen minutes of each other in the afternoon of the ninth day of the race. The rest of the bunch, Swenson, Peters, Riley and Honea, left for Grayling between eight and nine that evening.

The next morning Patty Friend reached Anvik near the point of exhaustion after slogging through the deep snow of the Shageluk wood lots. She said she'd felt that way for most of the race. "I made the choice to follow Jerry Riley's training schedule. And that's a really tough schedule. You're run through the wringer and so are the dogs. It's the kind of a schedule where the human being doesn't matter at all. If the schedule said I had to do a forty-miler today or a forty-five-miler, that's what I did.

"I just wanted to run the race and have fun doing it and do the best job I could. But even when we started we were exhausted, me and the dogs.

"So I got out on the race and I had this schedule and I had all this stuff I was supposed to be doing and it was just — I was so tired — emotionally."

She said she felt the pressure, not only of the race, but from the expectations of others. "Everyone had reasons for me to do well in the race that didn't have a thing in the world to do with me." Eventually the pressure from others began to bother her.

"It was just their attitude. I mean they had seen this team and it was a pretty good team." She had won the Cantwell 200, the first woman in recent memory to win any kind of a long-distance sled dog race, and that added to the pressure for her to do well. But by the time she reached Anvik she was running about a day behind the leaders and arrived in twenty-second place.

Shellie Vandiver, who was traveling the trail as health aide and general roustabout, had been encouraging her. "By the time I got to Anvik even Shellie had given up and just wanted to help," Friend said. "She went around town and found me a beaver to buy so I could feed my dogs."

While Vandiver looked through the village for dog food, Friend rummaged through her gunny sack to sort out the new gear and food. Her mother and father had come up from Oregon to help her prepare for the race and others had joined the effort. In the process of packing the gunny sacks for the race, they'd hidden notes of encouragement in with her equipment.

"My mom is really religious, not like ritual religious, kind of like spiritual. She had been writing me notes and I'd find them in my food all along the trail, in my drops. And my dad and different people would write notes to me. There was this little note from my mom. I found it at Anvik. It said something like 'Jesus Christ could call upon ten thousand angels.' And I thought, Oh, Mom.''

She tucked the note away in her gear and in her memory as she packed for the short trip upriver to Grayling.

Teams passed through Anvik over the next four days. The same day Friend was leaving, Pat Hurren, the twenty-six-year-old race marshal, who was from Whitehorse, in the Yukon Territory, stood talking with a group of people outside the community hall when one more musher drew up to check out. Hurren exchanged jibes with the musher while Demoski checked the gear. Hurren commented to a bystander how his feet felt a little cold. With his back to the dogs he chatted with the musher, and then the driver went back to the sled to hike the team out of town. Hurren looked a little perplexed as he realized his right foot all of a sudden felt warm. He turned around to see the team's wheel dog put his leg back down and run out of town in front of the sled, leaving the race marshal standing in a little circle of yellow snow. After the disappearing musher, Hurren yelled, "I'm going to buy that dog and make it die a thousand deaths."

While Hurren changed his socks and washed his foot he had to ponder a more serious difficulty. Time and checkers finally had caught up with Karl Clauson. When he was asked to produce his Iditarod cachets, the packet of postmarked envelopes he was supposed to be carrying, he couldn't find them and expressed as much surprise as anyone. Meanwhile, his family had found the packet at the bottom of the laundry bag he'd shipped home from McGrath and notified the trail committee. Under the race rules Clauson could have been disqualified for not carrying the cachets, and the decision rested with Hurren. The marshal didn't want to disqualify the musher and after some thought and discussion he decided to hold Clauson in Anvik until the cachets could be returned to him. Hurren reasoned the mistake was partly the fault of the checkers who should have caught the error earlier, since that was their job. In the interim, the bundle of envelopes was sent back out to the trail but got locked inside the Kaltag Post Office on a weekend and had to be searched for by the race people. Then the bundle had to be flown to Anvik. Clauson spent two days in the village waiting, but at least he wasn't disqualified from the race.

By the time the race reached Anvik, the teams were spread over five days and 200 miles of trail, the leaders heading up the Yukon River while those at the tail end were heading out onto the Kusko-kwim at McGrath. Ahead of them all lay 140 miles of the Yukon River, where they would go north into the teeth of a wind howling unobstructed into the teams' faces. The first stop on this section was Grayling, about eighteen miles upriver, and even that short leg would be treacherous for some.

14. Anvik to Grayling

FROM ANVIK THE TRAIL DROPPED DOWN A STEEP BANK, ONTO A SLOUGH, curved to the left, then curled back right to follow the slough around an island for a couple of miles before crossing the Anvik River where it joined the Yukon. The trail presented two left turns, one for each river. Then it crossed the Yukon. Winds had been howling down the river, and the trailblazers familiar with it had cut the trail on the east side where the winds wouldn't bother the mushers as much.

This was the first taste of those river winds that would buffet the mushers and dogs at a steady twenty to thirty knots, with some gusts reaching fifty and sixty.

Because the trail crossed the big river, it confused some of the drivers, particularly those who went out at night. On the evening of the ninth day of the race the leaders pushed down the bank and turned up the slough. Lindner, May, Honea, Swenson, Peters, Terry Adkins and Riley left within two hours of each other on a clear windy night.

Even for a trailwise team like Swenson's, with teams ahead of them, the maze of trails confused his leaders. There was supposed to be a haw turn to the left to turn up the Yukon and he knew that

— he'd been there before, won the race on the very same trail. But the angle at which the slough hit the opening with the Anvik and Yukon disoriented him for a time. "I went up the Anvik River a ways," he recalled. He reached a fish camp he hadn't expected and took a look at the stars. They weren't in the right place and he realized he'd gone the wrong way. Turning the team, he found the trail that headed across the Yukon.

The eighteen miles to Grayling had turned into maybe twenty-five because of his confusion on the Yukon. Despite the mistake, Swenson made the run in just three hours and ten minutes.

May, in front of Swenson, traveled the river in less than four hours. Along the way he kept watching the dogs he was pampering and recalled the way they had taken water in Anvik. As he thought about the drinking he began to carry the process a step or two further.

"Why couldn't you," he asked later, "take a rubber squeeze-bulb and go down the line and water those reluctant dogs? And, as a matter of course, give them some broth in the morning before breakfast. That would be real neat, to go down the line with a couple of gallons of broth in the morning. Give everybody a pint, then get up and go."

At Grayling he talked with race veterinarian Tony Funk and suggested his plan, maybe even as a solution to the tubing controversy. Funk listened while May explained his whole theory. Then the vet smiled. He looked at the musher and said, "You're a little late. Patty Friend's been doing it all along." During the race Friend had been using a squeeze-bulb food baster to water dogs that wouldn't drink. A dishwashing-detergent bottle worked even better, she found. She'd curl a dog's lips back and just squeeze a little broth into its mouth. May tried the same thing at Grayling, and it worked.

He and the other leaders, after four to six hours in Anvik and the short run to Grayling, stayed overnight before heading up the river in the morning of the tenth day of the race.

That afternoon, at about 2:30, Friend and her nine dogs headed out of Anvik for their first run on the river. But they went back. "We went out of Anvik and I don't know if it was a premonition or what, but it just felt like 'it's not right.' I went to the slough first and I wasn't sure I was on the right trail. I went out a little ways and then I turned around and came back. I wanted to make sure I was on the right trail."

A villager gave her directions and for the second time she left Anvik, heading for the Yukon River and the three- or four-hour trip to Grayling. For the short run she had decided to rest her leaders and put a couple of "glorified swing dogs" up front.

Ahead, Crazy Horse made one of his patented landings on the river in front of Grayling. He'd picked up on a photographer's term, *flat light*, for the diffused light that leaves highlights undefined. Several airplanes were parked on the river next to a line of tracks that marked where they had landed. When he brought the little airplane down, what looked like a flat landing strip turned into a series of jolting, bone-jarring hard-packed snowdrifts, and the plane hit violently, bouncing back up into the air and slamming back down several times until he could bring it under control. When he brought it to a stop, he turned a little sheepishly and said, "Flat light, bouncy landing."

Above the airplane a steep bank maybe fifty feet high rose to the village of Grayling, awaiting the mushers in the gathering dusk. A new village, it was built in 1963 after several families, tired of the annual floodings on the Yukon and Innoko rivers, abandoned the village of Holikachuk and moved to higher ground. The village consisted of log homes mixed with familiar government-designed, square, one-story frame dwellings. The village had electrical power and a big white dish antenna for the satellite telephone. Snow lay deep, the deepest that even some of the village elders could remember. In summer, it was two or three steps up to the doors of most of the houses, but now steps had to be cut down to the doors three or four feet through the snow.

At the long rectangular community center, a ham radio operator talked with other checkpoints, and several mushers' wives and other race followers chatted while nibbling dried fruit and raisins, all that was left for sale in the village store. Now and then a driver would check in or out. Gary Hokkanen stopped by for coffee. The conversation was light, but over the course of the day and into the evening, here and there the name of Patty Friend would rise out of the low din.

By 8:30 in the evening a tension had crept into the room. Friend had been on the trail six hours by then and phone calls from Anchorage added to the concern. Ken Chase checked in at 8:35. He had left Anvik about three hours later than Friend but hadn't seen her on the trail. Race marshal Pat Hurren, who had flown in from Anvik, decided her disappearance was serious enough to require action, and through the ham operator he called Anvik and asked folks to go out and search while he sent others out from Grayling on snow machines.

"I don't know why I didn't see the turnoff," Friend said later. "I think it was because there was a trail through a wood lot and another trail that turned diagonally and went off. That was the race trail and I missed it.

"I had the beaver in the sled and it was extra weight," she said — thirty or so additional pounds can add a noticeable burden.

"Pretty soon the trail petered out. There was nothing, absolutely nothing. It was windblown so what would happen was you'd have a flat surface and then a drop of maybe eighteen inches and then it would go up again and you'd have a stretch of maybe four feet and then it would happen again — the drop.

"There was no trail, and the straight and the drop and the strain — it wasn't flat. Pretty soon my dogs were feeling really sad. I started walking in front of them, but the sled kept hitting the wheel dogs because of the dropoffs. It was ever so sad and we walked and we walked. I kept asking myself if I could lead the dogs like this for eighteen miles.

"The trail was really rough; it was from all that wind. After a while there was no trail, absolutely no trail at all. There was this cliff and I kept weaving in and out, and in and out, trying to find the trail, and we kept going on these little blown areas and then they'd drop down. Really rough. It was from all that wind. The wind really whistled down the side we were on."

Ahead of her, as she plowed up the wrong side of the river, water bubbled up through open ice where warm springs came up through the river bottom.

"We just kept weaving back and forth," she said. "I kept thinking there's just got to be a trail. I kept looking across the Yukon. People think of the Yukon as just a river, but it's big and it's like a desert, just all wide and white.

"It was really frustrating. I mean there was no trail. It was eighteen miles, only eighteen miles."

By 9:30 P.M. the first snow machines had returned to Grayling, and the drivers hadn't found Friend or her team. Hurren by this time had dug out his heavy-weather gear and was gathering others to make a more thorough search. He had noticed the open water when he'd flown over the trail earlier in the day.

Out on the river, Friend and her dogs trudged on toward Grayling. "We went into this crap for the longest time. It was dark. It was cold. I was getting so tired and so cold and what I always did when I got tired and cold, was I'd give the dogs a snack and I'd eat something myself and I'd take a little sleep. So I had a snack and they did. I had fish sticks; I liked the grease. It's real important. Then I curled up on the sled. It was so cold. The wind was just whistling. I'd say conservatively it was forty miles an hour.

"So I took this little sleep and boy, I woke up, and the dogs, they were so sad. I was sad because I knew the moisture was being ripped away from their bodies out in that wind.

"But it was funny, I thought of Mom's note and I said, ' All right, Mom, I'll call for ten thousand angels.' And I called for ten thousand angels.

"All of a sudden there was this snow machine on the horizon, I mean immediately there was light on the horizon. And this person said, 'You want me to show you where the trail is?' And I looked at him and I said, 'Yeah, yeah, I'd like that.'

"And it took us — it probably took us forty-five minutes because it was still really tough going and the fellow would have to stop and wait for my dogs and then go ahead. And then we were fine, once we got on the trail and we went into Grayling."

With Friend and the dogs back on the trail, the man on the snow machine went on ahead and caught Hurren and the big search party before they left. He said he'd seen Friend at Charlie Wolf's point and that she'd be in town shortly.

Patty Friend's dogs moved quickly once they were on the hard-packed race trail. "I couldn't believe what it was like. I mean when we got on the trail there was hardly any wind. It's incredible how much wind there was on the other side, and how little, just a breeze, where they'd put the trail."

About twenty minutes behind the snow machine the exhausted musher and dogs pulled up to the community hall in Grayling. What should have been a three- to four-hour run had taken her more than eight and a half, and a crowd gathered around to hear the story. On many of the faces, particularly Hurren's, the enormous relief was obvious.

"The wind just took the soup out of us," Friend told the race marshal.

It hadn't taken all the soup out of them because while Friend and Hurren talked one of the lead dogs mounted the other. "It's okay," Friend told Hurren, "they're both males."

"They're both males," Hurren said louder for the crowd's benefit.

As the titters of laughter died, he said, "Calisthenics, Iditarod calisthenics," to another round of laughter.

The strain of the experience didn't leave much room for laughter from Friend, though, and she politely thanked everyone for the concern and asked where she was supposed to stay. A villager came forward to lead her toward a house.

Later Friend said of the experience, "It made me sick to think of all the time we lost there, plus we got so tired."

Tired as she was, she didn't want to break the schedule of four hours running and four hours of rest, and as she disappeared into the darkness of the village she said that she only wanted to stay an hour and a half or two. It didn't work. Once she had the dogs bedded down and fed she crashed and slept through the night.

Not until 10:30 the next morning was she ready for the trail again, looking fresher and rested. At the community hall, she stood in front of her team while veterinarian Funk stood on the runners, holding the brake. The dogs stood up, their tails high, a sign that they were ready to go again. "Who wants to go?" Friend called to the dogs. "You want to go? Who wants to go?" She turned and ran down the street toward the river and the team ran behind her, tails wagging, trotting comfortably, following, ready for another crack at the Yukon. Funk jumped off at the top of the bank and the red-snowsuited musher and her team disappeared over the edge on their way to Kaltag, 140 miles to the north.

The weather offered no respite from the day before. The sky hung grim and gray over the river and the wind howled again into the faces of the team — the kind of a day that set the stage for sorrow in the village of Grayling, where a village elder had died.

At Grayling, residents planned a potlatch for a wake in the community hall. The corpse was laid there and the race people moved out in respect. Realizing the ham operator would have a lot of trouble moving his equipment, the villagers offered to let him stay. He decided he'd just as soon not live alone with the dead man's body and disassembled his apparatus and moved to a small cabin where a new headquarters had been established.

The race people in Grayling had solved one problem. At many of the checkpoints the mushers' gunny sacks had been left outdoors for them to find. At one time or another many of the drivers couldn't find their bags, suggesting the possibility that someone had picked through them, hidden them or even stolen them. At Grayling the bags were kept in a storeroom at the community hall and each musher had to ask for his own. Then a villager would haul it out to him. The bags stayed in the storeroom even as the villagers prepared for the funeral potlatch.

The same day, Ken Chase checked out. A familiar face in the village, where his brother Ernie ran Grayling Air Service, Chase joked with the checker.

"Where's your snowshoes?" the checker asked, going down the list of mandatory equipment.

"In my back pocket."

"Where's your sleeping bag?"

"In my other back pocket."

"Where's your cachets?"

"Tied to my lead dogs."

With that the growing smiles broke into laughter and Chase, too, headed for the bank down onto the river.

As Chase left Grayling, the leaders were pressing toward Kaltag in the north. The mushers in the rear were four days behind, some just starting on the trail from McGrath to Iditarod, and the fifty-one teams still in the race would take more than five days to pass through the mourning village of Grayling.

15. Grayling to Kaltag

BACK IN MCGRATH, RON BRINKER HAD PREDICTED EMMITT PETERS WOULD make his move at Grayling. If Peters did, he wouldn't be alone. The six leaders had turned into a juggernaut, moving almost as one, and none of them was going to let anybody else get too far ahead. Lindner, May and Honea left Grayling within forty minutes of each other on the morning of the tenth day of the race. Terry Adkins, flirting with the leaders, had caught them at Grayling and, cutting his rest a little, ran out of Grayling after the first three. Swenson watched Peters. When Peters began packing his sled and harnessing his dogs, so did Swenson. Since Swenson packed and harnessed a little faster, he was out on the trail a few minutes ahead of Peters. Behind them, Riley's turn came: down the long bank and north. Less than two hours separated the first seven mushers as they pushed into the river's winds.

Ahead, what trail the blowing snow left visible followed the banks and lee sides of islands where the trailbreakers had tried to give the mushers shelter from winds that came howling down the open valley in gusts of more than fifty knots. Out of Grayling the trail cut between the western bank of the river and the first of the two Eagle Islands on the way to Kaltag. The teams passed Fox Point Island and several

158

smaller, unnamed islands, until they reached Blackburn Island, where a sign next to the trail advertised free coffee and a warm cabin for the mushers. An arrow pointed to the home of Clint and Vanita Thurmond, and many of the mushers took the opportunity to duck in out of the wind, camp, or just visit and give their dogs a break.

Then they were back on the trail, weaving through sloughs and around the small islands, many of them populated by moose browsing on the tender shoots of birch saplings. On one island, less than a mile long, twenty-three moose browsed among the leafless trees as the mushers passed. Winter can be tough on moose, what with the lack of forage, particularly when the snow is as deep as it was this year, and with poachers. Someone had shot a moose along this part of the trail but hadn't recovered all of the meat by the time the dog teams went through. Susan Butcher's dogs found the meat.

Driving up the river Butcher dozed on the back of her sled, dropping into sleep now and again. At one point she came out of her sleep and discovered that the dogs had stopped. "I woke up and they were chewing on something," she recalled. "I got them going and we passed what looked like a moose quarter on each side of the trail." The dead moose wasn't the only one to bother the mushers.

When the leaders reached the checkpoint at Eagle Slide, sixty-five miles and about thirteen hours north of Grayling, they found that an old bull had taken up residence behind the cabin. Eagle Slide was a gap cut through forest on the western river bank near the second Eagle Island. The clearing just accommodated the cabins that Ken Chase owned there. Steve Conaster and his father Ralph ran the checkpoint, with Steve, like other youngsters along the way, watching, planning, scheming and dreaming about running the race himself. His own team of dogs rested beside the cabin and several of the mushers admired them, some even offering to buy the whole team. The dogs had the build, and some even had the blonde coloring, of Ken Chase's breed, and as it turned out, Steve had worked with Chase and helped him train for the race. He wasn't selling any dogs, though. He would turn eighteen during the next year and he'd need the dogs for his own run at the Iditarod.

It was the old moose, though, that created the most interest at the checkpoint. He'd decided to bed down behind the cabin in a spot out of the wind that otherwise would have been a great place to rest a team of dogs. But there was no moving him. Rick Swenson was

particularly irritated by the moose. Swenson was constantly sensitive about the amount and quality of rest his dogs were getting, and
he complained that the mere presence of the moose kept his dogs
from sleeping well. For all the sympathy he got he might just as well
have gone and told it to the moose. He was invited to go shag it
away himself if he wanted. For his part, the old bull had found a
good place to lie down and wasn't about to leave just because some
crazy human wanted to rest a bunch of dogs. Several people went
back to try to chase the moose away, but for the most part he
ignored them. If the people became too irritating, he'd just stand up,
shake the snow off, lay his ears back, plant his feet firmly into the
snow and defy them to come any closer. No one particularly
wanted to be stomped by 1,500 pounds of angry moose, so eventually he was left alone in his bed, where he stayed for the better part
of three days.

While Swenson tried to get rid of the moose, Peters searched
through the pile of gunny sacks on the river for his bag of dog food
and supplies. Sometimes, with all the logistics of organizing the
race, the committee and support people make a mistake, and this
year one of those mistakes was misplacing the bag Peters had
tagged for Eagle Slide. His bag just never made it to the checkpoint.
It wasn't that there wasn't enough to eat — the bags awaiting those
mushers who had scratched were still in the pile and Peters was
free to go through and take whatever he wanted. But nothing he
would find could match exactly what he'd already been feeding,
and new foods could easily throw off the dogs' digestion. That in
turn might hurt his racing chances, maybe even giving the dogs the
sickness, which Peters so far had avoided.

So Peters fed his dogs some unfamiliar foods, but in that lead
group he got little sympathy; nobody was wasting time worrying
about somebody else. Though the front runners camped together
and joked when they met, the edge of competition underlined
everything, and after about an eight-hour stay at Eagle Slide to rest
and feed, the juggernaut moved out onto the river again, heading
for Kaltag, sixty-five miles to the north.

They were back on the trail and back in the wind. What the open
river and the wind threw at the mushers and dogs tested the determination of every man, woman and animal who ran into it. In
places the wind blew up huge drifts and in others it blew the ice

clear, leaving no footing. Howling out of the north, at times hitting the mushers and dogs at fifty knots, the wind tore into everything in its way. In temperatures around zero, even the slightest breeze can turn exposed flesh numb in minutes. And on the river, the temperatures at night were dropping to as much as thirty below.

The breeze generated by just the ten- or eleven-mile-an-hour pace of the dogs caused the wind-chill factor, at zero degrees, to drop to twenty below. Standing still in a fifty-knot wind at zero, a man is in a chill factor of minus sixty. The slightest bit of forehead or finger left to the mercy of that wind and cold is transformed to a headache and pain almost immediately, and then, if the person is unlucky enough, no pain. Mushers constantly checked each others' faces for the white spots that are the first signs of frostbite. Gary Hokkanen had put a canteen full of water inside his parky to keep the water liquid. Within two hours after he left Grayling the water had frozen solid, inside his coat.

If the wind hurt the mushers, it also tore into and demoralized the dogs. This was the place where the determined trail leader, the dog who would go through anything, became doubly important, more for his mental than his physical toughness. Going into a wind, a dog can decide very quickly he doesn't want to go. A day behind the leaders, Hokkanen saw his dogs developing this attitude. Between driving into the winds and slogging over and through deep drifts, Hokkanen knew he had to help the team. "I realized we weren't going to make it unless I got off the runners. I ran from Eagle Slide to Kaltag." Sixty-five miles.

When the going becomes difficult, the relationship between the dog and the musher becomes particularly important, even crucial. Because he was concerned for his dogs, Hokkanen ran sixty-five miles. A day behind, Ron Brinker actually had a dog show concern for him. Brinker had joked about his lead dog, Rabbit, the one with the same name as several others in the race, the dog he'd argued with about the trail going into McGrath. As Rabbit led his team up the Yukon River into that wind, Brinker, on the runners, occasionally would duck down behind the basket of the sled to give himself some shelter. Somehow, a good lead dog will know what's going on behind him, maybe just to see what he can get away with, or maybe just to make sure everything's all right. And at times a dog will sense misfortune. In any case, Rabbit, as he trotted up the river, checked back and didn't see the musher on the sled. So the lead dog turned back to investigate. There was Brinker, hunkered down out of the wind, his whole team stopped and curved around back toward him and his lead dog looking at him as if to ask, "What's the deal, Boss?" Once the dog saw that Brinker was there and everything was all right, he turned the team without command and pulled them back onto the trail heading north again.

All the way up the river the mushers helped the dogs, changing leaders to take the pressure off, stopping, resting, snacking, but still making demands, pushing toward Nome. As they drove into that wind, other, subtler aspects of the race were catching up with many of them.

Along the way, the front runners were averaging little more than two hours of sleep in every twenty-four. "The dogs get more sleep than the musher," Joe May pointed out. When a team pulled into a checkpoint or to camp, the dogs curled up and rested right away. But for the driver the work had just begun. Food had to be prepared and cooked. In camp sometimes a fire was needed. The musher had to check the dogs, their feet, their muscles, tend to them, take booties off, put them on, pack and unpack the sled and cook for himself. In a four-hour rest stop, the musher might take an hour and a half unpacking and feeding, and another hour and a half tending to the dogs and repacking the sled. That left him only an hour to himself, during which he might doze. Then again he might just eat and talk or, more likely, continue his endless cups of coffee. For Hokkanen the amount of sleep was maybe three hours a day. Friend, even after her harrowing trip into Grayling, wanted to sleep only an hour or two, even though it didn't work out that way. "You never get enough sleep," she stated. Among the leaders, over-sleeping could lose the race, and there were mushers who actually had yelled at friendly people who were trying to do right by letting an exhausted racer sleep when it seemed he needed to.

Even when there was the opportunity to sleep, more likely than not the mushers would linger over coffee or, if they crawled off into a corner for a few fitful minutes of dozing, they were awakened by noises around them, real or imagined. There were distractions, too, in the bustle of the checkpoints — some that didn't belong. Lindner, asleep at Grayling, had been awakened by a television crew and asked to roll over so they could film him sleeping.

In addition, for the leaders there was the added pressure of their competitors. The front runners worried constantly about their dogs, time, food, trail conditions and each other. And as they moved closer and closer to Nome, the pressure increased proportionately, keeping the racers working and their worries building at the same time their bodies were changing from the lack of sleep. The closer they came to Nome, the less of an edge anybody needed to break away. Early on, a half-day or even a whole day didn't put anyone too far out of reach, but by Kaltag even a couple of hours could make a difference. Just the watching alone cut into the quality, if not the quantity, of sleep. There would be no relief until Nome.

The race was a constant, twenty-four-hour day not only with very little sleep but, for many, a poor diet. After maybe years of experimenting and working with and agonizing over the perfect food for his dogs, more than one musher shortchanged himself with his own food. One driver shipped only frozen burritos for his trail food. Del Allison shipped himself Chinese dinners that a friend who owned a restaurant had prepared for him. As the saying goes, an hour later he was hungry again, and everywhere he went he tried to trade those dinners for anything that would stick with him a while.

Even those who had planned well discovered that the tremendous amount of energy put out was not being replenished even by the best of diets. Emmitt Peters sent himself Kentucky Fried Chicken, which, over the years, he had found sustained him successfully. Swenson liked the combination of pizza and cheese and steak — the steak cooked with as much as a quarter-pound of butter to add the fat that the humans needed as much as the dogs. Hokkanen, who was a friend of Swenson and had planned his race with him, shipped to the trail food containing 5,000 calories a day for himself. By comparison, normal recommendations for men between ages twenty-three and fifty range from 2,300 to 3,100 calories a day.

Even so, the diet was so deficient that Hokkanen ate raw sticks of butter just to keep up his energy, and he wasn't the only one. Added to the poor and irregular diets, the mushers, whenever they got a chance to sit down, tended to drink gallons of coffee or quarts of colas, both of which added to the dehydration already begun by the tremendous exertion in the dry, cold air. The result was a serious loss of body water. Even with the fine meals many villagers offered at checkpoints, most mushers lost weight as the demands of the race wreaked havoc on their bodies.

As the race wore on, the lack of sleep, poor diet, dehydration and pressure began to work on the mushers' minds as well as their bodies.

The long hours on the trail alone, coupled with everything else, began to tell, and after a time minds began to do strange things. There was Hokkanen, complaining of a deficient diet, conscious of it, moving on nervous energy, averaging maybe two or three hours of sleep a day, wired on coffee, eating butter, and heading into wind and cold that to his body felt like sixty degrees below zero. His canteen of water froze. And then when he thought the dogs might falter he stepped off the runners to run the sixty-five miles to get himself and his team to Kaltag.

How much can a man stand? Hokkanen found out. His mind wandered. He saw things. He was running up the middle of the river, a river a mile wide, bare of anything but snow — no trees, no branches, nothing except white that was lined a half-mile away on each side by dark banks. There in the middle of that river Hokkanen saw a sweeper, a low-hanging branch, the kind that would rip a musher right off the sled, and he ducked. He ducked so hard he smashed his nose on the drive bow. It bled, maybe a bone cracked, he didn't know. The shock of the blow brought him around and he realized he had seen a sweeper that hadn't been there. His mind had drawn a picture real enough to make him duck — but there had been no sweeper. The trail had gotten to Hokkanen as it had gotten to others before him and as it would get to still others before they reached Nome.

Jon Van Zyle at least could use the hallucinations in his paintings. One striking painting from his first race showed a large Eskimo face, a dog team moving across open snow coming out of the Eskimo's parka ruff, and lights on the dogs' feet flashing red and green as Van Zyle had seen them one night on the trail. Ken Chase in a previous race was approaching Koyuk, farther to the north, when he saw a giant neon light. Another musher remembered stopping and pulling his whole team and sled off the trail because a locomotive was coming at him. Hokkanen wore a bandage on his nose for the rest of the race as a reminder of how real the hallucinations could be.

Hokkanen continued on into the worst winds he'd ever seen in his life. Where others before him had found glare ice, Hokkanen found heavy drifts, and the wind hurled snow off the tops of them into his face, obscuring his vision. At times the wind drove snow through the ventilation slits in his ski goggles and he had to unpack the snow from his eyes. Because of the mist there were times when he could see only the sled and the wheel dogs, the other nine dogs disappearing into the snow ahead. His trip from Eagle Slide to Kaltag took him and his team almost twelve hours, which was faster than some of the leaders.

Other front runners on that stretch of river took between eleven and thirteen hours as they played their cat-and-mouse game of watching and moving in relation to each other, although some of the more independent ones — May, Lindner and Honea — refused to play. Some of them camped on the ice south of Kaltag. A trophy had been offered for the first team into the village and the mushers discussed who was going to win it. Finally Honea, who had led much of the way up the river, made the decision: "I'll go." And he left. Ahead of him Rich Burnham, who had run a previous race, drove a snow machine while he stuck birch saplings into the snow to mark the trail. Later he admitted he could barely keep ahead of Honea's dogs.

Behind the first group of teams, the wind left few of those trail markers standing. Rick Mackey, whose dogs had begun to come back from their illness, ran into the wind and drift and missed the saplings and the trail. Instead of following the packed, straighter Iditarod Trail, he ended up crisscrossing the river on snow machine trails. Slogging through the deeper snow on the lesser-used trails, Mackey worried that he was going to wear the team down again. As it was, he was having trouble bringing them out of the five-miles-an-hour pace they'd fallen into while they were sick.

Perhaps the worst the river threw at the dogs and drivers came as they rounded the corner at Twenty-two Mile, a point that far south of Kaltag that exposed the mushers to a length of river that offered no shelter. Ron Aldrich, a veteran of four previous races, ran into what he called maybe the worst he'd ever seen on the Iditarod Trail. "Winds and drifts," was all he could say to describe it.

A day behind Aldrich, four mushers experienced a hallucination of sorts but one that was reality. On the bank at Twenty-two Mile was a shelter, a six-by-eight-foot log-walled cabin with a canvas roof. Snow had piled up around the door, so there was only a small window open that the mushers could crawl through to sleep out of the wind. One night four drivers went in there: Bill Rose, Bud Smyth, Rome Gilman and Steve Adkins. Rose kept his eye out for a while to spot John Barron, with whom he was having a private race. Eventually Rose joined the others asleep on the floor, the four bodies filling the tiny space. But when they woke up in the morning there was another lump. "Who the hell is that?" somebody asked. "I don't know how anybody that big could have got through that window and found a place in there without waking anybody up," Rose marveled later. "I thought it was Barron, but he must have gone right on past." Out of the red bag, crammed into a corner of the cabin, emerged Del Allison, laughing. Shortly afterward they all crawled through the window and pushed on into the wind toward Kaltag, the last stop on the Yukon River.

By the time the race was stretched along the river, the leading teams were going faster and the slower teams were falling farther behind. Dog teams forged their way north on the river for nine days until the last team, driven by Gene Leonard, passed through Kaltag. The anticipation of getting off the Yukon must have driven many of them on their way. As bad as it was, the river claimed only one victim. Terry McMullin, the trapper from Eagle, scratched at Eagle Slide, suffering from pneumonia.

As the mushers came off the river exhausted, the town of Kaltag prepared to meet them exhilarated. Kaltag stands on a high bluff at a gentle bend in the Yukon, exposed to winds that pass down the river from the northeast. In places the wind had blown both snow and dust away from the bank, laying lines of brown through the openings between graying log structures on the river front and more modern ranch-type homes farther away. Iditarod airplanes, including Larry Thompson's, lined the airstrip on the southwest corner of the village.

There was an air of excitement and anticipation as the two hundred residents awaited the first teams to come off the river. And out on the river, dog drivers also felt anticipation — anticipation of getting away from the ice and wind and into the protection of the village.

Later a resident of Kaltag asked Swenson how the trail had been.

"The trail's good where the wind blows hard, bad where it only blows," Swenson said, his face bright pink where the wind had left it almost raw. "A typical Yukon River trail. I ran into some water in different places."

The questioner asked him if he'd lost any weight lately.

"I haven't lost any lately," Swenson answered and then, rolling his eyes, added, "I'm standing on the back of the sleigh eating."

The questioner almost took him seriously and asked if that was true.

"On this river? God, I hate this river."

16. Kaltag

THE CENTER OF IDITAROD ACTIVITY IN KALTAG WAS THE HOME OF LARRY Thompson, the colorful race pilot. There in Thompson's frame house, bright red with white trim, was gathered the entourage that was following the race. The two-story building looked as if it belonged more on an Ohio farm than on the high bluff overlooking the Yukon River in Alaska. The river as it passed Kaltag had finished its westward course and now flowed south. The Iditarod Trail rose off the river directly in front of the house, ascending a steep bank about sixty feet high. Throughout the day the officials, reporters and race followers moved in and out of the house, now and then casting watchful eyes toward the river for a first sight of the approaching mushers.

In a cold storeroom at the rear of the house, a pile of beaver carcasses awaited sale to the incoming mushers. One of the women flying along with the race had appropriated two of them and began building a stew in the propane-fired oven. Steve O'Brien, a trapping partner of Crazy Horse's brother Frank, winced at the sight. He was asking twenty-five dollars apiece for the beavers and watched fifty dollars go into that stewpot. Judging by the pile of carcasses, though, he would make plenty of money — money he wouldn't have received in the years before the race, when there wasn't much call for beaver meat and a trapper ate what he could and discarded the rest or used it for lynx bait.

The long, rectangular main room of the house served as kitchen, dining room and living room. At the back, where counters and a stove and refrigerator formed a white L, two women worked on the beaver stew, which was sending up a delicious aroma. Connecting the kitchen with the living area was a plank table, long and white, flanked by benches. Completing the furnishings was another L, couches in the living end of the room and, parallel to the table, a double Yukon stove — two fifty-five-gallon drums, one on top of the other, that heated the house. Multipaned windows lighted the parlor area and offered a view of the river. First stop for anyone entering the house was the table, where it was difficult to avoid a cup of coffee. During the afternoon Larry Thompson napped on one of the couches while the women busied themselves at the back with the stew, Jello and other dishes they planned to serve the already assembled group and the mushers to come.

Outside, villagers went about their business with, apparently, little interest in the activity at Thompson's. Kaltag is an older village than Grayling or Anvik. Old log and board houses stand along the river bluff, gray from exposure. As it had along most of the river, the snow lay deep here, and it was a few steps down to most of the houses. Each house had a small sign tacked near the front door identifying the occupying family. Even an old church, now converted to a house, its steeple still tall against the wind, carried the name of the family living inside. A group of men worked outside one house clearing snow from the doorway. Winds had compacted the snow so much that the workers used chain saws to cut it into blocks. Between 225 and 250 persons lived in Kaltag, most existing on a semi-cash, semi-subsistence economy, fishing in summer, trapping in winter, and taking jobs with government agencies when they're available.

Punctuating the life of the village, the diesel generator at Edgar Kalland's store and post office chunk-chunk-chunked in the background, sending black exhaust smoke in rings out a tube behind the log building. The Kallands showed a movie every Friday and Saturday evening and used their own generator rather than the newer power plant that served most of the village. Their chunker didn't quite put out the current that was needed and as a result the movies ran a little slower than they should have. For the people of Kaltag all the actors and actresses had bass voices, the result of a slow-moving sound track. The week's movie was to be "The Longest Day."

Edgar Kalland, who, with his wife, owned the store, was one of the four men surviving from the original serum relay to Nome. In 1925, Kalland as a youth had carried diphtheria serum about thirty miles from Nine Mile to Kokrines during that dramatic run to save the children of the gold rush. Kalland died in 1981.

Kaltag has a brand-new hexagonal log community center and a modern, out-of-place high school. The school officials had offered the school's home-economics room to those race followers who didn't have a place to stay. Near the school was a dog lot belonging to one of the villagers who'd found a novel way to recycle an old boat — he'd turned it upside-down and cut holes in the gunwales for the dogs to crawl through into the shelter.

Toward late afternoon anticipation heightened and people wandered over to the river bank now and then to see if anyone was coming. Rich Burnham, Thompson's son-in-law, came up the bank on a snow machine after marking trail in front of the leaders. An electricity began growing in the air. It happened at every check-point: the race was a festive occasion breaking up a long, hard winter. For all the beauty an outsider sees along the trail, winter for the people who live there can be severely depressing, particularly in March, the traditional cabin-fever season, when winter has gone on long enough and thoughts turn to spring long before the snow and ice have left.

Winter in Alaska takes its time seeping into the mind. In the fall there's an air of anticipation. Snow falls, the rivers freeze and the trapping's about to begin. For most, winter supplies have come up on the barges, there's food cached, fish dried, wood cut and the hunting season to look forward to. The days grow shorter and shorter to only about four hours of dim daylight by the time of the solstice in December. But the true cabin-fever season doesn't begin until the days grow longer. By March, when the equinox brings twelve hours of daylight, people have had enough of winter, but the snow and ice remain well into April, sometimes May. The change in the mind from winter to spring comes sooner than in the rivers — breakup hasn't taken the ice out yet — and there's a feeling of being trapped. The cold and the snow hang ominously over the land and depression manifests itself in violent ways. The rate of suicide is particularly high among the young people of the Yukon River villages. The state, in addition to leading in suicides, also leads the nation in violent deaths per capita, and both statistics show a bulge during the days of late winter. While cabin fever can't be blamed entirely, it certainly adds to the situation. The problem concerns many Native leaders as well as state social agencies. Among those concerned is Ken Chase, who, as a corporation president, has been working for a solution. Chase views the Iditarod at least in part as a chance to lift that boring and depressing atmosphere in the villages and provide something in the way of festivity to take minds out of the late winter doldrums.

Kaltag did take on a festive air as the residents awaited the arrival of the mushers, and there was a feeling that the event drove out at least some of the mental cobwebs and gave relief just when it was needed most.

Once Rich Burnham had driven up the river bank, the villagers knew the mushers couldn't be far behind. Gradually the residents moved toward the bluff, looking across the mile or so of snow-covered river ice to catch the first view. Village youngsters, playing along the bank in their colorful parkas, used anything they could find, from plastic sheets to garbage-can lids, to sled down the steep bank to the river below. Out on the ice a pile of plastic bags held the village's trash, waiting for the river to carry it out with the ice at breakup. As a crowd gathered, Edgar Kalland walked to the bank alone, his shock of white hair moving in the breeze as he scanned the river through dark-rimmed glasses. The serum-musher-turned-storekeeper took a special interest in the Iditarod. His name was on the trophy given to the first musher into Kaltag each year, and I wondered if Edgar Kalland, if he were a generation younger, would be running the Iditarod. Maybe not. In Kalland's youth there was little time for anything beyond basic survival, let alone a race like this. Even the serum run, in his recollection, was simply another chore to be done, and few of those participating had felt anything like the heroes the world made them out to be. In any case, whether he would have run in the race or not, Edgar Kalland stood and watched and perhaps remembered.

Earl and Madeline, two of the children who had been sledding on the bank, came running up the bluff at 5:48 P.M. yelling, "Dog team! Dog team!"

How they saw the team before anyone else was a mystery, but over on the east bank of the river a pencil line moved across the expanse of white. To the north the skyline disappeared in haze but a line of light on the southern horizon illuminated the almost imperceptible movement of Don Honea's dog team. As the crowd grew on the bluff, he came closer, pumping behind the sled, then turning the team westward toward the village. In the excitement, several of the children roared down the hill on makeshift sleds at the same time, followed by a riderless sled that caused titters in the crowd that now had grown to maybe a hundred.

The kids kept yelling, "Dog team! Dog team!" the thing to shout to gain the approval of the adults in the crowd, who also were excited by the arrival.

"Who is it?"

"Honeadon, Honeadon."

The musher disappeared behind a snowdrift for a moment, then reappeared over a rise. Chatter and laughter rose as the villagers awaited the too-slow team. Cameras came out all over the place and Edgar Kalland lifted his battered old 35-mm for a picture of the first man into Kaltag.

As the musher came closer the kids began whistling, calling the dogs. By 6:01 Honea's voice, talking to the dogs, floated across the ice. "Hike. Come on. Hike." The dogs, anticipating a village and a rest, appeared to pick up the pace.

"Look at that leader."

"Yeah, look at it."

The dog appeared to be limping, perhaps favoring a tender foot.

By then all the kids were whistling. The team reached the bottom of the bluff and the crowd moved to form a chute at the top for the dogs to run through. Just off the river, Honea stepped off the runners to trudge up the hill, easing the load for the dogs. Soon he was at the top and into the crowd, which collapsed around him. The villagers clapped and cheered. Iditarod at Kaltag had begun.

At 6:05 Don Honea officially checked in, and the kids crowded around him and the sled and the dogs, jumping, touching the sled fondly, dreaming, and the adults, a few with dreams in their own eyes, circled around behind the children.

"How far to Unalakleet?" Honea asked, only half seriously, creating a question as to whether he'd just keep on going, without a break, to the next checkpoint. The question, one of a series to come from the mushers, was meant to unsettle the others and leave them with doubts about his plans. Perhaps the least ruffled of the leading mushers, Honea still looked almost dapper with his pencil-thin mustache and the yellow-tinted dark-rimmed glasses.

Soon renewed shouts of "Dog team, dog team" outweighed interest in the musher already in town, and the crowd, grown by now to about two hundred, rushed for the river bank again. If the river bank had been a boat it would have been listing precariously as the passengers rushed from side to side.

By 6:11 three more pencil lines were approaching on the far side of the river. Twilight hung gray, but the teams stood out on the pure white of the Yukon. The village dogs had picked up the excitement and throughout the town dogs were yammering and yowling

A man in the crowd scanned the incoming teams. "First one, fourteen dogs," he announced.

"That's Swenson."

One of the youngsters asked, "Where's Sonny Linden?" He got the name a little wrong, but there are no bubble-gum cards to teach the young people of Alaska the names of their sports heroes.

Conversation buzzed among the smaller groups along the bluff. With a knowledgeable air men and women talked about dog racing, who looked good, who didn't. Some could be heard referring to times a generation ago: "When I ran this river . . . ."

Swenson reached the bottom of the bluff and he too ran up the hill. Everyone rushed to the port side and the boat listed again. The children picked up their whistling, and claps and cheers greeted the musher. The youngsters ran behind the sled and a village puppy, lost in a forest of ankles, jumped through the crowd, yapping excitedly.

Someone asked, "Still got the shoes?" sounding as if he had given some shoes to the musher or at least advised him.

"Same pair I started with," Swenson answered. He was referring to boots that were a new design of an old faithful, the shoe-pac, which have rubber bottoms and leather tops and are lined with felt. The new ones Swenson wore were all tan, with wrap-around Neoprene soles and large loops for quick lacing.

Violet Burnham made the necessary checkmarks on her sheets and Swenson said, "Guess I better go put these huskies away." He had had his faster trail leader running in front and now, while Edgar Kalland held the team, he moved the dependable Old Boy into lead to steer through the intricacies of the village. Swenson walked to the back of the sled, clucked through his teeth, and the team jumped up and headed off to town just in time to make way for Emmitt Peters, coming up the hill.

Peters, who didn't have to change leaders, stopped just long enough to check in. With Digger and Diamond up front he probably had the best tandem of lead dogs in the race. The team looked strong; the dogs didn't even lie down. They'd just come sixty-five miles into the wind on the Yukon River and had had to eat unfamiliar food at Eagle Slide. Yet they just stood there waiting patiently to go again. Someone asked Peters if he planned to stay the night. "Oh, yeah," he answered jokingly. From here on there would be no straight answers; if a musher could keep the others guessing he might get them off balance, gaining a little edge somewhere that might get him a few precious hours ahead. Peters moved his team off into town just as the youngsters began whistling again and the deck listed back to starboard.

Now it was Sonny Lindner who came running up the hill. The dogs cast back and forth, looking for the way. The leaders took them into the crowd and amid the laughter people extricated themselves from the tangled lines. Lindner ran forward to take the leaders' necklines and lead them to the checker. When the dogs were finally untangled, he told Violet Burnham, "It's hard to steer with the leader in wheel." He moved forward to put his gee-haw leader back up front for the trip through the village streets. The youngsters lined up around the sled, touching this and pointing at that. One stood on the runners and gave the brake a few tentative pumps. Lindner, changing dogs, watched the kids with his air of shy surprise at the attention. With his leaders back in front he moved on into town.

Behind him, Joe May worked his way up the bluff. He checked through quickly, saying he'd stay the night and heading into town. But the dogs, exploring, wandered in a couple of directions and he had to yell, "Somebody's got to show the leaders where to go." The owner of the home where May was staying gathered in the leaders' necklines and took them off toward his house. With May's arrival the first rush of mushers had ended, and for the next six days dog teams would climb the long bluff into Kaltag, last stop on the Yukon River.

With the excitement over for the moment, the villagers returned to their homes and the race crew headed back into Thompson's house for a taste of beaver stew. The meat was surprisingly good, not comparable to anything else, dark, rich and juicy. Trapper O'Brien, however, only picked at his, perhaps thinking of eating something he usually discarded, or more likely looking at the dollars going into the mouths of humans rather than into paying customers' dogs.

Within a couple of hours the mushers had settled and fed their dogs, had a bite themselves and, though they must have been feeling tired, wandered into the house one by one for conversation.

Swenson, the first to drop in, maintained his confident swagger. In a chair near the end of the table at room center, he sat with his coat off, revealing heavy wool trousers with nylon windbreak patches on the front. His fair-skinned face had turned a reddish pink in the wind and his cheeks looked puffy. He wore small wire-rimmed glasses made smaller by his broad Scandinavian face, the contact lenses he usually wore gone for the moment.

Emmitt Peters and Don Honea were staying in houses at the far southwest corner of the village, near the trail to Unalakleet, and this bothered Swenson. He kept asking if anyone had seen Honea and no one had. He worried: "Two towns you don't sleep in — Kaltag and Shaktoolik. It's too easy for somebody to sneak out of town."

A member of the household where Peters was staying came in

"Tell Emmitt I already left," Swenson told the visitor.

"He said to tell you he's gone two hours," came the answer.

"I'll be there at Old Woman with a fire going," Swenson responded, referring to a cabin that was once a relay station for the telegraph system.

Swenson wanted to know who'd come in and how far behind the others were. He spent a long time reading the checksheet. In particular, he asked about Herbie Nayokpuk. But the report, confirming earlier rumors, was that Nayokpuk's dogs were sick and he was looking for a place to scratch, anyplace where a plane large enough could land to haul his dogs home.

Swenson took a walk to the storeroom to look at O'Brien's beavers but he didn't buy. Returning to the living area, he went into his speech. He didn't like to feed beaver because for one thing the dogs wouldn't want to eat anything else once they'd tasted it. It would be like putting high-test gasoline into a car designed for regular, then tuning the engine for the higher octane. The car just won't run on regular anymore. He said his dogs were doing fine on lamb chops, and by the end of the race Swenson would have fed only three beavers to his team.

The trail appeared to have taken little toll on Swenson so far — maybe just a little off the edge. Still completely sure of himself, he had lost some of the brashness of Farewell, but none of the intensity. He seemed a little tired, but the excitement and pressure of the race were keeping him wired. He gave the impression that he sleeps twelve hours a day for the rest of the year so he can stay awake for the two weeks of the Iditarod.

Talking with race marshal Pat Hurren, he said, "I know what my strategy is, but I've got to remember to stick to my plan. It's easy to get psyched out. For a while." He winked. He had a strong, fast team and had yet to drop one dog from the fourteen who'd started. His strategy appeared to be to stick with the people he felt had the fastest dogs, letting them know he had that strong team right behind them, and forcing them to push too hard to stay in front of him. They knew that if they faltered, he'd pass and be gone, but all the while they were breaking trail. They had to stay with him and be pushed. Then, on the stretch into Nome, he'd rely on his dogs' strength and speed up and pass the few mushers still around, who, he assumed, would have pushed their dogs hard enough that they couldn't take the increased pace.

So far his race had been geared to Emmitt Peters. Swenson had left checkpoints just minutes behind the Ruby Indian and arrived within minutes of him at the next ones.

Lindner joined the group, picking a chair slightly behind Swenson. His face also had reddened, or at least pinkened, adding to his cherubic expression with the bright blue eyes and shy smile. Lindner talked about leaving town shortly. He already had checked out for 10:30. He said he'd camp about eight miles out.

"Yeah, you'll go eight, somebody else'll go ten, somebody else'll go twenty," Swenson said. "Why don't you go get some sleep?"

"Hell, I get more sleep here than I get at home," Lindner answered.

Joe May walked in and sat on the coffee table facing Hurren, who told him about the beaver for sale. "I'm bludgeoned with beaver. Too much to carry in the sled," May said, but he did allow as how he would like some at Shaktoolik and Koyuk, another couple of hundred miles up the way.

Talking about the place he was staying, May told Hurren, "I'm pulled up over there," and he pointed with his thumb. "They pulled everything out of the sled. Boy, things really got done. The guy's got some really good-looking dogs over there. I'd like to put about six of them in front of my team."

May was still favoring the dogs that had picked up the sickness. He still wasn't running the way he'd like, resting longer and feeding more often to bring the sick dogs back. The sickness had affected the musher, too.

"I don't have a plan anymore, Pat," he said to the race marshal. "The dogs get paranoid, I get paranoid. One sneeze and the whole thing stops."

"Have you caught up with Number One anymore?" Hurren asked.

"Yeah, I'm talking to him more and more. I told him, 'I caught you again, you s.o.b.'"

"Does he ever answer you?"

"Oh, yeah," May said. "All he tells me is to go faster."

Perhaps uncomfortable with the subject in front of so many people, he turned to Lindner and asked, "Why do you wear different color shoes?" then, aside, "I ought to get a good answer to that."

Lindner smiled and looked down at the mismatched fur on his mukluks. The answer to May's question didn't come. Instead he asked, "You going to stay in town? Got a good place?"

"Yeah, they're resting good," said May, a little disappointed.

"There's some good camping places out there," Lindner said, still hinting at leaving.

About this time Jerry Riley drove his team up the bank and stopped outside the house. Only Violet Burnham went out to greet him, but he became the subject of the talk in the room. Everyone agreed that he was tough and that even if he had to go with only five dogs he'd finish well. He was already down to seven. Hurren commented that Riley was not popular in the villages along the river. "He manages to alienate people wherever he goes."

One of the mushers added, "Riley don't like dogs."

Talk turned back to the trail. Swenson, looking ahead, said, "Dogs do better out on the coast. They're in good shape now. They can go forever now — the good teams. They do better out on the coast, it's colder. Snow's different, it breaks up, like crystalline or something."

And there was talk of the equipment problems: something was always breaking, something was always jury-rigged.

"I had to run a dog over here on the neckline without a harness," Swenson said. "They chewed up three. I borrowed two."

He paused a second, then looked around, particularly at Lindner and said, "Well, I guess I'll go camp at the end of the airstrip. Then some guy'll go camp on the other side of the berm."

Swenson made sure Violet had him checked out for 11:30. Lindner smiled, almost laughed, toward Swenson and said he himself was checked out for 10:30. "I'm leaving in half an hour. The dogs don't get any sleep sittin' around town and neither do I." He could sleep well enough outside of town, though — the previous year he fell asleep with his foot out in the trail and Eep Anderson ran over it.

But nobody moved to go, and Swenson picked up an Anchorage newspaper that was full of stories about the race. He read for a minute, then told everyone he'd found a story about bar odds on the race: 15 to 1 on him, 3 to 1 on Peters, and 4 to 1 on May.

He turned to Lindner: "You better go back to town and bet — on me." The next day a quick perusal of the paper found no such story.

Someone offered the mushers some of the beaver stew, but the idea of eating the same thing they fed the dogs brought refusals. Swenson said he didn't eat lamb chops, either. Nothing else offered seemed to raise any appetites until someone mentioned Jello. At the sound, Lindner perked up and asked for a bowlful. "Jello's gotten to be one of my favorite foods," he said as he dug in.

Gradually the conversation filtered to a lower pitch and people began drifting off. Swenson chose to sleep upstairs at Thompson's rather than go back to the house where he'd been invited. He explained that he couldn't sleep with all the people over there, but it could have been that, with Peters and Honea on the other side of town where he couldn't see them, Swenson wanted to be at the checkpoint when they came to check out. It was easy to picture him sleeping fitfully with his ear to the upstairs floor, waking every time a door opened and closed.

One after another the drivers drifted out of the room, leaving open the possibility somebody might try to sneak out of town. Swenson, at least, was worried at the prospect. After all this time on the trail, each musher knew about how long any other wanted to rest his dogs and how long he'd stay in a checkpoint or a camp. Swenson had to know that Lindner would stick to his promised departure time. But he also had to know, or believe, Lindner wouldn't go too far before he camped. A mere four-hour lead at this point might mean the difference between winning and losing.

The planes of the Iditarod air force roosted in a line along the airstrip on a cold, clear night as the village slowly went to sleep. About 11:30 the light of a snow machine bobbed through the village. Right behind it were Sonny Lindner and his team. He had meant what he said, and consistent with his philosophy of getting out of town to rest his dogs, he was on his way. He disappeared into the darkness of the trail and would camp a short way out of Kaltag. A short time later the snow machine returned and the driver stopped to talk. Obviously thinking Sonny had made the correct move, he talked about 1974 when, after he led Carl Huntington out of town ahead of the others, a snowstorm came in behind him and Huntington went on to win the race.

Later on, Huntington himself told a slightly different story of that run out of Kaltag. "Sure I went first," he said. "I camped down in a draw and on the hill above me was a fire where Herbie and Jerry Riley were camped, watching." Huntington went on to win the race, though, the only musher to have won major sprint races in Alaska and the Iditarod.

Back at Thompson's house the race crew slept in various-colored lumps on the floor of the living room, at least until 5:25 A.M., when Jerry Riley emerged in a noisy rustle demanding to know where the checker was. No one could tell him and that annoyed him. He charged into a bedroom and rousted someone who could check him out, and quickly was gone into the sleepy mist.

By morning the leaders had all left — Honea at 3:30, May at 5:00,

Peters at 5:30, Swenson at 6:00 and Riley at 7:15. Ernie Baumgartner, the electronics technician from McGrath, and Terry Adkins, the air force veterinarian, had passed through during the night.

With the leaders gone, a new wave of mushers filled the vacuum. Shortly after sunup Joe Redington and Susan Butcher drove up the bank, followed closely by Rick Mackey.

Young Mackey wanted to talk with his father, who already had gone on to Unalakleet. Rick's dogs had come back from the sickness, but he couldn't get them to move fast enough, and the trip up the river on the snow machine trail through deep snow and drifts had worn them down again.

"I'm going too slow. They've been too many times — no enthusiasm." Some of the dogs in his team had made the trip to Nome four times already. "Maybe I'll have to get the whip out. Joe Garnie just pulled in and two or three days ago I was faster than him. I don't know. I sure wish I knew what it was."

Later his father, Dick, who had won the race the year before, would say the dogs' slower gait developed when Rick eased up on them during their bout with the illness. They fell into a five-mile-per-hour pace, became used to it, and wouldn't go faster unless he did something to push them out of it.

Despite the depression and fatigue, Shellie Vandiver noticed that Rick Mackey didn't seem any the worse for wear. "You still look chipper," she told him.

Mackey removed his fur hat, soaked with perspiration. "I don't feel chipper."

He was caught in a trap only the son of an accomplished father can know. If he won the race, people would say it was because he used his father's dogs, the ones that had won the race the year before. If he lost, they would say he was a poor musher because he couldn't win the race even with his father's top dogs. No win.

Redington and Butcher stopped by for a moment. Her round face bright red, Susan Butcher, with her long black braids, could have been a pioneer woman winning the west in the 1800s. No one would guess that until she came to Alaska a few short years ago, she lived in the more refined atmosphere of Cambridge, Massachusetts. Still animated, she was talking constantly — the moose quarters she found on the trail, a dog who wouldn't work, a female in heat.

Redington listened, smiling almost paternally. Toward the end of her monolog he asked her, "Did you see me fall off the sled?"

Redington was concerned about reports that a representative of the American Society for the Prevention of Cruelty to Animals might be watching the race in Unalakleet. "A special investigator," Redington said. "The mushers ought to be warned." The ASPCA had come out repeatedly against the Iditarod Trail Sled Dog Race, claiming the event was cruel to dogs. The mushers and others involved with the race bridled at the criticism. There was no question that dogs got sick on the trail; there were injuries, there were deaths and perhaps even some cruelty by individual contestants. Not every musher treats his dogs the same way and there are those who treat the dogs badly. It has become general knowledge, though, that those who finish the race in high positions year after year are the ones who treat their dogs the best. The dogs, bred for work, aren't Park Avenue poodles, and they are, in the most literal sense, trained as beasts of burden. After miles and miles on training trails they are as toughened as any human long-distance runner for an Olympic competition and, as many have pointed out, can handle the rigors of the trail better than a man. They would be of no use, wouldn't even exist, otherwise. The food they receive is better than any commercially prepared dog food, being the product of years of study by mushers intent on giving the dogs all the nutrition they need. The ingredients in canned dog food compared to the race mix of any of the leading mushers shows how well these dogs are treated. Where commercial foods offer meat byproducts, horsemeat and bone meal, the mushers are going broke feeding beef, lamb chops, beaver, calves' liver, beef heart and salmon, along with a wide variety of high-energy trail snacks.

The health care the dogs receive on the trail is better than that available to any musher; the best of modern medicines go to the dogs, while a musher gets by with aspirin and a pat on the back. And there's that veterinarian at every checkpoint with the authority to make a musher drop a dog if need be.

Despite all the care, dogs do die on the trail, but seldom if ever can the deaths be tied to cruelty. The death of a dog needs to be put into perspective. Most of the trail deaths are caused either by pneumonia or heart attack, not by beating or injury. Since there were eight hundred dogs in the race, four or five deaths seems a low

mortality rate, considering the strain, a testament to the condition-
ing the dogs had received. In any population of eight hundred dogs,
whether they're running the Iditarod Trail or chained in a dog lot or
living in an apartment in New York, five or so could be expected to
die during a given month, and that's all that would die by the end of
this race.

Those involved with the race felt the ASPCA had made a judg-
ment without understanding the situation. Even the state chapter
disagreed with the national and had favored the race, honoring Joe
Redington and his wife Vi with the organization's Humanitarian of
the Year Award in 1978 for their work with the Iditarod.

Still, Redington worried about what an investigator might see and
assume in Unalakleet, knowing what bad publicity at the national
level might do to the race. He asked those race officials remaining in
Kaltag to pass the word among the mushers to be on the lookout for
the investigator and watch what they said in Unalakleet.

Redington and Butcher left to take care of their dogs. More teams
had arrived and many houses had dogs sleeping outside along with
their sleds, and here and there a few curious onlookers talked with
a musher or looked over the dogs.

Near the southwest corner of town Howard Albert, the young
Indian musher from Ruby, put booties on his dogs' feet for the long
trip to Unalakleet. Race veterinarian Tony Funk looked over the
dogs and asked Albert if he'd had any problems with them. Both
agreed the dogs' health was good. If there was a problem, Albert admitted, it was in himself. In his second Iditarod, the year before, he
had finished seventh, and now he hoped to improve his position.

"Got to do at least as good as I did last year. Any of those teams I
can beat?" he asked the vet.

"Yeah — Jerry," Funk answered, referring to Riley.

"Might sell most of these dogs at Nome. It costs too much to be
competitive. Boy, they're forty miles over, huh?" He was referring
to the front runners' lead.

Funk nodded confirmation.

"Swenson. How do they look?"

"Good, strong."

Albert shook his head. "How do they make them so tough?"

Not knowing what to say, Funk looked at the twenty-year-old
sympathetically and said nothing.

"I plan on beating *somebody*. I messed around down the trail. Made the same mistake I made last year. I let them get too far ahead."

With booties on all the dogs, he put the rest of his gear in the sled, pulled the cover tight and strapped it down. Once on the runners he thanked Funk, said goodbye and hiked the team up toward the airstrip.

A few houses over, Redington and Butcher fed their dogs. "I've got to catch up sometime," the sixty-one-year-old Redington said, but it wasn't going to happen right away. Joe Redington had a unique difficulty along the trail, one that had to do with his popularity among the villagers.

Two men stopped and asked him if he had eaten. Redington smiled noncommittally. They invited him for a hot meal. When they left he said, "They're all so nice. And you have to be careful not to offend anyone. We were invited over there, and . . ." his voice trailed off as he nodded toward two more houses. "I've eaten more than a few meals on the trail that I didn't need." The extra meals take valuable time and add another burden as well. Redington and Ron Aldrich, two of the most popular regulars in the race, were among the few who actually gained weight along the trail while everyone else lost.

Butcher walked up, still talking, this time about a dog who chewed necklines. "I think it's because Ivak got to her." Ivak was a male dog on the team. "Now she just wants to make a nest and if she can't pull out far enough, she chews the line."

Redington nodded. "Who'll win?"

He talked about Don Honea. "Nice guy, looks like he's got the dogs. Looks like they'll hold up. Well, Rick's got the power, too." He turned back to his chores and perhaps another meal before he could leave on the trail to the coast.

Throughout the morning the sky had been clearing, bringing good flying weather with it. The time had come to think about the flight over the Kaltag portage to Unalakleet and I returned to Larry Thompson's house to wait for Crazy Horse.

Throughout the day as mushers in the village tended to their teams others pulled up off the river, part of a parade that would go on for seven days. While Redington and Butcher prepared to leave, Mel Adkins sat at the white table in Thompson's house flipping through the pages of the checksheet. In his first race, with borrowed dogs at that, he was happy he'd been gaining on some of the others. With fifty-five mushers in the race, the checklist covered four pages and as Adkins read the names a happy realization spread over his bearded face.

"You know," he said, "I've come seven hundred miles in this race and I finally made the first page."

At the top of that first page were the leaders, already well on their way to Unalakleet.

Rick Swenson had put the status of the race into focus the night before just before he went upstairs to sleep. Looking around the room he said loudly enough for all to hear: "Well, now we're all together, ready to race. All the sick dogs are shipped home. All the preliminaries are done."

17. The Kaltag Portage

THE ROUTE THE DOGS TOOK OUT OF KALTAG FOLLOWED THE OLDEST
connection in a web of gold rush trails that joined the remote gold
fields and villages. Centuries before the first white men arrived,
Eskimos and Indians used the portage at Kaltag to cross from the
Yukon River and the Interior to the Bering Sea Coast. The Kaltag
portage follows a natural pass through the Nulato Hills, rising gently
to a thousand-foot divide in the low mountains and then dropping
almost as gently through a series of ridges called the Whalebacks.

As fur trading and then gold mining created a need for transportation routes and communications, the white men followed this well
worn trail between Nome and the Yukon, bringing mail, supplies,
fur and gold as they came and went. Later the pass provided the
easiest route to string telegraph wires to and from the Interior. In
1925 the diphtheria serum for Nome went via the Kaltag portage.
Leonhard Seppala set out from Nome intending to cross the portage
and meet the relay coming the other way at Nulato, about thirty-six
miles north of Kaltag. But the first mushers were faster than he expected and met Seppala even before he left Norton Sound on the
sea side of the pass. A fellow named Jackscrew, whose real name
has not survived, carried the serum out of Kaltag forty miles to the

185

telegraph relay station at Old Woman. There he was met by Victor Anagick, who took the fur-wrapped package as far as Unalakleet and to the next man in the relay.

On that same trail, the Iditarod Race meets the serum route for the first time when the race follows its alternate southern route. On the same trail as Jackscrew and Anagick, Don Honea now had the fastest time, crossing the portage in a little more than sixteen hours, as did the rest of the six racers in the juggernaut: May, Peters, Swenson, Riley and Lindner. This was the twelfth day of the race.

With sleds heavily laden for the ninety-two mile leg, they traced the old route along the Kaltag River as its frozen path led them through spruce forest until they rose above tree line near the river's source. They left the river, slipped over the top of the pass and began the descent into the valley of the Unalakleet River, passing the old telegraph relay station at Twenty-two Mile. The Unalakleet snakes its way along the north side of a broadening valley as it drops through the Whalebacks. At Old Woman, where a creek of the same name joins the Unalakleet and a mountain named Old Woman shadows the telegraph building, the mushers found shelter to camp and rest and feed their dogs.

The few trees in the valley cling to the river banks as the trail drops toward sea level. Twenty-two miles east of Unalakleet the trail passed Whaleback Cabin, at the site where a small Native community stood when the first white men arrived. Early white travelers reported that both Eskimos and Indians lived in the village, a rare occurrence because the two groups regularly fought each other. This was the farthest east many of the white explorers encountered Eskimos regularly. All that stands today is the telegraph cabin, once a maintenance shack for the line and now a trail shelter for those passing through.

The trail over the divide brought the teams and drivers into another world, the third of the climatic and cultural areas of the race. From the bitter cold of the broad Interior, the trail now came under the influence of the Bering Sea. From Unalakleet the trail would follow coastline and salt water all the way to Nome.

The portage also brought the race from the Athabascan Indian culture of the Interior to the Inupiat Eskimo culture of the coast. "When you come through Unalakleet, you open the door into a whole new world," Joe May observed. "The customs of the people

are worth the trip. It's a real eye-opener." Where the Indians tradi-
tionally have looked to the land for sustenance, the Eskimos looked
to the sea and the ice, bountiful with seals and walrus, whales and
salmon. May noted one difference in particular between the two
cultures: the attitude most of the Eskimo mushers have toward
their dogs: "They care too much about their dogs, maybe. Those
guys really have something going with their dogs."

During the crossing the wind gave the teams little relief. It blew
hard, but this time from behind. Lindner said that didn't help much
because the high valley caused the wind to swirl, and no matter
where it came from the wind kept blowing snow up into the dogs'
faces.

That same wind gave Crazy Horse another scary landing at
Unalakleet, where he had to fight the little airplane down the
runway in a thirty-five-knot crosswind that threatened to flip the
plane even after he fought it to a stop.

Behind the leaders, others fought wind and storms, too. Keith
Jones, a commercial fisherman from Ambler, battled his way in
wind and drifts and later said that without the snow machine trails
that wound through the valley he might have been in real trouble.
Where the leaders took as little as sixteen hours to drive the portage,
some of those toward the rear took almost thirty.

Ahead of them, Unalakleet, the salmon capital of the arctic,
awaited the Iditarod Trail Sled Dog Race. The largest village along
the trail, Unalakleet had a population approaching five hundred.
Aside from the commercial salmon industry, the largest employers
in town were government agencies. Some years the people of
Unalakleet supplemented their incomes by fishing for king crab,
but that fishery depended on wide expanses of shore-fast ice.
Fishermen drop crab pots through holes in the ice, but over the past
few years, the town and much of the rest of Alaska had been expe-
riencing mild winters, leaving no ice close to shore for crabbing.
Though winter had been colder this year than the previous two, it
hadn't been that cold at Unalakleet. Little snow lay on the ground
and much of the trail to the north was over gravel blown clear.

The checkpoint in Unalakleet was the Lodge, a three-story struc-
ture offering rooms and a small restaurant. The proprietor was
George Brown, who had attended Mount Edgecumbe School in
Sitka with Crazy Horse. At the time the two attended the school,

which was run by the Bureau of Indian Affairs, there were no schools in the villages beyond the elementary level, and any Natives who wanted to attend high school had to go to Sitka in the far-away southeastern part of the state. More recently students have been able to board in Fairbanks and Anchorage for their schooling, and a court decision now requires the state to build high schools in any villages that have seven or more students and request a school. Still, many continue to travel to Anchorage or Fairbanks or Mount Edgecumbe.

Brown and Crazy Horse discussed their school days over coffee in the Lodge whenever Brown could get away from the business at the grill. "There's no economy in Unalakleet in the winter," he complained, but added that the Iditarod was helping. In just the two days people had been coming in for the race he'd sold seventy-two cheeseburgers. On any other day of the winter, he said, he'd be lucky to sell ten. Iditarod people had filled all the rooms in the Lodge, as well.

As afternoon turned to evening the race watchers began filling Brown's restaurant awaiting the first mushers.

At just before eight the village's siren and church bells sounded to announce a musher heading into town across the ice at the mouth of the Unalakleet River. A crowd gathered in the darkness to watch the bobbing headlamp come across the snow, led by whining snow machines. Don Honea pulled up the slight rise off the ice and onto the street in front of the Lodge, with Emmitt Peters' lead dogs almost between his runners, and Sonny Lindner right behind Peters. The three were quickly adopted by the owners of the homes where they were to stay and moved along into the darkened streets as spectators leaned again into the wind to peer out and spot another team. About half an hour later a fourth light bobbed across the ice and another team arrived: Rick Swenson's. Swenson's face looked serious, if not in pain, under the peak of his black hat with the DOG logo. Swenson moved around his team, hobbling a little, and told of a tumble he'd taken out on the ice that had hurt his knee. Carl Huntington had suffered a similar injury the year he won the race, finishing in Nome with a knee swollen to the size of a cantaloupe.

Race manager Dick Mackey, Swenson's rival from the year before, greeted him to check him through.

"How'd those guys look?" Swenson asked of the teams who'd arrived ahead of him.

"Good," Mackey said. "Strong."

"They perk up when they get over that hill and start coming down into Unalakleet," Swenson said.

Someone asked him when he planned to leave. Swenson looked up toward town where the others already were feeding their dogs.

"I'll be right behind those guys when they go." Then he clucked to his dogs and followed the man who would be his host for the night.

No one expected another musher for at least a couple of hours so the crowd dispersed, many heading back to the Lodge for coffee. Some would have liked a drink, but Unalakleet, like many villages, had voted to stay dry, so there was no drinking, at least in the open. Rumors of a bootlegger filtered through the race party but no one actually ever located one.

At each checkpoint the racing became more intense. In earlier races, it had been pretty much a camping trip as far as Unalakleet, and then it was all out for Nome. But as the quality of the teams and care and feeding improved, the race had become more competitive. Joe Redington had complained the year before that the camping trip ended at Farewell. By this race, with runners like May, who pushed out in front and dragged the rest of the race with them, there was no doubt at all that the competition had begun right at Lake Lucille and had never let up, just increased.

Mackey, speaking from the vantage point of a winner, sat in his room in the Lodge talking about what would happen from Unalakleet to Nome.

"Now they're looking at dogs. They'll look them over and start to drop the slow ones. Swenson looks good because he has the most to choose from," Mackey observed. "The winners usually finish with seven or eight."

Swenson reached the Bering Sea with all fourteen dogs who'd started. Among his competitors, Honea and Peters were down to eleven each, Lindner had ten, May had twelve, and Riley had seven.

Swenson said he had planned to drop two dogs earlier but they'd all looked so good he left them in the team. At Unalakleet he left the first two behind. Peters dropped a dog and so did May. The dogs dropped from here on weren't necessarily injured or sick, but a team can only go as fast as the slowest dog and the racers wanted speed for the three-hundred-mile dash to Nome.

"From here they're going to do in two and a half days what it took them five to do coming out of Anchorage fresh," Mackey said. "From here on, you've got to drive the dogs like they're going to cross the finish line in Nome and drop dead. They won't, of course, they're tougher than the men, but that's how you've got to drive them."

If the mushers planned to drive the dogs hard, they meant no less punishment for themselves. There would be even less rest and no relief from the pressure.

"If Honea doesn't ruin it, they're all gonna take off about five in the morning," Mackey said. Ruin it how?

"If he starts earlier they're all gonna go. You don't let nobody get that far ahead. Emmitt and Lindner want to wait as long as they can, but when somebody goes they're all gonna go," Mackey said.

As Mackey talked, word passed up through the Lodge that Riley had checked in, and the race manager went out for a moment to talk with the musher. He returned in about ten minutes.

"I asked Riley how he was doing," he reported. "He said 'I've got seven dogs, five good ones. That's enough.'" Mackey laughed. "He'll do it, too. That's all he needs.

"The dogs are always tougher than the men," Mackey's monolog continued. "Riley comes closer than anyone to being as tough as the dogs. He can take the deprivation and it drives him all the harder."

Throughout the race Riley had been the subject of controversy, partly because the fierceness of his competitive nature tended to alienate others and partly because of his reputation for being particularly hard on dogs. His defenders, like Mackey and Patty Friend, pointed to his successes and the quality of his breed of dogs, which was first developed in the 1920s and '30s by his father. He had won the race once and finished second twice. That kind of record can't be attained with poorly trained and cared-for dogs. Mackey was saying Riley simply pushed himself harder than anyone else did. He pushed his dogs just as hard, asking no more of them than he did of himself, yet what he asked of his dogs was perhaps more than the other racers might. Even with only seven dogs he wasn't giving up, either.

One of the group suggested maybe the intense drive and single-minded pressure in Riley was what offended people along the way.

"Yeah, exactly," Mackey said.

Mackey's prediction about someone ruining it almost came true, but it wasn't Honea who left early, it was Lindner, the one who hated to stay in towns anyway. Lindner had planned to leave with Honea because his headlamp was malfunctioning. But as they were preparing in the early morning hours, Honea got to talking with some folks who were watching, and the next thing he knew Lindner had disappeared out into the darkness, without a light, at about 4 A.M. Honea finished his conversation and followed shortly. At 5:30 Peters, Riley and Swenson turned their teams north and at 9:00 May, still favoring a couple of dogs, chased them up the coast.

That day was a holiday in Unalakleet. The schools let out so youngsters could watch the racers pass through and someone stood by the bells and siren all day to announce the arriving mushers. Crowds stayed downtown near the Lodge to watch. Daylight presented another view of the town. A deep canyon cut through what snow the wind had driven into town, and the dogs passed through the canyon after they came up off the ice. On one side stood the Lodge, on the other, the modern Alaska Commercial Company, the town's main store, still offering cash for furs. Next to the trail where it came off the ice, a sign proclaimed "The City of Unalakleet Salutes the Iditarod Trail Race. Welcome Home Duke and Junie." The welcome was for Victor Katongan and Clarence Towarak.

In midmorning the crowd grew larger, surging toward the ice. Katongan was due any time, and the gathering of his family, friends and acquaintances grew larger every few minutes. Women wearing their best intricately decorated fur parkas and brightly colored kuspuks watched the ice. The colorful kuspuks, cloth overdresses hemmed and ruffed with fur, relieved the otherwise gray scenery. Children ducked through the crowd as Eskimo eyes tested by years of looking for game across broad expanses of ice scanned the horizon for a dog team. Snow machines buzzed every whichway across the ice. Before long someone spotted a team and shouted. The call went up for the Duke, but the musher was Rick Mackey, weaving around spots of glare ice. Mackey's dogs pulled him into the canyon and he stopped to talk just a moment with the checker before taking the leaders' necklines and leading the team farther into town.

Behind him the villagers turned back to the ice and searched for a sign of Duke Katongan. Again the tested eyes picked out a team far in the distance. This time the children ran out onto the ice calling out dogs' names — the team was Katongan's, and the youngsters seemed to know all his dogs. After staying out front with May for part of the way, Katongan had fallen behind. Some of his dogs were sick and he reached Unalakleet with eight of the twelve who'd started. The children even knew which dogs were missing, recognizing the remaining dogs and calling to them along with the musher. "Duke, Duke," they shouted as he drove the team up into the crowd. Everyone pressed in on him and behind his dark sunglasses he laughed and smiled at the almost embarrassing reception, grinning through a wispy dark mustache. After the depression of falling behind, the welcome obviously pleased him.

He turned to someone in the crowd and said, "Thought of quittin'."

"You keep going," a shrill feminine voice shouted back.

An older Eskimo woman in a bright kuspuk, her round face ringed in fur and accented by wire-rimmed glasses, embraced him, and they both grinned into the cameras of the photographers nearby. After a hug, the Duke hiked his team up into town toward his house. The crowd trailed along behind, with shouts here and there of "Duke! Go, Duke!"

Behind him by a little more than an hour, Hokkanen came into town. Hokkanen bedded his dogs down, then, in screaming hunger despite his 5,000 calories a day, just about ran for the Lodge. Before he was done, he had devoured three of the biggest steaks the place had on hand. "I felt like I could have eaten more, needed more, but I was full. You can't carry enough food to eat," he said while he patted the lump in his stomach.

Still up on the portage, Herbie Nayokpuk and Joe Garnie struggled with their fading dogs. The ninety-two-mile stretch proved to be the limit for Nayokpuk's team. He pulled into Unalakleet after twenty-four hours on the trail from Kaltag and confirmed the Kaltag rumors by calling it quits. Garnie, whose dogs were in a little better shape, decided to try one more run, the short stretch to Shaktoolik. Behind them Clarence Towarak, Junie, reached his home town and scratched, perhaps remembering two years earlier when he went all the way and finished twenty-sixth. There was no money for finishing that far down and he didn't want to have to drive his team 230 miles back home again.

For seven more days mushers and dogs dropped down off the Kaltag portage, fighting winds and snow and drifted trail to the Bering Sea. The campers at the back of the pack reached the village a day after the winner had been decided in Nome, but that didn't matter. They had made it to the sea and there would be no stopping. Ron Gould led the group most of the way. In a previous race he'd come this far and scratched. At Unalakleet, the group changed leaders. Harry Harris, who had lived several years in Nome and knew at least some of the coast trails, led the rest of the way.

18. Unalakleet to Shaktoolik

IN THE LIGHT OF A BLOSSOMING DAWN THE RACE'S LEADERS PRESSED northward on the forty-mile leg to Shaktoolik. They passed Unalakleet's cemetery and airstrip and found themselves on a trail that paralleled hills sloping to the sea. The packed snow of the trail made a line of white through hillsides turned brown by winds that had blown away the looser snow. Gravel on bare spots of the trail tore at the plastic and P-Tex of the sled runners. To the east the ridges of the Whalebacks rose into mountains; to the west, the waters of Norton Sound extended all the way to the horizon. To their left the drivers could see Besboro Island and farther north, Cape Denbigh; way off in the mist of the northwest was the dim outline of their goal, the southern shore of the Seward Peninsula, and somewhere along the western part of that shore, Nome.

A short way out of Unalakleet the trail wound behind the first ridge of coastal hills, steep rocky bluffs that stood in defiance of the violent Bering Sea. As the mushers passed, the water lay calm. The trail turned to follow a creek bed up to a low divide in the hills. Over the divide the trail descended to cross the North River, then Egavik Creek, where a few weathered old buildings once served as a reindeer slaughterhouse. Victor Katongan fished here when the salmon came in the summer.

The descent out of the hills to the beach disoriented some of the mushers. Maybe it was because of being so far north or maybe because of wandering minds, but Gary Hokkanen, a day behind the leaders, said, "There's a feeling you're always higher than you actually are. It's a gradually descending series of hills but you have a feeling you're going higher — disoriented. It's a real surprise when you come to Shaktoolik and you're at sea level."

The descending trail crossed Junction Creek and then followed the shoreline. Just north of the creek a spit that almost looked like a man-made causeway fronted the ocean. The trail followed the lee side of the spit across Beeson Slough. Ahead in the distance a low ridge called the Reindeer Hills appeared to be an island out in the water, although in fact the hills were connected to the mainland by a wide frozen area of muskeg. On the eastern side of the bog the land sloped upward again into the Nulato Hills. On a map, the Shaktoolik Peninsula looks almost blue because of all the muskeg ponds that dot its low surface, but as the mushers crossed, it merely presented a slightly raised extension of the snow-covered ocean ice. Only here and there did slight depressions and rises present occasional shadows. In the low winter sun the land looked barren, but in reality it was just the opposite — the proud Eskimo people who lived there had for centuries taken their living from the land and the ocean, hunting and fishing, gathering and trapping, raising herds of reindeer. It was only barren to the untrained eye of the inexperienced Outsider. Villagers at Shaktoolik maintained a reindeer herd that foraged, almost wild, across the peninsula and into the low hills behind. The seal hunters of the village were famed throughout the arctic.

As the dogs pulled the mushers along the spit, the first sign of habitation was the weathered gray buildings of Old Shaktoolik, abandoned in favor of a newer village three miles to the north. The deserted buildings, half covered with snow, still withstood the Bering Sea storms, but a wrecked airplane near the old landing strip hadn't fared as well and a propeller, now attached to an old windmill, was turning in the wind.

Sonny Lindner's dogs led the rest of the teams toward the old village. Seeing the buildings, the trail-wise team turned up the short bank of the spit, headed toward shelter and stopped to lie down. A village was a village as far as they were concerned and it was time to rest and eat. "They were so used to it, and the villages are so far apart," Lindner said, "they'd never expect to go through one." After a short talk, Lindner convinced the dogs that this wasn't the place, and he led them back down to the trail where once again they headed toward the populated village to the north.

There Lindner pulled in first after a little more than five hours on the trail on the morning of the thirteenth day of the race. Within two and a half hours Peters, Swenson, Honea and Riley followed. They came up off the ice on the inland side of the slough, behind the spit and into the new village of Shaktoolik: two precise rows of government-blueprinted one-story frame houses, a post office and a school, all with a look of newness and impermanence after the older buildings back down the trail.

Across the street that ran between the neat lines of buildings, snowdrifts higher than a man's head had built up over the winter. At first impression the drifts looked as if they'd been thrown up by bulldozers, like giant speed bumps to slow down the snow machines that roared around the village. But that was a city impression. What had happened was the engineers who'd laid out the village had not considered the prevailing winds that came out of the northeast across open Norton Bay. Those winds had funneled snow between the buildings, leaving giant ridges perpendicular to the flow of traffic and obstructing anything moving down the street. No such drifts blocked the way past the old buildings of the abandoned village the Eskimos had built back down the coast.

The dog teams rested in the warm midday sun out of the wind next to several of the village homes. The temperature was too warm to run in and the dogs could rest well in the sun, so the drivers took advantage of the break. A dog uses valuable energy just keeping warm in the cold, even while he's sleeping, but in this warm sun the dogs could have been on a beach, sprawled every whichway, soaking up the warmth and getting sleep that did not eat up their energy.

In the home of Lynn Takak, the checker, a buffet was laid on a round table for the mushers and crew of followers. Reindeer meat in roasts and stews, and delicious arctic char, one of the northern species of fish related to trout, were offered to all who stopped.

As the shadows began to grow longer toward afternoon, Lindner trudged up and down the drifts through the village looking for Don

Honea. He wanted to leave but he didn't want to go alone. "Too boring for the dogs," he said. They had to cross ice-covered Norton Bay to Koyuk, sixty-two miles, with not a single tree to relieve the eyes. "If we take turns leading we can go a lot faster," Lindner said. "I'm looking for Don to go."

With the coming of afternoon, colder temperatures and better running conditions, other mushers were stirring, too. Emmitt Peters came out of the house where he had been napping, carrying water for his dogs.

His drawn dark face showed the pressure of the race trail. "My leader's hurt. Hurt since Skwentna," he said almost blankly. He had another leader, Diamond, but Diamond didn't take the commands, the *gee* and *haw*, as well, "especially in that wind."

"Gonna leave in an hour . . . get some rest . . . long haul," he said and then disappeared back into the house.

Two drifts to the north Swenson was changing sleds. He'd driven the fast, racy toboggan as far as Shaktoolik but now was picking up a more conventional wood and rawhide model for the run into Nome. Swenson too had begun to show the strain. He was distracted, bothered by almost anything that could affect his chances. He complained to me about "you guys."

"Can't go anywhere without a camera pointing at you, or somebody writing things down or somebody turning on a tape recorder. Then that girl writes about all the cruelty and problems with the bad teams. Nobody writes about how good the good teams look."

He was still hurting from an incident sometime back, when he was feeding his dogs while a television crew filmed the process. All the strangers milling around the dogs had disturbed them and when one of the cameramen moved in for a close-up, two of Swenson's dogs had stood up and walked away from their food, refusing to eat. That had been too much for the musher and he'd chased everyone away. Two dogs off their feed could slow the whole team, and Swenson wouldn't tolerate the intrusion.

As one competitor said in another race, "Every minute you spend talking with someone or posing, you're not paying attention to the dogs, you're losing your concentration." The travel involved in the race threw everyone together at the checkpoints: racers, spectators, sportswriters, photographers and members of television crews. Like it or not, everyone ate, slept and lived together.

For the most part, the person who runs the race doesn't enjoy the public scrutiny media coverage gives. It takes a certain kind of personality to enjoy the loneliness of the training trail and accept the day-after-day grind of preparing a team for the race. The musher in training lives a solitary life, preparing for one big event a year, and even when that event begins he still spends most of the race alone with his dogs, far away from spectators and press. The mushers just weren't used to being watched or being around crowds. That was part of the make-up that made them mushers in the first place.

Still, in the context of Alaska, these were the sports heroes, particularly the leaders, the serious racers. They were the Reggie Jacksons and O.J. Simpsons and Arnold Palmers, the superheroes. People wanted to know about them and about the race. But where the stars of the big spectator sports Outside were used to performing in front of thousands and being interviewed and photographed everywhere they went as part of their job, the mushers at best could only make the best of a difficult situation.

And even Reggie Jackson didn't have to tolerate reporters in right field with him, or in the dugout or in his bedroom. In the case of Swenson's dogs not eating, the reporters had actually come out of the press box and had an effect on the game. And even if somebody at a checkpoint just walked by a sleeping team and a couple of dogs woke up, their sleep had been disturbed and the racer's chances affected. Lindner didn't stay long in the villages because the distractions kept the dogs from resting well. For an intense competitor like Swenson, the potential for distraction of his team, not to mention his own distraction at the constant feeling of exposure, was enough to make him chase away almost anyone.

Swenson finished watering his dogs and looking them over, then went back inside the house, casting a wary eye around to make sure nobody was too close to his team. Somebody was looking the team over, though, somebody who bore watching.

A young resident of the village named Bruce watched the drivers and the dogs intently. Like the rest of the children in his third-grade class, Bruce had the day off to watch the race pass through. He'd lived his whole life in Shaktoolik and planned to grow up to be a strong hunter. Every now and then the report of a rifle echoed across the ice from the edge of the sea. "Seal hunter," Bruce said, with the air of a hunter who understood these things. He talked about his older brother who hunted seals and about the time he shot a seal himself. Somehow the seal escaped, "but I know I hit it," the youngster said as he looked at two frozen seal carcasses lying in the snow behind a house. Bruce talked about the wolves that attacked the village's reindeer herd and how some of the village dogs were part wolf and how some of the older men drank and fought.

Round-faced, smiling, and happy that the race was in town, Bruce looked over all the dog teams as he walked down the street. Some he stopped to examine more closely.

"That dog in Sonny Lindner's team, the white one, I want to skin it," he said.

At the house where Don Honea was resting, Bruce walked into the living room. Honea was sitting on the floor pulling on his socks getting ready to leave with Lindner. Perhaps the most relaxed of the leaders, Honea was talking with Crazy Horse when Bruce walked in. Looking up, he smiled and said hello.

As he worked on the second pair of socks, Honea and Crazy Horse talked about the use of dog fur for clothing. Honea wore wool socks but he knew of better ones. In the villages, at least in recent times past, nothing went to waste, not the dog hair shed in the spring or the hide of a dog that had died. Honea said dog hair made particularly good socks, to which Crazy Horse agreed.

Bruce listened to the conversation until he had to speak.

"I'll skin a dog for you," Bruce said.

Recoiling in mock horror, Honea said, "Don't skin one of my dogs."

"You don't have any white dogs," Bruce said, standing his ground as if that were the only consideration in the matter.

With that response the group in the room looked at him and then began coaxing.

"I want a white dog, to make mittens." Then his voice dropped as he admitted, "so people will think I got a polar bear."

He looked befuddled, almost angry, when everyone in the room laughed. The expression on his face said people didn't laugh at a great hunter.

Honea finally interrupted the laughter and said to Bruce, "Go down there and skin one of Rick's dogs. Tell him I said it's okay."

"Does he have any white ones?" Bruce asked as he turned

toward the door. He left, apparently, to take a closer look. But Swenson escaped Shaktoolik with all twelve dogs, so Bruce probably didn't find the right one.

As the first five prepared to leave Shaktoolik for the ice of Norton Bay, Joe May drove his dogs along the hard-packed snow behind the inland row of houses. Takak met him on a snow machine to guide him to the checkpoint and the two men stopped to talk. Up front a village puppy stood nose to nose with May's leaders, yapping a challenge. With the air of old men listening to and tolerating the overconfident ramblings of a noisy teen-ager, the leaders looked ahead, ignoring the insignificant challenge, not even dropping their muzzles for a sniff. May, back on the sled, yelled, "Hike," and the dogs took off again, almost running over the poor pup, who scurried to the side with his tail between his legs. But once the team had passed and the danger was over, the pup picked up his yapping again and chased after the sled.

As May passed the checkpoint and pulled across the street next to a snowbank, the village youngsters ran behind him shouting, "Jomay, Jomay, Jomay!" The lead dogs stopped, and before May could hit the brake, some of the team dogs overtook them and bunched up. Instructing the kids to hold the leaders, May pulled the sled back until the gangline came tight again. He wanted to turn the team around so they'd be facing the right direction out of town, toward the marshes rather than the open sea. He stood still, holding the sled, and talked to his leaders. "Haw, haw," he said in a low voice. The leaders turned 90 degrees for a normal left turn, keeping the line taut. May said, "Come, come, come," and the leaders turned back toward the sled until, with a shove on the sled by May, the whole team was facing the right direction, 180 degrees, perfectly executed, from where they'd stopped.

May was falling behind. He had left Unalakleet four hours behind the others and reached Shaktoolik four hours behind, an unrecoverable four hours. As his dogs napped and he cooked their food, the front runners, after seven hours of rest, repacked their sleds, hiked up their dogs and left within an hour of his arrival.

Lindner followed Honea out into the frozen marsh at 4 P.M. Within an hour Peters, Swenson and Riley joined them on the trail toward the ice of Norton Bay. Lindner and Riley had each dropped a dog at Shaktoolik, leaving Lindner with nine and Riley with six.

They were leaving on a clear day to cross under a starry night and northern lights. Around them the winds were blowing up another storm, and by the time the middle bulge of the mushers reached Shaktoolik it had blown up full force.

A day later Joe Garnie tried crossing into the storm with fading dogs that had taken twenty-four hours to cross the Kaltag Portage. Garnie was going to give the dogs one more run, one more try to see if they could make the next two hundred miles into Nome, but a short run toward Koyuk showed him the inevitable. "The dogs wanted to go, but they just couldn't," he said. Out of eleven, only four could pull. "I stopped for twelve hours to see if the rest would start pulling. I could have pulled out and forced them across but I didn't want to do that. They were already running on their reserves. Their body weight was just down." When he saw how the dogs were doing he turned back to Shaktoolik, where he dropped out of the race.

Right behind Garnie, Patty Friend was feeling the strain. She'd been sticking with her four-hours-on, four-hours-off schedule and while it suited the dogs fine it left the driver exhausted. For perhaps the tenth time she observed, "There's never enough sleep." She stayed with a friend of a friend in Shaktoolik. "They kept telling me 'you've got to take a shower. You'll feel better after a shower.' And, like a shower is the last thing I wanted . . . on my mind. I mean I just wanted to lay down, just a couple hours, just a couple hours, maybe even an hour. 'You've got to have a shower, you've got to feel clean because you'll feel better.' I felt fine filthy. I felt great."

But she acquiesced and took the shower, and between that and caring for her dogs found no rest during the four hours she spent in the village. She and Ernie Baumgartner drove out into the brunt of the storm. They fought the storm in the dark for a couple of hours but finally gave up. They, too, returned to Shaktoolik and stayed for what was left of the night. They left again at 8:30 in the morning of the fourteenth day of the race.

Behind them the forty-five teams still struggling up the trail, some as far back as the Yukon River, would take another four days to pass through the village.

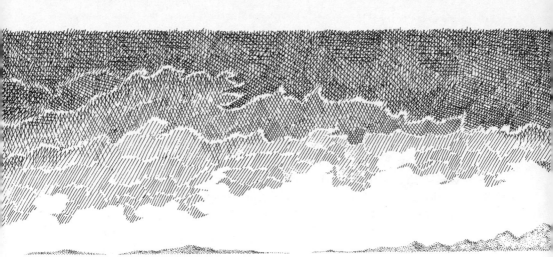

19. Shaktoolik to Koyuk Across Norton Bay

THE TRAIL FROM SHAKTOOLIK TO KOYUK, THE FIRST STOP ON THE SEWARD
Peninsula, took a path twenty miles farther than usual because
Norton Bay hadn't frozen completely and the teams had to hug the
shoreline to avoid open water. For seventy-two miles all that lay in
front of the lead dogs was the wide open white of what sea ice
there was. The teams first crossed the snow and ice of the marshland behind Shaktoolik on a long, lonely, featureless trail with
nothing on it but here and there a tuft of grass. The trail rose a bit
to cross a bump of a hill, but except for that one slight incline and a
large boulder at the water's edge nothing until Koyuk stood even
three feet high. The sunken shapes of the marsh ponds disappeared almost to invisibility in the flat light of dusk. Just as the
sun dropped into clear sky under the heavy cloud cover, the slight
ridges that faced west lighted up, reflecting the low angles of the
rays.

After the marsh the trail left the land, crossing a barely discern-
ible line onto the sea ice of Norton Bay, a hook of an inlet at the
northeastern corner of Norton Sound. Winds had blown up drifts
on the ice in some places but in others had blown it clear, leaving
slippery, unsure footing for both dogs and men, and making sleds

difficult to steer. Fractures made the ice look like rocks cut in geometric patterns, and where it was blown clear the ice had turned green to the color of light jade. Pressure had pushed some of the fractured sections up over others, leaving jagged little ridges. Mountains bordered the bay to the east and north; off to the west the Seward Peninsula stretched toward the Bering Strait.

Driving his dogs in temperatures near thirty degrees below zero, Leonhard Seppala had carried the diphtheria serum across Norton Bay as he raced to Nome. He had met Myles Gonangnan near Shaktoolik. Turning around immediately, Seppala went back out on the ice and took the medicine ninety miles back to Golovin. The racers, as they worked their way across the broad expanse of ice toward Koyuk, were taking a longer route than Seppala did.

In the wind, all of the leaders cast about on the ice trying to find the trail and avoid the bare spots. Lindner worried about the effects on his dogs as they wandered around looking for the trail. "Damn," he said later. "Spent more than an hour back and forth on the ice out there. They've been running into the wind for five days now. Bored. It slows them right down." He said nothing about the effects the wind had on him.

Swenson had an easier time, even though his headlamp wasn't working. He said he liked the trail, that it had good traction. But whatever gave Swenson and his dogs good traction worked against others. Del Allison, crossing a few days later, said it felt as if the ice had salt in it that was tearing out his plastic, and he thought for a time of stopping and removing the runners and going on bare wood.

For a while, Peters was ahead of Swenson, but somewhere on the ice his dogs missed the trail so he too spent some time wandering back and forth, much of it on glare ice. Swenson was met by a man on a snow machine who led him the rest of the way into Koyuk, but Peters and the others had to find the trail themselves.

Riley, crossing with only six dogs, pushed hard to keep up. When Lindner saw him he thought maybe the team was done. "Saw him out on the ice pushing his sled into one of the dogs," he said.

Part of the frustration of that section of trail, particularly at night, was that from as far as forty miles out the drivers could see the lights of Koyuk as it leaned up a hillside on the banks of the

Koyuk River. As they searched for the trail and worked around icy spots, the lights never seemed to come any closer.

At the beach line in front of the village a lantern shone to guide the mushers toward the checkpoint and, in houses that almost all faced the water, villagers occasionally stood in their doorways to look out toward the ice for signs of the first arrival. The sky had cleared somewhat, with another cloud bank building in the west. An almost full moon cast its light over the snow and the northern lights made a hazy but failing attempt to blaze among the stars. Wind whispered from the east off the mountains.

Most of the buildings in Koyuk were old, gray and weathered, in contrast to a new school and recreation center. A rectangular corrugated metal armory of the Alaska National Guard served as the checkpoint. The building was headquarters for a company of the First Scout Battalion, "the eyes and ears of the arctic." The Eskimo Scouts had been formed during World War II as a reconnaisance unit when the Japanese invaded the Aleutian Islands. Decommissioned after the war, the various units reformed into the Alaska National Guard and were the only reserve units in the United States that trained where they would be deployed during wartime. But even in peacetime the guard served a function since members often were called up for arctic rescues. In a village where jobs were at a premium, many of the men and women augmented a subsistence lifestyle with dollars from the military.

In the armory the furniture had been cleared away for the mushers. A sign on a blackboard said in large letters, "Welcome to Koyuk." Someone had written below it, "Only 150 miles to go, go, go." A large sheet of brown paper listed all the mushers, with spaces for their times in and out and the number of dogs they had. Roger Nassuk, the first sergeant of the scout company and the official checker, said that in previous years he'd made the list in chalk on the blackboard, but mushers trying to confuse each other had changed times and numbers of dogs, so this year he'd gone to paper and an indelible Magic Marker. Youngsters in cross-country ski boots milled around waiting for the teams to arrive.

Near midnight bobbing lights showed out on the ice as the first teams approached. A snow machine pulled up to the armory and the driver announced that Emmitt Peters was in the lead. Then more snow machines drove off the ice and right behind them came Swenson's team. Swenson pulled into the circle of light at the front of the armory and stopped. Even after about a thousand miles and the boring run on the ice, his dogs stood up, none of them in a hurry to lie down to take advantage of the stop. When Swenson finished checking with Nassuk, he asked some of the youngsters to lead his team around into the bushes across the street, where they'd be out of the wind. "Don't grab the tuglines," he admonished a boy who then reached for the necklines of the leaders. But the boy started taking the team the wrong way and Swenson had to leave the sled to lead the dogs himself. As he disappeared around a house into the darkness, Emmitt Peters appeared in the light.

Running up to his leaders, Peters looked at Digger, petting the dog and running his hand over his leg. "Don't know if he'll make it. Been on three legs since Skwentna." Peters had been ahead of Swenson out on the bay but at some point had missed the trail and ended up on glare ice. They both reached Koyuk just after midnight on the fourteenth day of the race. Within an hour and a half, Lindner and Honea drove up to the armory. Where Swenson and Peters had picked up snow machines to lead them, the second two had had to find their own way.

Swenson and Peters, and then Lindner, unpacked their sleds and hauled their cooking gear into the armory, and soon the room was filled with the familiar smells of Blazo stove fuel, melting fat, beaver, lamb chops and all the other ingredients that went into the five-gallon cooking pots. Honea stayed at a villager's home. Tired but still going strong, Swenson talked as he worked, while Peters sat quietly watching his pot. To no one in particular Swenson said, "It's my one big trip of the year. Other people get vacations. After this I go home. I'm broke. I've got six months to recover and six months to get ready for the next one." Lindner smiled a knowing agreement. It was a sentiment echoing one Richard Burmeister of Nome had expressed earlier. "I don't give a damn where I finish. I just want to come in with the dogs in the best shape I can. I've got $7,500 in bills to pay when I get home."

As the competition intensified, little time was left for anything but the dogs. The mushers fed their teams, talked, napped a little, and stayed just about five hours, all four of them leaving between five and six in the morning.

During the night Jerry Riley passed through, leaving behind a dog that snoozed unmoveably, curled in a ball tied to the bushes outside the armory. Riley had dropped a dog at Shaktoolik, too, leaving him with only five — the five good ones he had told Dick Mackey were enough. But even the good ones were giving him trouble. Those who saw him leave said the dogs hadn't wanted to go; they had tried to run into the armory, and when he dragged them off the steps and turned out of town, they ran under a house. Nevertheless, the man many considered the toughest on the trail was still driving toward Nome with enough dogs to finish.

May also passed through in the night, arriving a good five hours behind the leaders, but his dogs, he said, were coming back. He'd crossed Norton Bay in a little more than eight hours, within minutes of the times of the five in front of him. He had nursed his dogs back to health, and though he liked to say he had the big tough trapline dogs that weren't as fast as Swenson's or Peters', he was turning in just as fast times as they were, now that he could pick up his schedule again. He still thought his dogs could go a hundred miles in twenty-four hours and he was looking for some dirty weather to push into if the others stopped.

While the first four had almost six hours in Koyuk, May took four, which fit into his schedule, but Riley stayed only an hour and a half, leaving within an hour of Swenson, Peters, Honea and Lindner. No one could waste time anymore. Checkpoints had become temptations, warm beds and hot meals beckoning like the Lorelei to the tired mushers and dogs. But there was no giving in; an extra hour somewhere and the race could be won or lost. Nome and Front Street beckoned, too, and there would be plenty of rest after the race, and no hurry to get up in the morning and get back on the trail.

Everyone cast wary eyes to the weather. Banks of clouds built up in the sky and as the leaders left for Elim, the next checkpoint, the winds picked up again, the northerlies hitting from the side while throwing up snow and drifts into the faces of the teams still crossing the Norton Bay ice.

A day behind the leaders, Bob Chlupach, driving his team of registered Siberian huskies, headed out onto the ice from Shaktoolik only to run head on into the storm. Leaving just before noon, he ran until the storm pounded his dogs with too much. "It was the worst part of the trail. I finally had to stop. I slept behind the sled to keep out of the wind. During the night the wind changed and I had to get up and change sides. In the morning the dogs were just lumps of snow." The section of trail that had taken the leaders just over eight hours to cross, took Chlupach almost twelve.

Patty Friend and Ernie Baumgartner, following Joe Garnie, who had gone into the storm and scratched, turned around to wait it out.

Ron Aldrich tried it in the morning. The veteran of five previous races fought the storm all day long and into the night. He pushed and walked and coaxed his dogs as they plunged into the wind through the daylight hours and on into darkness. At night he could see the lights of Koyuk but couldn't push the dogs any longer. "I was walking faster than the dogs and I thought, 'This is ridiculous.' I just made camp and went to bed." Early in the morning he pressed on again reaching Koyuk after more than twenty-five hours on the ice.

John Wood left Shaktoolik fourteen hours behind Aldrich, driving into a storm that was now abating, but the winds slammed into his team just as hard, hard enough to knock over four of the dogs. "I loved my leaders," he said. "They just stood up and went on. We could see the lights of Koyuk forty miles before we got there." Aldrich and Wood arrived at Koyuk within twenty minutes of each other.

Except for the first few teams, those who crossed Norton Bay remembered it as the worst the trail threw at them between Anchorage and Nome. And it came at a time when the deprivations of the trail, the expended energy, the poor diet, and the lack of sleep had exacted a great toll from the drivers. It also came when the goal almost had been achieved. Nome was within two days' run. The area was one where hallucinations were common in the eerie blank white surface and the dark sky and beckoning lights of Koyuk. On Norton Bay the year before, Ken Chase had seen "a whole church lit up and everything, neon."

The winds of Norton Bay had come when the racers were drawing on their last reserves of energy, when they most needed that energy to make the 150-mile dash into Nome.

20. Koyuk to Elim

WASTING NO TIME, THE LEADERS TORE DOWN THE NORTON SOUND ICE TO-
ward Elim, the next stop, forty-eight miles to the west. Emmitt
Peters arrived first, followed twelve minutes later by Swenson.
They had taken just six hours for the trip. A similar distance earlier
in the race — Nikolai to McGrath — had also taken Peters six
hours, whereas it had taken Swenson eight, and Swenson's dogs
had been resting for twenty-four hours. These two teams were
running at their earlier speeds or even faster. Lindner wasn't doing
as well. The short leg to Elim took his team seven and a half hours;
Honea, eight. Riley, with just five dogs and only a short rest in
Koyuk, also made the run in eight — and that probably included a
rest stop. May made it in eight and a half.

The trail from Koyuk began on sea ice on the shore of the Seward Peninsula. The mushers had worried about open water, but
soon the trail ran up on a coastal plain, mostly an extended beach.
Low hills rose gently to the north, and spruce boughs every hundred feet or so marked the trail. The teams drove around steep
rocky bluffs for about fifteen miles out of Koyuk, then curved inland through the low hills. Although the hilltops were only six or
seven hundred feet above sea level, their rounded crowns were

bald just the same. At this latitude the trail ran close to the northern timber line, and even low hills reached far enough into the sky to prevent growth of anything but tundra grasses and mosses. The hilly trail led behind Bald Head, a prominent point on the north side of Norton Bay, then down onto the frozen sea ice and marsh of Kwiniuk Inlet.

Across the inlet, the abandoned buildings of a former Federal Aviation Administration installation offered shelter at Moses Point. Later in the month, this would serve as a staging area for the annual two-week training of the Eskimo Scouts.

From Moses Point, the trail stayed on the ice of the sea and beach, divided only by a line of driftwood. The teams passed a reindeer-slaughtering corral, abandoned, knocked-down aircraft-beacon towers, and several of the local residents' fish camps.

The trail continued along the shore, rounding another series of rocky bluffs until Elim, nine miles from Moses Point, appeared along a slightly curved beach guarded by two large rock faces.

On a bluff ten to twenty feet above the beach the village was a scattering of weathered board and log homes mixed with newer painted plywood structures. Dirt exposed at the beach line had been pushed in plumes through the town, much as in Kaltag. The overturned boats of local fishermen lined the shoreline. Ice stretched a mile out into the sound to open water.

Too late to welcome the leaders, but well ahead of most of the teams, two schoolgirls tacked a welcome sign to an old building near the beach.

About a hundred families lived in and around Elim, and the race was popular there; everyone wanted to entertain a musher. In order to give everyone a chance, village officials held a lottery, with each family placing a number in a hat. Those whose numbers were drawn accepted as an honor the chance to open their homes to the mushers they'd drawn.

Welcome or not, the leaders weren't staying long. Swenson and Peters, now running strongest, stayed five hours and forty minutes. Lindner and Honea, who were traveling a little slower, cut their rest stop to less than four hours in order to keep up with the other two.

Outside a villager's home Swenson's dogs rested and ate while he repacked his sled. Mellowed a bit since Shaktoolik, he allowed an ABC television crew to attach a remote microphone to his sled to pick up his words on the way down Front Street in Nome. Swenson's wife, Kathy, walked around the team and talked, asking onlookers who might see Peters to find out when he was leaving. Swenson was still gearing his race to Peters and wouldn't go until the other team moved.

Farther west, a fraction closer to Nome, Peters was outside another house standing in the snow, almost vacantly looking over his dogs. Now and then he'd stoop to pick up a leg and examine a foot. He touched Digger's leg gingerly because the dog was still favoring his injury. Peters, tired and puffy, showed the trials of the trail, almost rambling as he spoke. "Got to work on Swenson. Don't let him sleep too much. . . . He wants to sleep. I won't let him — I'll rest here five more hours then run to White Mountain. I'll rest there five hours . . . then into Nome. Tomorrow afternoon." He talked not to people but through them, addressing the mountains or himself, as if drilling into a mind he knew might fail the plan that would keep him going, to win the race.

Swenson dropped two dogs in Elim, leaving him with ten. Peters and Lindner each dropped a dog, leaving them both with nine. May and Honea now each had eleven and Riley had five, the minimum he was allowed to finish with.

At midday on the fourteenth day of the race and about 1,017 miles from Anchorage, the drivers and dogs faced a 120-mile sprint — tired men and tired dogs driving to give everything they had left to give. To say the race had started anywhere but Anchorage would be a mistake. No one could allow himself to be left very far behind and still expect to win. A team had had to stay fairly close to the front-running group all the way. To be six or eight hours behind on a fast trail anywhere after the twenty-four-hour layovers was enough to lose the race. To catch up, a driver would have to push his dogs too hard time after time and cut short the rest stops, and sooner or later they'd falter. The pace had to be kept right from the start and the dogs still had to have enough left by Elim to make that sprint. The race was getting faster, not slower. In order for the dogs to be able to make this last run they couldn't have been worn out on long catch-up runs farther back on the trail. Howard Albert, the young Indian from Ruby, was running in seventh place. He was eleven hours behind May, who was sixth at Elim, and Elim was the dividing line. May was still there, within reach of the leaders, and with a little luck and maybe some of that dirty weather, he had a chance to win. Albert was too far behind.

The leaders weren't faltering. Their dogs were running strong, just as fast as they had in the early part of the race. When Swenson and Peters rattled their sleds, their dogs, as far as they'd come, came up eagerly once more and leaned into their harnesses ready for another run down the ice.

Winds from the north at thirty and fifty knots continued to pound those teams behind the leaders. Gary Hokkanen, driving out of Koyuk, wanted to change a pair of damp gloves for a dry pair he was carrying in the zippered front pouch of his big blue parka. The new pair didn't come out easily. Snow had been driven so fiercely through the small holes between the zipper teeth that Hokkanen found he was carrying a rock. He had to pound on the pocket to free the gloves from the hard-packed snow.

As the leaders pressed toward Nome, the last-place teams were still struggling up the Yukon River toward Kaltag.

The evening after Hokkanen left Koyuk, Patty Friend, running twentieth, struggled toward Elim. She had stayed in Koyuk only three and a half hours and as she stood on the runners, the exhaustion and the pressure were beginning to overtake her. She nodded, fighting to stay awake, but eventually the nervous energy gave out and she fell asleep riding the runners. As her grip relaxed she fell off, and before she was startled awake by the cold snow, the team had gone on down the trail. She jumped up and ran, then slowed to a walk as she pursued the driverless team across the ice. Keith Jones, who had left Koyuk minutes behind her, caught up and offered her a ride. They followed Friend's team for two hours before they found the seven dogs curled up in balls and catching a nap.

Along the coast trail, Ron Aldrich took a wrong turn. When he didn't show up at the next checkpoint within a reasonable amount of time, people began to worry and snow machiners went out to look for him. Somehow they missed him and the race marshal called an airplane into service. In Nome, Aldrich's wife Dottie heard that he was missing. A delightfully irreverent woman, Dottie said, "Oh, Ronnie gets lost every year. Nothing to worry about."

Nevertheless, the airplane made the search and the pilot located a musher and team, but identifying them from the air was difficult. An observer in the airplane dropped a note reading: "If you're Ron Aldrich raise both hands." Aldrich retrieved the note and returned to his sled where he read it. Complying with the request, he raised both hands to the circling airplane. Seeing the movement, Aldrich's team read the arms as a signal to go and took off, leaving the dumbfounded musher standing in the snow. But Aldrich has a bellow that could knock down the walls of a barn and in that voice he hollered the leaders' names. They stopped at the sound and he ran to grab the sled, lucky he hadn't had to chase them farther.

Aldrich followed Friend, and others followed them, and four days behind the leaders, Ron Brinker dropped in to enjoy the warm hospitality of tiny Elim. He had wanted to stay for just a short time, but he sat down to an immense breakfast while his host family fed his dogs. Two hours later there was talk of dinner, and as he looked at the array of steaks and other foods on a big table Brinker decided he could eat another meal. That called for another nap, and when he finally left, about six hours behind his schedule, he had a bag full of sandwiches, a Thermos of coffee and the cheers of the folks who'd shared their home. "I wanted to turn around and spend the rest of my life there," he said. But the race had to go on, even for someone in thirty-fourth place.

21. Elim to Safety

AFTER ONLY ABOUT FIVE AND A HALF HOURS' REST, EMMITT PETERS attached the tuglines to his dogs' harnesses and drove down the bank onto the Bering Sea ice. Five minutes later Rick Swenson followed, Sonny Lindner and Don Honea leaving at five minute intervals behind him. For Honea and Lindner the rest had been only a little more than three and a half hours, but by this time they had to cut short the rests in order to stay with the two leaders. Peters left a dog in Elim, Swenson left two and Lindner, one.

Once on the ice they turned west toward Golovin, twenty-eight miles distant. They followed the shoreline for eleven miles tending generally to the southwest, in sight of each other until Swenson and Peters began pulling away. To avoid a long run around Cape Darby, the trail took the teams inland across a portage through the Kwiktalik Mountains, a ridge of peaks rising 1,300 to 1,700 feet that pushed seaward to the point of the cape. The pass through the north-south ridge offered protection from the wind until the mushers dropped down to sea level, crossed McKinley Creek and turned northwest toward Golovin. There the wind blasted off the land from the north, tearing into the mushers and dogs when they came out of the protection of the hills.

On the flight to Golovin Crazy Horse had to fight the stick against the wind, trying to act casual about possible danger. Where the land sloped gently and evenly down long valleys to the sea, the wind had maintained a constant direction and velocity, allowing the pilot to brace the airplane against it and fly an even course. But the uneven coastline forced the airplane around steep rocky bluffs close enough, it seemed, for the wingtips to touch the rocks. On the eastward side of those bluffs the plane flew smoothly, but rounding them, the engine noise would change ominously, deepening into a throaty roar, noticeably lower than the normal whine. That was the first indication the air had changed, that turbulence was coming. Another pilot called the sensation "the airplane getting tense." The sound produced a fear centered in the abdomen, and then the wind hit. The wind that had flowed smoothly out of the valleys now roiled off the tops of 300-foot cliffs, slamming the little airplane down like a giant hand crushing a fly. Then the pressure of the irregular force would lift, and the airplane would sail upward again, leaving viscera close to the cabin floor. The approach of each rocky bluff brought a new fear tickling around inside the rib cage. Then the airplane would tense and the slamming would start again as Crazy Horse, with a stoic grin, fought the wind until Golovin materialized out of the growing dimness of the gathering snowstorm.

Another scattering of weathered, gray buildings with a few of the HUD government-blueprint houses mixed in, Golovin lies on a spit of land at the north end of Golovnin Lagoon. Martin Olson's large white general store dominated the low skyline. A one-lung Whittey power plant thudded its reassurance that electricity flowed through the wires connecting the village homes like a black airborne nervous system. Crazy Horse recalled a Whittey diesel that ran for seventeen years straight in Ruby. Seventeen years it ran without so much as a cough, and then one day the generator stopped, never to produce electricity again. Few people moved about Golovin, and the clerk in Olson's store said most of the residents had gone to White Mountain for a church conference. Only the clerk and former mayor Ralph Willoya and his son remained.

Martin Olson, in his red and white Cessna 206, dropped out of the storm to land at the small airstrip. He told Crazy Horse the flying weather was bad all the way to Nome and the airport there was closed. Olson was part of a family that had been established in Golovin for a long time. In 1925 Leonhard Seppala had passed the diphtheria serum to another Olson — Charlie — who carried it as far as Bluff, fifty-three miles from Nome. Martin Olson, who owned the store and a flying service and was a leader in the area's regional Native corporation, had been flying the Seward Peninsula since the late 1940s. But even years of experience can't always avert tragedy and, sadly, two years later on a flight from Shishmaref, where he'd gone to search for a missing friend, Martin Olson's plane went down and he perished in a snowstorm.

A storm built over the race trail, the catalyst of a growing drama. As darkness began to fall, Peters, Swenson and Lindner began to pull away from Honea. The leaders slipped across the portage through the Kwiktaliks, ran up Golovnin Lagoon and headed on for White Mountain after only a short rest stop. For Honea the trail began to turn sour. During the night, as Honea's team worked its way down the west side of the pass toward the lagoon, his leaders missed the trail, and instead of following the Iditarod, he came down in one of the washboard, bouncy snow machine trails that crisscrossed the area. Snow machine drive belts create crosshatches in a trail that, when frozen into ridges, have a corduroy effect, giving the driver a bouncy ride and the dogs poor footing. In addition, snow machines can make tighter turns than are comfortable for a dog team and sled. When there are trees and rocks in the area, those tight turns make steering the sled difficult, putting more pressure on the driver.

Honea, working hard behind the sled, removed his mittens, then his parka. He was warm from all the effort. As the team careened down the ravines, his headlamp began to fade, the battery losing power from the cold. On one of those tight turns, the sled skewed sideways and slammed into a rock or a chunk of ice — he went by so fast Honea couldn't make it out. The collision broke a runner off the sled and Honea screamed the dogs to a halt to examine the wreckage. The damage was severe; the sled needed either major repairs or replacement — hardly what he could get out there on the trail. Honea wasn't even on the right trail, and the chance of anyone even seeing him in the dark, particularly without his light, was slim. He anchored his sled and tied down the eleven dogs, then set off on foot to find the correct trail. Still warm from the physical exercise, he left the parka and mittens behind. There on the lonely, snowblown west slope of the Kwiktalik Mountains, the unknown quantity, the musher Swenson and Peters had continued to worry about, had lost his chance. He might have won the race but he wouldn't now. His lost victory suddenly was of little concern to Don Honea. The problem was to find his way to the trail and get the damaged sled to Golovin.

For two hours Honea plodded through the incessant wind that piled snow against anything in its way, including a sled and eleven dogs immobilized by sleep.

Eventually he located the Iditarod Trail. Returning in darkness and the storm, and with the snow covering the dogs, Honea was greeted by a landscape devoid of team and sled. His simple search for the trail now turned into a vital search for the survival equipment in the sled, particularly his parka and mittens. Although he searched for some time, not even a lump was visible to show him the way, and growing fear crept into him like cold driven by the wind. The ravines and holes that had led to the accident helped slightly by giving him places to take shelter from the wind, but the cold could still reach him without his parka.

Jerry Riley passed with his five dogs but could offer little help. Riley traveled light and the only clothes he carried, he was wearing. Others would pass, the stranded musher hoped, and he stayed close to the trail while he searched for the team, but the fear had begun to take hold, and by the time Joe May drove out of the mist, Honea wasn't sure he could survive the night.

May gave Honea his down pants and a pair of heavy mittens. They talked, getting a grasp on the situation, and discussed what they could do, particularly how to resolve it without Honea being forced to withdraw from the race. They decided May should go on into Golovin and alert race officials while Honea, now better protected with the pants and mittens, stayed by the trail and looked for the dogs. Ironically, just one hundred feet from where the two mushers talked, the dogs lay buried in the snow, sleeping, oblivious to the drama around them, grateful for the rest.

Two hours before daybreak May moved toward Golovin to send out a search party. Honea again began looking for his dogs, and in the growing light finally located his team. He jury-rigged the sled and turned toward the checkpoint. On the way in, he met four snow machiners who were coming out to help him. In town he was able to borrow a sled that would carry him and his gear to Nome, but it wasn't a dog sled. Instead, he had to use a welded metal sled made to be towed by a snow machine. Heavy and slow, it was supported by steel runners that picked up snow and didn't slide like plastic or P-Tex, thus putting an extra burden on the dogs and slowing them as effectively as if another couple hundred pounds had been added to the load. Honea pushed on, nevertheless, toward the White Mountain checkpoint that the three leaders already had left.

Swenson, Peters and Lindner made the trip from Elim to White Mountain in about nine hours. All three planned a good rest before the sprint to Nome, but now, only seventy-seven miles from the finish, Front Street was just too close. They spent only five hours. Swenson and Peters by then knew what Swenson had suggested all the way along: the race was between the two of them. From the fifty-five who started in Anchorage, the competition for first place had come down to two. For all the hard work Lindner had put in behind the sled, he didn't have the dogs to sustain the speed of the other two on those last few miles. Each leg of the trail along the coast had taken him as much as two hours longer than either of them. There was no time now for him to pull out of checkpoints ahead of the others to give his dogs a rest away from noise. Jerry Riley, tough as he was, couldn't do it with just five dogs and he was well behind, anyway, about six hours. Honea's threat had ended on the hills into Golovin. May's team was tough and steady and even fast, though May was loathe to admit it, but it didn't have the speed to catch the leaders. Time for dirty weather had run out. First place would be decided in a race between Emmitt Peters with his injured lead dog, Digger, and Rick Swenson with Old Boy, a leader people had told him was too old and too slow. For Peters, the anticipation was like trying to go to bed before reading the last chapter of a spy story. The reader, in this case, the musher, just couldn't sleep without finding out what was going to happen.

They fed their dogs and let them rest, and talked and watched, nervous, wanting rest themselves but not daring to shut an eye for fear someone would get the jump.

"That damned Emmitt," Lindner later said. "We were all in the same place, in White Mountain. We had our bags out. He jumped up and said he was too nervous to sleep. So we all picked up our bags and off we went." They could have stayed and rested a while. Their nearest competitor, Riley, arrived a half-hour after they left. And Peters and Lindner with nine dogs each, and Swenson with ten, could have easily outrun the five-dog team Riley had. But when the intensity became too much and Peters had to test his team on that last mile, they all had to go with him. Eleven hours down the trail Peters would read the last chapter. Shortly after eight on the fifteenth morning of the race the three of them pushed out onto the trail again.

Riley soon arrived in White Mountain, followed by May an hour later, Both stayed only briefly. Honea, with his dragging sled, came in two hours after May.

The trail now crossed frozen muskeg for almost ten miles before it rose and dropped through seven low hills separating several creeks that emptied into the Topkok River. The teams ran southward down the Topkok until they reached ocean ice again near Topkok Head, a bulge in the coastline that created its own bone-jarring winds, sending air currents crashing and boiling toward the ocean.

Through the gathering storm, the storm that was still pounding Norton Bay, the leaders passed, seemingly untouched, around Topkok Head and through the Topkok funnel, a valley that channeled and compacted the winds into wind-tunnel proportions, testing the aerodynamics of dog and musher. As Riley crossed the ridge on the Nome side of the funnel, May dropped into it from the east. They were close enough that May could see Riley as he disappeared over the ridge, but as short as the distance looked, May had a long way to go. Down into the funnel he plunged, perpendicular to the wind and snow coming at him from the north. The weather that day saw winds gusting to fifty knots and hurling snow — just the kind of dirty weather May had been hoping for early in the race, the kind of weather his dogs could go through while others had to stop. But the Topkok funnel threw more at May and his dogs than even he was prepared for.

"Things were going to hell. I was a little scared out there," he admitted later. As the team worked its way through the funnel, the snow blew so thick and so hard May couldn't even see the first six dogs of the eleven out in front of him. Eventually they balked, hesitated, and then stopped. "I couldn't see them. They were laying down flat," he said. As much as he might want to go, a musher learns to trust the instincts of the dogs. When they stopped, May walked forward and those first six already had laid down. The whole operation had come to a halt and in that blizzard, May worked to protect himself.

A man doesn't go against the elements in the arctic. He reads them and goes with them. To fight the elements leads to greater complications. The true test of the survivor is to know when to go and when to hole up and wait out the weather, and the dogs and the wind had told May the time had come to hole up.

Once he stopped moving behind the sled, the cold came creeping through May's clothes, no matter how heavy they were. "Circumstances can pile up on you out there," he said. Maybe he'd been working hard and there was a layer of moisture along the skin, helping that cold. In any case, with the cessation of movement, the body ceases generating precious warmth. What little warmth clothing holds dissipates all the faster in the wind. Every wet spot on the cloth becomes an opening for the wind, and every opening — zippers, buttonholes, sleeves — becomes a traitor giving entry to the cold and exit to the heat. May had left his heavy mittens with Honea. Now he had to work with thinner gloves, damp ones, at that. The gloves separated his fingers, leaving more surface exposed to the cold and wind, more surface that would allow heat to escape. At first his fingers began to ache, then stiffen, making the simple work of unsnapping dogs and opening the sled bag a painstaking process. Every movement turned to agony, every brass snap became a challenge to be overcome. The simplest task took on monumental proportions. The difficulty of the physical movement caused frustration, creating first anger then, slowly, fear.

"Things just kept going one thing to another — really I didn't know if I was going to make it or not." Within hours of Nome, May found himself in a battle for survival.

"I've told them a shovel ought to be required," May said. "On the coast a man can't save himself with snowshoes, but he can with a shovel. They ought to require a shovel from Unalakleet on."

With numbed fingers he finally tore the sled cover open and took out a snowshoe. As his fingers stiffened around the tail of the shoe, he began digging down into the snow. A lesser man might have panicked by this time, but May kept his head. One foot, two feet, three agonizing feet of snow he dug out, widening a hole to accommodate a man, a hole May wasn't all that sure he'd leave.

He returned to the sled for his sleeping bag. The down pants, the ones he had given to Honea when Honea was in trouble, were part of his sleeping gear, an inner liner to the sleeping bag. Honea still had the pants. One more layer of insulation to contain that precious body heat was unavailable, another reminder of the seriousness of the situation.

May took the sleeping bag and crawled into it, in that painfully carved-out snow cave. The cold came with him, the wind driving snow before it pounded the cave, filling the openings, covering the man. The driven snow even worked its way into the sleeping bag itself. In the cave, May waited out the storm.

May had talked, even joked, about catching up with Leonhard Seppala earlier in the race, but here in the land where Leonhard Seppala, so many years before, had raced and hauled freight and carried diphtheria serum, May came closer to Number One than anywhere else on the trail.

A painting by musher/artist Jon Van Zyle shows a man driving a dog team under a broad blue sky. In that sky is the hazy face of one of the old-time dog drivers watching almost Godlike over the team's progress. Perhaps somewhere in the sky above the sleeping Joe May, Number One watched now, looking benevolently upon a musher who had been following in his runner tracks.

How much time he spent in that snow cave, May didn't know; minutes can become days in the mind of a man caught in the clutch of the arctic. He guessed he was there about eight hours. On the official time sheets of the race, May took about seventeen hours from White Mountain to the next checkpoint, compared with Swenson's eight and a half, a difference of eight and a half hours. Another guess would place the time in the cave nearer four hours: that's how far behind May Don Honea left White Mountain. The time would have been longer had it not been for him.

Honea left White Mountain heading into a lessening storm, moving slowly because of the steel sled, but with rested dogs. As he dropped down into the Topkok funnel, the wind had abated. Moving through the lowland he neared the spot eight miles from Topkok Head where May was sleeping out the storm, buried. He came upon May's sled and his dogs, who moved at the sound of the approaching team. He saw no musher and he shouted. After poking around and looking for tracks, he called again. Eventually he roused May from his cave, and the other musher emerged from the snow, awakened from that cold overwhelming sleep that has left many another northern traveler a frozen stiffened shell under a small mound in a wide expanse of cold, cold white.

May shook off the snow, stomped his feet, took the mittens offered to him — his own mittens — and a bond was established, a bond as strong as any can be between two men who had rescued each other from the very edge. The race mattered little anymore. It was something to finish, to get over with. It was insignificant in the face of what had happened between the two of them on the trail. Together they headed for the next checkpoint, Safety, a roadhouse at the last stop before Nome.

Meanwhile, Swenson and Peters pushed their dogs for all they had left to give. Lindner tried to keep up but the two up front kept putting distance between him and them. And Riley tried valiantly to catch all three.

Behind, forty-one mushers, some as far back as Unalakleet and Kaltag, struggled up the trail facing their own races, probably not even knowing first place would be decided within the next few hours.

22. To Safety and Beyond

SWENSON AND PETERS RACED ACROSS THE TUNDRA-COVERED HILLS OUT OF White Mountain toward Port Safety with Lindner right behind them, at least at the start.

In the shadow of a range of three-hundred-foot hills, they crossed marshland, the Topkok River and several feeder creeks. They passed within a few miles of Bluff, where Charlie Olson had handed the diphtheria serum to Gunnar Kaasen, who carried it the rest of the way into Nome while Seppala followed slowly to rest his dogs.

They raced through the funnel and along the sea ice until they reached a spit of land that served as a sea wall protecting Safety Sound from Norton Sound. Along the way the signs of habitation become more evident as they passed fish camps and summer cabins belonging to the people of Nome.

They stopped once to rest and snack the dogs, maybe for a couple of hours, the last any of them, dogs or men, would have before they saw the lights of Nome. Then the sprint began in earnest. They had been traveling together since Ophir. At this point, as they prepared for the deciding run, there was nothing left to say. "He started going and I started going," Swenson said.

Swenson reached Port Safety first, driving into the checkpoint at the Safety Roadhouse at 4:43 P.M. on the fifteenth day of the race. At this, the first bar since McGrath, there was no time for fun or rest, no time for guff or kidding or even for talking. Swenson ripped everything out of his sled except the mandatory snowshoes, ax, sleeping bag, dog booties and packet of postmarked envelopes. Food, stove, cooker, clothes and anything else that would lighten the load flew out of the sled as checker Dave Harding slipped the Number-12 bib over his burnt-orange parka. Swenson unhooked a wheel dog from the team and left him, then clucked, shook the drive bow and raced out of Safety looking over his shoulder for some sign of Peters. He had taken just five minutes at the last checkpoint, leaving at 4:48. He never saw Peters, who came in only four minutes later. Peters, too, jettisoned everything he could, slipped on the Number-21 bib and raced after Swenson three minutes after he'd arrived. They had made the forty-five miles from White Mountain in eight hours and thirty minutes, an average of a little more than five miles per hour, but the race was speeding up now. Two miles out of Safety they passed a sign on the road: "Nome 20 miles."

Lindner followed them into Safety an hour and forty-three minutes later. He wasn't as rushed. He knew he wasn't going to catch them and he stayed ten minutes, dropping a dog before pushing on again for Nome. Riley arrived three hours and fifty-nine minutes behind Lindner, but he knew that he was out of it and that May and Honea were too far behind to catch him. He stayed almost an hour, leaving at 11:12 that evening.

May and Honea reached Safety within minutes of each other in the middle of the night. They had tried to run together, but Honea, with the heavy snow machine sled, kept falling behind. May's trip through the funnel had taken him seventeen hours. While they were resting almost three hours at Safety, Dave Harding reminded them there was quite a difference in money between fifth and sixth place, fifth paying $3,000 and sixth, $2,500. May said it didn't matter. "We had decided to run together. An experience like that is something you'll never forget. There's a bond formed. Prize money meant absolutely nothing after that experience."

The two left Safety within a minute of each other, shortly after 6 A.M. on the sixteenth day of the race. They stayed together for a while but May's dogs kept drawing ahead of Honea's, who were pulling that borrowed sled. They talked about it and Honea told May to go on ahead.

May's dogs gradually increased the distance between them. As he rode the sled and watched the dogs, one of them, as tired as the musher, began to waver. The dog's unsteadiness brought a chuckle.

"When you get tired, humor is in a different dimension," May said. "What might not be humorous to someone wide awake might seem totally funny. In '76 Swenson passed me about two miles out of town. We were both in the same kind of shape and we both stopped and he had a tangled dog. He weaved out there, untangled the dog and shook the handlebar to go and the wheel dog did one of these Laugh-In things, just keeled over. He went back and set the dog up and went back and shook the handlebar and the dog fell over the other way. He looked at me and he said, 'You know, Joe, that's the third time that guy has fell over on me.' He went back and took the dog out of the team and laid him on the sled and the dog was snoring by the time he hit the top of the sled and he slept all the way into town.

"Now that was funny, but it wouldn't have been funny to someone from the SPCA. But, hey, there's a difference between running a dog to exhaustion and running a dog that's tired. These dogs, most of 'em, are in good condition — the physical condition is fine, but they're pooped. They haven't had much more sleep than the driver.

"I've got this one little guy — he's been to Nome three times already. He's done it every year. On the last day he goes to sleep on the way into town. He comes back on the neck line and he's paddling along and that feels pretty good, too. Pretty soon his front feet stop going. He forgets and one of them won't go and down he goes on his chin and that wakes him up and he goes and then it starts all over again. I have to talk to him all the way into Nome just to keep him awake." May, relaxing and talking to his sleepy dog pushed around Cape Nome and headed for town.

A day later, in twentieth place, Patty Friend drove five dogs out of Safety following Keith Jones.

"We headed out of Safety after him," Friend said, "and I could — I just knew he had a strong team. He had more dogs than I did and I could see after we ran, oh maybe, I don't know how many miles, but I could see we couldn't catch him.

"One of my dogs, Tiger, had been weaving just a little bit before I stopped and I decided, 'you know this isn't worth it. I don't want to lose that dog,' meaning I didn't want him to fall over. I knew I could go to Nome with five dogs but it wasn't worth it to push him to the point of — I just decided, 'Hey, Patty, this isn't worth it.'

"All the planes and this helicopter were flying around watching the race and I just sat down on my sled. I had all this squaw candy, these strips of fish. They'd kind of been accumulating. I gave each dog a share and I had a little share and I sat on my sled and there was this helicopter flying over me. They were watching the race and I was just sitting down."

She had felt pressure throughout the race from others and "part of me was tied into what they were saying. I was going to finish twentieth and there was no honor in that, no honor whatsoever. And a part of me was saying 'Patty, twentieth is fine. You did the best job you could do under the circumstances. You did the best job you could do and that's respectable. You're finishing the race and that's fine.'

"It was really a significant time because I decided, 'I'm not going to play. I'm going to do this for Patty Friend.' What a toughie. It took me to Safety to decide that.

"So we sat down and we let those guys fly around and we had our snack and took a little rest in the sun and pretty soon we went along.

"We were traveling along and there were people there and they wanted to talk to us. And they came down, so I told them about my dogs and what it had been like." ·

After more than 1,100 miles, Friend relaxed and took her time, reaching Nome after dusk, to the dismay of friends armed with cameras.

Mushers and teams passed through Safety for eight days, many stopping for the first taste of a tall cold one at the bar before heading on toward Nome.

Ahead, the final twenty-two miles of trail lay along the sea ice, a trip of between three and five hours around the cape that had given Nome its name. Back in the late 1800s, when the United States Geological Survey was just getting around to mapping and naming parts of Alaska, a young cartographer had been working on the map of the Seward Peninsula. When he came to the outcropping just east of what is now Nome, he could find no name for it. Next to the cape he scribbled the question: "(Name?)," meaning for someone to look it up. Apparently the next person in line couldn't read his writing because when the map was published there was Cape Nome. Later, when gold was discovered on Anvil Creek, the town that formed on the beach was named for the cape with no name.

Closer to Nome the trail passed more fish camps and farther on, the Fort Davis Roadhouse, the end of the road system in winter. In summer the road went eastward past Solomon. Two miles past Fort Davis, the trail went up off the Bering Sea ice and onto fabled Front Street. A siren sounded announcing the arrival of each musher, and the townspeople and visitors poured out of bars and houses and businesses to watch the tired mushers cross a finish line marking the end of the great race, and the Iditarod Trail.

Out on the ice Swenson and Peters raced toward that goal. Swenson, out front, lost his last chance to see Peters as darkness fell, but he took a calculated risk and stopped to change his leaders. His fast trail leader went back into the team while he called on the reliable command leader Old Boy to lead him through the intricacies of the town. The exchange made, Swenson shook the drive bow and raced off again, not knowing just how far behind him Peters was.

23. The Winner

THE LARGEST CITY ON THE TRAIL WAITED FOR THE RACERS, AND THE wait had taken all day. Nome's 2,800 citizens had been joined by at least that many more, and the town bulged to the corners of its hotel rooms, waiting to see the arrival of the winner of the Iditarod Trail Sled Dog Race.

Throughout the day, as Swenson and Peters raced toward them, the townspeople worked and celebrated and cast occasional glances eastward down Front Street toward where the teams would come up off the Bering Sea ice.

Workmen unrolled snow fence that would line the chute to lead the mushers under the arch that marked the finish line, the end of the trail. "Red Fox" Olson had built the arch some years before, sawing a large spruce tree in half lengthwise. Huge burls ballooned in the wood at each end of the log and Olson had carved between them the words, "End of Iditarod Dog Race, 1049 Miles, Anchorage to Nome" in the richly finished wood. This was the goal. To pass under that arch meant the culmination of all those dreams, justification of all those reasons to run, and the joy of having made it across more than a thousand miles of Alaska by dog sled.

The arch stood near the western end of Front Street in front of

Nome's city hall where, in the council chamber, the race committee had established its headquarters. For more than a week volunteers answered phones, answered questions, solved the little problems that nagged a project of this complexity. And in that room on the fifteenth day of the race moved the bundles of nerves who were waiting. Friends, sponsors, wives, girlfriends, reporters, photographers, race officials, anyone with any interest in the race passed through that nerve center at least twenty times a day. Others spent their time wandering through town or glued to radios or sitting in one of the saloons along the street.

Even with its Iditarod population of more than five thousand, the town was small compared to what it once was. At the turn of the century, when gold fever was strong and people were panning gold right on the beaches, more than thirty thousand people lived in Nome and most of them had spent days like this one, anticipating the winning teams in another sled-dog contest, the All-Alaska Sweepstakes, a four-hundred-mile winner-take-all race to Candle and back. Front Street looked different then, jammed tight, with false-fronted buildings squeezed together on a much narrower street. Front Street eventually had been widened to four lanes and some of the buildings burned or taken down.

As the day dragged on, the stools in the bars filled and so did the standing room. Outdoors, visitors posed under the arch while others took their pictures. Press conferences defined rules — where photographers could stand, where mushers would go to be interviewed, ropes and fences, rules of civilization. Television technicians laid their wires around the finish line, setting up cameras and microphones. Shortly before 5 P.M. word rippled through the headquarters and then through the bars and town; Swenson and Peters had passed through Safety. The winner would cross the finish line in about three hours. Eight o'clock would bring the mushers into Nome. As dusk turned to dark the technicians started to hang lights from poles and trucks and even the arch that marked the end of the wilderness. With darkness, the lights were turned on and tested, illuminating the chute to the proper f-stops.

Bars along Front Street, full most of the day, overflowed as seven o'clock came and went; outdoors, the crowd leaned into the snow fence, listening to announcer Dick Mackey talk to them through a squawking public address system.

Photographers elbowed for position, basketball players fighting for the rebound. One camera-holder stood suspended in the sky by a utility company snorkle for the overhead shot.

The crowd filled the street and sidewalks all the way back to the buildings, shoving those in front into the snow fence. About a quarter after seven the sound of a siren blared through town. A musher had passed the Fort Davis Roadhouse — two miles to go. Swenson or Peters? The television lights came on. Those not blinded by the surprise of the lights turned toward the east, the end of the street where the dogs would show first, but it was too dark to see that far. No one could see even when the flashing red lights of the police escort car came on as it followed the winning team down the street. Mackey speculated as to who it was but no one knew for sure. Waves of applause rose and broke along the crowds as the winner, whoever it was, passed.

As the police car stopped, two, then four dogs appeared in the range of the television lights. Then they stopped. From behind, somewhere out in the darkness, emerged the big burnt-orange parky. Rick Swenson grabbed his lead dogs' necklines and, running ahead of them, led them down the chute. A sign on the city hall told him the students at Romig Junior High School back in Anchorage were cheering. The wave of applause reached along the snow fence and toward the arch.

Swenson let the dogs loose and ran to the arch, leaped and slapped his hand on the flat wood. His momentum carried him farther than he expected and he landed on his knees facing the team. The lead dogs launched themselves toward the musher and Swenson went down in a tangle of happy, tail-wagging huskies — a team that had accomplished. Ten of them, nine dogs and a man, had won the Iditarod Trail Sled Dog Race. Officially they had traveled about, 1,137 miles across Alaska in 15 days, 10 hours, 37 minutes and 47 seconds and they'd made the last 22 miles from Safety in 2 hours, 59 minutes, 47 seconds, better than 7 miles an hour. Rick Swenson was the first person to win the race more than once.

Freeing himself from the dogs and lines, Swenson walked to his sled and rummaged inside the cover for a moment. Then he turned to Nome Mayor Leo Rasmussen. "I brought you something," he said. A microphone picked up an "Oh, oh." Then Swenson said,

"Here's the mail." Near the spot where Gunnar Kaasen had delivered the fur-wrapped package of diphtheria serum, and as hundreds of mail drivers had done before him, Swenson handed the mayor of Nome his packet of postmarked cachets, carried to Nome by dog sled.

Officials guided Swenson through the crowd to a platform, a flatbed trailer. Microphones materialized in his beard.

"It's really great to be here," he said into them.

"How do you feel?"

"Well, I'm not tired. . . . I guess it's just a rush to win, a rush to get here. We've been pretty much going steady since Kaltag."

A Native woman in a big fur parka yelled, "I got to give him that Eskimo kiss," and enveloped the musher for a moment.

"What did it for you?" a questioner interrupted.

"I guess it was lamb chops."

About his competition he said, "Emmitt and me, we pretty much knew who was going to be racing since Ophir. We're friends. We camped together and when we got ready to race out there today there was nothing said. He started going and I started going and I was lucky and I got ahead and I never had any trouble and I won."

As race officials began to extricate Swenson from the crush on the stand, the siren wailed again. Another musher. Emmitt Peters. More quickly, it seemed, than Swenson's team, Peters' dogs appeared in the lights, Digger still in lead running on all fours as he crossed the finish line while another wave of applause broke over the arch. After almost 1,200 miles Peters finished within 42 minutes of Swenson to become the only person to have placed first, second, third, fourth and fifth in the race. His time was 15 days, 11 hours, 19 minutes and 7 seconds.

He answered questions into the microphones, told the crowd he was going to get out for a year or two to raise and sell dogs and then accepted the helpful ushering off the stand. He had known he wasn't going to beat Swenson, at least that's what he said later in the week. "Skwentna. When my lead dog was hurt. I've got the faster team, but with my lead dog hurt? When I saw Digger was hurt I wanted to cry.

"Your dogs are your children. Treat them right and they respond to you. Treat them badly and they look at you and won't go. I kept going but I knew I'd get beat."

Three hours after Peters finished, the siren sounded again. By this time many of the spectators had spent a good deal of time in the celebration atmosphere of Nome's saloons and more than a few lurched rather than walked to the snow fences. By the time the bars emptied, eight dogs and a sled were in the chute and Sonny Lindner came into the light behind them, running up to the finish line and an embrace from his wife, Sharon.

The officials checked his sled for the mandatory gear, then took Lindner to the stand, but the interviewers lost interest quickly after a few of Sonny's *Yups* and *Nopes*.

Somewhat embarrassed by the attention, he looked about for help and finally found a trailbreaker to clear the way through the press of the crowd so he could descend the steps out of the limelight. At that point he was accosted by a short red-faced man who'd just come out of one of the saloons after perhaps staying a little too long. There had been a writer from a national magazine covering the race and along the way he'd picked up a bushy marten hat similar to Lindner's.

The barfly lurched up to Lindner, Instamatic in hand, and said, "Hey, lemme take your picture." One look through the viewfinder and he put the camera down. "Hey you're not a musher, you're the guy from *Playboy*." That brought a laugh from Lindner and then someone explained to the man with the camera that this was indeed Sonny Lindner, who had just finished third in the Iditarod Trail Sled Dog Race. Unconvinced, but not willing to take a chance, the man stepped back and launched a flash in Lindner's direction. Friends escorted the musher toward the warmth of race headquarters and other friends escorted the photographer back to the bar. As he was leaving he turned to Lindner and said, "There's a *Playboy* writer here, no kidding. I'll introduce you."

The crowd around Lindner ferried him into headquarters and the crowd along the snow fence returned to previous pursuits. Another team wasn't expected until early morning so it was time to get down to the serious business at hand. Iditarod Week had begun in Nome.

24. Nome: Iditarod Week

DURING THE NIGHT JERRY RILEY FINISHED THE RACE, ARRIVING UNDER THE arch at 4:29 A.M. with the five dogs he had told Dick Mackey were just enough. He came into town just as he'd run the race, almost invisibly. He'd been out there, he'd been seen, but he'd kept mostly to himself and run alone much of the time. He'd had his troubles but had finished the race and placed very well, fourth, well ahead of many of his critics and with only five dogs. His time in the early morning limelight was brief, and he passed quickly again into the darkness of Nome.

For the next forty-eight hours mushers arrived at irregular intervals, filling out the top twenty places, those that paid some prize money. And for each arrival, Nome's fire siren wailed people out of the bars and houses to watch the tired but happy men and women cross the finish line.

Behind Riley came Joe May, who had pulled away from Don Honea for the last time. May finished at 10:09 in the morning of the sixteenth day. Honea followed more than an hour later at 11:21.

Behind them, matching his seventh-place finish of the year before, Howard Albert drove his dogs under the burled arch at

232

4:26 P.M. All had their moments with the microphones on what amounted to a reviewing stand for the sporadic parade. But the crowds had thinned and at least some of the interest had waned. The winner had won, and it would be almost two weeks before the last musher drove his dogs down Front Street.

Favorites were still out on the trail, though, and on the evening of the second day of arrivals the crowds began to gather again. Two of the most popular mushers in the race were due to be coming up Front Street: Joe Redington and Susan Butcher.

Out on the road to the Fort Davis Roadhouse spectators gathered to watch their approach. Shortly after seven a musher in a blue parka drove a team past the line of cars. A woman bystander, mistaking the driver for Redington, yelled, "Where's Susan?"

"I hope she's a long way behind me," came the answer.

The dogs slowed, glancing sideways, then pulling laterally toward the cars along the road. "Go, you dang dogs," the musher yelled. "Don't stop to look at cars now." Rick Mackey had passed Redington and Butcher, and at his urging his dogs passed the cars and continued on to Front Street. After he finished he told reporters how he got on the "wrong dang trail" and went through Solomon by mistake, about a four- or five-mile detour.

While he was talking the siren sounded again, signaling the arrival of Susan Butcher. As they waited by the chute, the people with microphones talked with Butcher's mother, who had come to Nome to see the end of the race.

"I told Lolly," Mrs. Butcher said, referring to Lolly Medley, one of the first two women to finish the race in 1974, "about the day Susan was born. I never thought this was going to happen, but I'm very proud of her and it's wonderful she and Patty are in this race and that women are getting into the race."

Butcher's team entered the chute between the snow fences, and about half-way to the arch she stopped the eight dogs and rushed ahead to catch the leaders to pull them across the finish line. Most of the mushers had to do this because the dogs, unused to the crowds, would otherwise wander about in confusion. Throughout the crowd, women cheered and whistled. She crossed the finish line, her round red face broken by a wide grin. The right side of the ruff of her parka was white where the wind off the sea ice had blown and frozen her breath. Susan Butcher, who the previous year became the first woman to finish in the money, had now become the first woman to finish in the top ten.

On the stand after her welcome, she said, "It's good to be here. My dogs are pretty tired."

"I'm gonna cry," her mother said as she moved toward her daughter and the microphones. "I think it's wonderful."

Butcher looked at her mother a moment and responded through the mikes. "We're totally opposite people. My mom could never do anything or think anything like this."

"That's true, but I'm proud of her anyway," Mrs. Butcher said.

Someone asked about Joe Redington. "When we came out of Safety, I left in front of him, and after a quarter of a mile he passed me and when Rick passed us both, I passed him again."

When the next, inevitable, question came, she was ready.

"Well, I'm not much of a women's libbist," she said, "I just think women can do whatever they put their minds to and I wanted to do the Iditarod." A loud cheer rose from the women in the crowd below the flatbed trailer. When it subsided she said to even louder cheers, "I don't see why a woman can't win it." Just as the round of cheers began subsiding the siren wailed. This time it was for Joe Redington.

The Father of the Iditarod brought his team across the finish line in tenth place, to the applause of the crowd lining the fences. On the stand, Howard Farley of Nome, who had run the trailbreaking race in 1973 and helped Redington with the Nome end during the formative years, said, "Welcome home."

"Thank you," said the grandfather from Knik.

Then came the microphones. "What about working with Susan?"

"I couldn't keep up with her here. When she got close to Nome she got in a hurry. Couldn't do much about it."

"Was Susan really your leader?"

"Well, that's pretty well true. Feets" — Redington's famous lead dog — "had a heart problem and could only run to Knik. After that it was Susan."

Someone asked if a product he endorsed in advertisements worked for him on the trail. Redington, wearing an orange knit hat with an emblem bearing the product name, laughed. In imitation of an announcer's inflections he said, "Hot Tang. It's convenient and it tastes great."

He was asked about this year's competition. "The competition's quite a bit tougher. Bud Smyth said there were fourteen teams in the top ten this year and I think that's about true."

"Has the Iditarod become what you thought it would when you were conceiving it back in Knik?"

"Even greater. It's something Alaskans look forward to even more than I do. I expect a hundred mushers in the race pretty quick, and more international mushers."

"What about being called Father of the Iditarod?"

"I don't know who gave me that title but I accepted it. I guess it took quite a bit of fathering to get it going. . . . I'm glad to be here." That last sentence was the signal to let the tired musher go, and amid the crowd's shouts Redington descended the stairs and moved with his friends into the headquarters office.

Redington rounded out the top ten finishers in the race. Early the following morning Gary Hokkanen brought nine dogs through the chute to capture eleventh place and the rookie-of-the-year prize. Behind him came Terry Adkins and Dick Peterson.

Crowds poured forth to see them all, but the number of onlookers had diminished — until another favorite approached the finish line. Ken Chase, who, with his blonde lead dog Piper, was the only one to have run all the Iditarods, approached Front Street, and people came out to cheer. Chase always finished fast, and had hoped that he might win the $500 prize money for the fastest time from Safety to Nome. Early in the twenty-two-mile run somebody told him he was well behind Swenson's two-hour-fifty-nine-minute pace, and he hadn't bothered with it. But, as he drove closer to Nome, an onlooker yelled that he was close. Then he started pumping on the sled, pushing. When the dogs came up the ramp onto Front Street he ran off the runners and sprinted down the street. In his heavy insulated one-piece snowsuit, he began to perspire as he ran next to the sled. He ran the length of Front Street to the chute until his dogs crossed under the arch. Once across the line he was told he'd missed Swenson's time by only eight seconds.

He took several minutes to catch his breath. Still panting, he said "Darn it. I could have cut ten minutes off that time if I'd known."

"This has been a bad year for me. What number did I come in? Fourteen. Two days ago I was twenty-one."

But Ken Chase's bad year hadn't quite ended. After almost 1,200 miles on the trail, in driving winds and temperatures sometimes thirty below zero, he'd overheated on the run down Front Street. Then, after standing around outside for an hour or so, he went to a round of parties and by morning he woke up with the snuffles and a sore throat. After all that time on the trail, he caught a cold in the last hundred yards.

Through the rest of the day the remainder of the top twenty teams finished. Ernie Baumgartner came in fifteenth with six dogs, then Mel Adkins with his borrowed team. Bob Chlupach finished seventeenth, then Victor Katongan. Rounding out the paying positions were Keith Jones and Patty Friend.

Of the experience Jones later compared it to his climb of Mount McKinley: "They're both the kinds of things you only do once."

Said Friend, "The worst problem is sleep — lack of it. It's tough. I'm glad to be here."

The first twenty mushers finished within two days of each other and shortly after Friend, Brian Blandford, first of the Nome mushers, arrived as the twenty-first. He told the home folks, "It's good to be back." Having trained his dogs on the nearly treeless Seward Peninsula, he said, "I learned a lot just camping out with trees around. I think I'll give it a rest for a couple of years."

Swenson had won the race on a Sunday. Blandford arrived on the following Tuesday and through the rest of the week sixteen more teams made Nome in time for the Friday-night awards banquet. In the meantime, the days of inactivity became a trial for those who'd spent at least two weeks out on the open trail, which was never far out of mind. Riley talked with Redington on a street corner the day after Redington finished. "Too old," Riley was saying, "too old. The dogs were just too old."

After they talked Redington turned and walked down Front Street looking almost sad, although several people greeted him with smiles and hellos. After his sixteen days on the trail he finally had had a good night's sleep. "Slept too much. Then I got up and didn't have any place to go. Strange feeling."

Redington, like the rest of the mushers, after shedding heavy parkas, pants and bushy marten hats, had resumed human proportions and had the same no-place-to-go re-entry problem that most of the others had. Now of normal size and disoriented for a day or two, they seemed almost vulnerable despite the magnitude of their recent accomplishment. The private people from the lonely training trails were in the public eye again, and after the shared experience of the trail found the notice uncomfortable and each other's company comforting.

With the better part of a week until the banquet, many had little to do but sit around and talk, while others bartered, traded, bought and sold dogs.

In the headquarters office one day, just passing time, Hokkanen and Peterson, who had become friends along the trail, traded jibes. Peterson looked at Hokkanen's hat, made of marten fur.

"That hat looks ratty," Peterson said touching the fur. "If I caught that in a trap, I'd let it go." They both laughed.

Hokkanen turned the hat over in his hands. "I sold all my good furs," he said. "I kept all the ratty ones so nobody'd steal my hat." He noted that Rick Swenson, for the same reason, had a marten hat made only of the yellow fur from the throats.

Nearby on a bulletin board put up for the mushers, a note from Howard Albert asked if anyone had found a marten hat he'd lost along the way.

Peterson and Hokkanen had entered the race with serious intentions, hoping for the rookie prize to help attract sponsors, and hoping to learn the trail well enough to compete seriously the following year.

"I should fly the trail once," Hokkanen said. "I just got into it to see what it's like."

Peterson wanted to get back to Anchorage as quickly as possible to find a sponsor for the next year — "while the interest is still hot."

Hokkanen felt he should have done better. "My dogs were faster than eleventh place, maybe third or fourth place, but I didn't know where the trails were."

Around them the headquarters was in constant motion as mushers walked in and out, wives checked on husbands' progress and various onlookers and reporters moved through, most of them stopping to admire the impressive array of trophies on the long table or look at photographs of previous races along the walls and on the windowsills.

The bulletin board, in addition to Albert's note, carried several messages as well as hastily scribbled advertisements offering dogs for sale. The notes told readers that Swenson, Peters and Terry Adkins were selling pups. Howard Albert was offering his whole team: "three-year Iditarod finishers."

Periodically the siren announced another arrival and the room's inhabitants would troop outside to welcome the latest finisher. One team, Eep Anderson's, managed to sneak past the siren sounder, the only one to reach Nome quietly.

At 3:22 in the morning of the Thursday of race week, Myron Angstman crossed the finish line with Nick, the setter, still out in single lead. As Angstman passed the Board of Trade Saloon a drunk came out on the sidewalk and began doing jumping jacks. Nick tried to follow him back into the B.O.T. Somehow the jumper beat the team to the end of the chute, and Nick tried again to chase him, but Angstman managed to regain control and lead the team under the arch to finish in twenty-fifth place.

Behind Angstman, at 7:23 that morning, quiet Walter Kaso drove his team down the chute and under the arch to share a record. Throughout the race mushers had been dropping dogs at checkpoints for a great variety of reasons. In the history of the Iditarod only two mushers had gone the entire trail with every dog who started: Terry Adkins and Eep Anderson's brother Babe. Kaso became the third, complementing the feat by bringing in the biggest team ever — sixteen dogs. Of the accomplishment Kaso, with a trace of Flatbush in his voice, said, "Well, everybody got up every day and we kept going."

Behind Kaso, Jim Rowe, the second of the Nome mushers, drove his team along the shoreline on the sea ice as friends yelled from the bank to cheer him on. Rowe's dog lot was on the east end of town and the dogs, deciding they recognized home, tried to go up the bank. But after a short tussle of wills, Rowe turned the dogs back toward Front Street and the arch, happy to be finishing and looking toward home himself.

By Friday morning, the day of the banquet, thirty-three teams had reached Nome. Cliff Sisson and Ron Brinker pulled up onto the street in a race for thirty-fourth. They tore down the street as if first place was at stake until they encountered a plough that was pushing snow around. Sisson's dogs went one way, Brinker's the other, and Sisson's leaders emerged first, running toward the calls of his wife Anne who was standing under the arch. Sisson beat

Brinker to the line by a mere sixteen seconds, then pulled far back in the chute to leave room for the other team.

Brinker finished with his humor intact. As if they had just raced for first prize and they were the only ones in Nome, Brinker asked the checker, "Where's everyone else?"

A moment later, as race officials cataloged his mandatory equipment, he said, "I didn't even know it was a race until I heard Rick won it. I was out there havin' a good time."

A ruddy-faced man stumbled up to Brinker and asked, "I don't believe it. How'd you do it?"

Brinker, not knowing the fellow, turned to a bystander and winked. "I just stood on the runners."

Brinker had turned in the fastest time between Safety and Nome, beating Swenson by more than nine minutes. The $500 prize, though, could only go to those in the top twenty. Throughout the race Brinker had been relaxed, jovial, always ready with a wisecrack and a smile. When so many others had been serious, some complaining, over a particularly difficult trail, Brinker always had been able to interject humor. He faced the race with a love of life that perhaps came from an experience when he had almost lost it: in Vietnam a land mine had nearly killed him, tearing up his abdomen and destroying ligaments and tendons in his leg. He had spent nine months in a body cast, and when he was released from that white prison doctors had told him he might never walk properly again. He had played with pain. Across nearly 1,200 miles of Alaska he had worn a metal brace fastened at midcalf and midthigh to keep his knee, which had no natural lateral support, in place. He had faced death before and no matter what the difficulties of the Iditarod Trail, they paled, they were a celebration of life in the face of that land mine.

Brinker and Del Allison had left Safety together after enjoying a couple of drinks at the roadhouse bar. Allison, though, didn't get very far. He had to return claiming two flat tires. Two dogs just weren't up to that last mile. He dropped one and carried the other part of the way in the sled, finishing thirty-sixth, with twelve dogs left from the twenty-one that had started. He too had approached the race cheerfully, and when he crossed the finish line just an hour before the banquet he said that's all he'd wanted to do — "get here in time for the party."

Thirty-six mushers made Nome in time for the awards banquet. Late on Friday afternoon all the mushers, officials, reporters, fans and families began filing into the National Guard Armory near the east end of Front Street for the ceremony. As the people lined up outside, a dog team suddenly wound through the crowd, tangling people and dogs as the team tried to file right on in for the banquet, too. John Barron had come up onto Front Street in the most timely finish of all, and his dogs had decided they might as well go to the party with everyone else. Barron managed to extricate the nine dogs from the crowd and continued down Front Street calling back, "I never thought they'd find their way here."

Barron was the last to arrive in time for the banquet. Still on the trail were Karl Clauson; Richard Burmeister; Jon Van Zyle, who would go on to complete a series of twenty paintings from his experiences; Jerry LaVoie; Gayle Nienhueser; and Mackey's campers: doctors Ron Gould and Jim Lanier; Don Montgomery; Harry Harris; and finally Gene Leonard, whose booze hounds would win him the red lantern, traditional prize for last place in a sled dog race. Where Swenson spent fourteen days on the trail, Leonard took twenty four days, nine hours, two minutes and twenty-four seconds. And the late arrivals didn't miss the party. The people of Nome always held a second banquet for those who didn't make the first. For Jim Lanier there was another prize: the satisfaction of having raised more than $10,000 in pledges — over $10 per mile — for the Providence Hospital thermal unit.

The main banquet provided a festive reunion for the trail people and their families and friends. A free flow of drinks mellowed the crowd over hors d'oeuvres. Each musher, from thirty-sixth place to first, had his moment before the microphone. Each received a belt buckle and certificate signed by the governor commemorating the accomplishment, and each took the opportunity to thank friends and supporters and, most specially, sponsors for their help. Swenson's lead dog Old Boy was brought in to be presented with a garland of flowers. After a joke about Susan Butcher and Joe Redington, the Golden Harness Award for the best lead dog went to Peters' determined leader Digger.

The sportsmanship trophy, given in the name of Ken Chase by the Alaska Native Brotherhood, went to Sonny Lindner for his generous time given to obliterate the false trail out of Farewell.

Honea and May were mentioned as contenders for the trophy because of their mutual aid during their trials near Golovin and the Topkok funnel. Hokkanen accepted his trophy and $1,500 for rookie of the year.

But the night was Rick Swenson's. The first musher to win the race twice, he received his trophy, his check for $12,000, a special belt buckle handmade by a Native artist, a beaded belt sent by another Native artist in Canada, a bottle of champagne and the cheers of all in attendance.

In his speech he thanked his sponsors and those who had helped him prepare for the race. He also noted the resurgence of dog teams in Alaska and the place the Iditarod held in that resurgence:

"I think that, pretty much, all of us know that the Iditarod has been responsible for the revival of dog mushing in Alaska, and I think that all of you people here tonight are part of the Iditarod and you can lift your heads up high and think that you're part of the people that are bringing dog mushing back — and not only to this state but all over the world. This race brings the people of this state together from all over, from southeast to way up north. Everybody in this state for probably two weeks or a month works to put together a successful Iditarod and once again I think they've brought off the biggest and best Iditarod ever. So, I'd like to say again how great it feels to be up here and I really feel that I'm representing a team effort of hundreds of people. . . . All their help and support is what brought me into victory.

"I've kind of left out until last probably one of the main ones. I think this year I had one of the greatest camping companions, one of the best caretakers of dogs there is anywhere in the world. I spent a lot of time with Emmitt Peters and it was kind of a good thing to keep track of each other. We had a lot of fun together. It's going to be hard not having Emmitt there next year but he's just like me — he might be there, too. I'd sure like to thank Emmitt. I think in the four years I've run the race I probably learned more about taking care of dogs from Emmitt Peters than anybody else. He's not a selfish person. He's always willing to help out.

"So thanks a lot and I hope I can be back next year, and I'd like to be back as number one, but there's a lot of guys out there want to beat me and I'd sure wish them the best of luck."

After Swenson's speech the ceremony stretched on toward midnight, and when it reached its conclusion no one was ready to quit.

Down Front Street at the Bering Sea Saloon the Dr. Schultz Last Frontier Band, which had been designated the official Iditarod band, played its Alaska-tinted brand of soft, folksy rock music, and many of the banquet-goers filled the tables to listen, at least sometimes. Loud laughter, conversation and shouts across the room occasionally drowned out the band despite its amplifiers. A happy crowd celebrated a great event. The trail had been forgotten for the moment and mushers joked with each other and their families. Partying had taken the place of driving dogs and keeping track of the race.

In the midst of the noise of the Bering Sea Saloon, a lull developed, one of those moments at a party where someone's been talking too loud and admits something personal to everyone in the room instead of the person to whom he's talking.

Into that lull Ron Brinker's voice rose: "Swenson's hooking up."

Around the room a head jerked here, a backbone straightened there. Involuntarily, muscles tensed. The trail had made its impression. Swenson was going. Everyone else had to. The race, the trail, the experience had seeped into the very nervous systems of those who had been involved, and for that brief moment Brinker's joke, while it hung in the air of the Bering Sea Saloon, took everyone who'd been there back out, back, somewhere on the Iditarod Trail.

Epilogue

EVEN 1,200 MILES OF TRAIL WEREN'T ENOUGH FOR SOME OF THE mushers. During the race, more than a few said, "You have to be half crazy to do this sort of thing." Crazy or not, some hadn't had enough and for them the season didn't end after they crossed the finish line.

Del Allison and Ron Aldrich rested in Nome for the better part of two weeks, then hitched up their dogs again and turned north toward Barrow, on the North Slope, another 1,200 miles distant. They spent more than five weeks on the trail, following the coastline and passing Eskimo whaling camps on their way. In Kotzebue, Allison's wife Jeanette joined them with another team, traveling with them for the rest of the trip. Along the way one of Aldrich's dogs, the one who'd been caught in Mulcahy Park at the start of the race, gave birth to pups, which they wrapped in furs and carried with them. They reached Barrow in late April, Allison and Aldrich now having traveled approximately 2,400 miles, believed to be the longest trip by dog sled ever completed in a single season.

Behind them, Dennis Kogl and Laurie Larson, who with their tandem sleds had joined the Iditarod Trail at McGrath, also pushed for the North Slope, beating breakup and eventually reaching Prudhoe Bay on the Arctic Ocean east of Barrow in late May.

While those teams pushed on to the north, Joe Redington and Susan Butcher fulfilled one of Redington's dreams. With the help of mountain guide Ray Genet, Redington and Butcher climbed Mount McKinley with their dog teams. They reached the summit in April 1979 with a combined team of four dogs, a larger team being impossible because of the difficulty of controlling more than four dogs on the tricky ridges of the mountain.

243

When race time came in 1980, all the players returned for another go at it, including Emmitt Peters, who'd said he wouldn't. In his third running, Joe May won the race, beating Peters' record by about 7 hours, finishing in 14 days, 7 hours, 11 minutes and 51 seconds. Of the accomplishment, May, who'd said in 1979 he couldn't see why the trail couldn't be done in 11 days if conditions were good, said, "Oh, I wasn't racing, I just got here first."

But May's record wasn't to stand for long. In 1981, under almost perfect conditions and on a slightly shorter trail, Rick Swenson won his third Iditarod, cutting the time to 12 days, 8 hours, 45 minutes and 2 seconds. By now the purse had fattened to $100,000, with $24,000 going to the winner. Swenson won his fourth Iditarod in 1982 in a race that saw storms stop the mushers at several of the checkpoints along the way. After the intense pace of the year before, Swenson said the 1982 race was much more relaxed and that he enjoyed it more. In previous races he'd been criticzed for not breaking trail, but in '82 he took the lead several times. He'd also been kidded that he couldn't win on the north trail through Ruby, his previous three wins having all been through Iditarod. His winning time on the northern route was 16 days, 4 hours, 40 minutes and 10 seconds.

Susan Butcher continued her pursuit of first place. In 1980 and again in 1981 she finished fifth. Then, in 1982, she made her best effort to date, finishing second, a bare three minutes behind Swenson.

In his sixth attempt, Rick Mackey won the race in 1983 at a near-record pace, finishing in 12 days, 14 hours, 10 minutes and 44 seconds, only about 5½ hours off Swenson's record. The 1983 race followed a slightly longer trail than in 1981.

In 1984 following a race plan similar to Joe May's, commercial fisherman Dean Osmar from Kenai, Alaska, won the race over a trail plagued by warm weather and even rain. Osmar had trained in the warmer climate of the Kenai Peninsula, and when the temperatures rose, his dogs fared well, running so far out front that Osmar covered the last 500 miles of the race without seeing another musher. The winning time was 12 days, 15 hours and seven minutes.

Then in 1985 the face of the Iditarod Trail Sled Dog Race changed. Libby Riddles of Teller, Alaska, braved a vicious storm on Norton Bay to widen her three-hour lead and became the first woman to win the race. Riddles's victory catapulted her and the Iditarod into the national spotlight as no other aspect of the race had done. Riddles was named national Sportswoman of the Year, appeared on television talk shows across the country, wrote a book, *Race Across Alaska*, and even entertained movie offers, becoming in the process a national spokeswoman for the Last Great Race.

Early in the 1985 race a moose kicked its way through Susan Butcher's team, killing two dogs and injuring several others, and forcing her to withdraw from the race for the first time in her eight years of competition. From that low point in her career, Butcher began laying the groundwork for a record unequalled in sled-dog racing. She won the 1986 race in record time, blasting into Nome in just 11 days, 15 hours, and six minutes. It was no fluke. In 1987 she set another record, reaching Nome in 11 days, two hours, and five minutes. Then in 1988 she beat everyone to Nome again, this time in 11 days, 11 hours, and 41 minutes, thus winning three straight Iditarods in the three fastest times. Her husband, David Monson, himself an Iditarod veteran, was meanwhile fielding a second team for the Yukon Quest, a thousand-mile sled-dog race between Fairbanks and Whitehorse in the Yukon Territory. He missed victory by minutes in the 1987 running and then returned to win the race in 1988.

Even as the racers compete for faster finishes and better dogs, time continues to catch up with some of those who had provided the heritage for the event. Shortly after the 1979 race, Harry Pitka, one of the original serum mushers, died in Anchorage. Two years later, after attending the banquet for the 1981 race, which was dedicated to him, Edgar Kalland also reached the end of the trail. In the summer of 1987 Charlie Evans died, leaving at that time only Billy McCarty of the original mushers who had carried that precious diphtheria serum from Nenana to Nome in 1925.

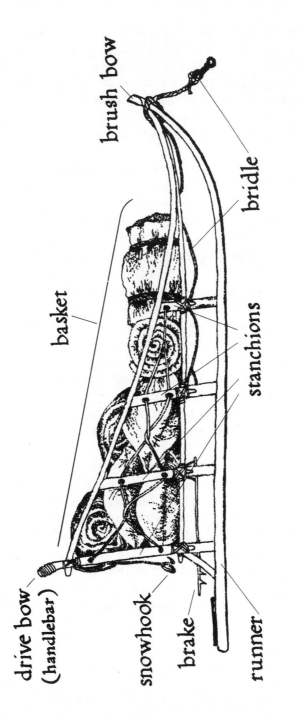

brush bow

bridle

basket

stanchions

drive bow
(handlebar)

snowhook

brake

runner

Sled typical of those used in the Iditarod Trail Sled Dog Race.

Finishing Times, 1973 to 1988

FINISHING TIMES, 1973

	Days	Hours	Minutes	Seconds	Prize Money
1. Dick Wilmarth, Red Devil	20	0	49	41	$12,000
2. Bobby Vent, Huslia	20	14	8	46	8,000
3. Dan Seavey, Seward	20	14	35	16	6,000
4. George Attla, Fairbanks	21	8	47	53	4,000
5. Herbert Nayokpuk, Shishmaref	21	11	0	19	3,000
6. Isaac Okleasik, Teller	21	18	21	25	2,500
7. Dick Mackey, Wasilla	22	4	3	49	2,000
8. John Komak, Teller	22	4	36	34	1,800
9. John Coffin, Noorvik	23	6	43	29	1,600
10. Ron Aldrich, Montana Creek	24	9	58	36	1,400
11. Bill Arpino, Tok	24	12	12	0	1,000
12. Bud Smyth, Houston	26	11	25	35	950
13. Ken Chase, Anvik	26	11	45	35	900
14. Ron Oviak, Point Hope	26	16	54	1	850
15. Victor Katongan, Unalakleet	28	23	41	4	800
16. Robert and Owen Ivan, Akiak	29	11	34	25	750
17. Rod Perry, Anchorage	30	1	39	21	700
18. Tom Mercer, Talkeetna	31	?	35	45	650
19. Terry Miller, Palmer	31	4	20	7	600
20. Howard Farley, Nome	31	11	59	11	500
21. Bruce Mitchell, Esther Dome	31	12	5	6	
22. John Schultz, Delta Junction	32	5	9	1	

SCRATCHED

1. Dr. Hal Bartko, Palmer
2. John Schultheis, Knik
3. Darrell Reynolds, Anchorage
4. Barry McAlpine, Goat Creek
5. Slim Randles, Talkeetna
6. Raymie Redington, Knik
7. John Luster, Chickaloon
8. Alex Tatum, Anchorage
9. C. Killigrock, Point Hope
10. David Olson, Knik
11. Herbert Foster, Kotzebue
12. Ford Reeves & Mike Schrieber, McKinley Park
13. Casey Celusnik of Fairbanks, one of the mushers in the double team with John Schultz of Delta Junction, also scratched. But Schultz stayed in the race and came in 22nd.

FINISHING TIMES, 1974

	Days	Hours	Minutes	Seconds	Prize Money
1. Carl Huntington, Galena	20	15	2	7	$12,000
2. Warner Vent, Huslia	21	11	18	42	3,255
3. Herbert Nayokpuk, Shishmaref	21	18	28	42	2,449
4. Rudy Demoski, Anvik	21	21	32	2	1,627
5. Dan Seavey, Seward	22	11	43	55	1,224
6. Ken Chase, Anvik	23	1	3	50	1,023
7. Raymie Redington, Knik	23	1	55	1	821
8. Ron Aldrich, Montana Creek	23	3	1	10	728
9. Joe Redington Jr., Knik	23	3	25	19	651
10. Dick Mackey, Wasilla	23	5	21	20	573
11. Joe Redington Sr., Knik	23	10	15	57	465
12. Tom Mercer, Talkeetna	24	8	18	22	387
13. Jamie "Bud" Smyth, Fairbanks	24	9	52	23	372
14. Rod Perry, Anchorage	26	18	34	30	341
15. Dave Olson, Knik	27	4	17	29	325
16. Reuben Seetot, Brevig Mission	27	4	29	22	310
17. Robert Ivan, Akiak	27	7	2	49	279
18. Victor Katongan, Unalakleet	27	9	35	26	248
19. Dr. Terry Adkins, Anchorage	27	13	28	8	232
20. Tim White, Taylor Falls, Minnesota	27	17	35	0	196
21. Desi Kamerer, Anchorage	27	23	53	30	
22. Clifton Jackson, Noorvik	28	5	9	6	
23. Mary Shields, Fairbanks	28	18	56	30	
24. Lolly Medley, Fairbanks	28	19	25	30	
25. Joel Kottke, Anchorage	29	6	34	49	
26. Red Olson, Fairbanks	29	6	36	19	

SCRATCHED

1. Dr. Steve Murphy, Anchorage
   (prior to the race)
2. Carl Topkok, Teller
3. Richard Korb, Tok
4. John Ace, Palmer
5. Bernie Willis, Gambell
6. Ward Olanna, Brevig Mission
7. John Luster, Chickaloon
8. Don Rosevear, Knik
9. John Coffin, Noorvik
10. Wilbur Sampson, Noorvik
11. George Attla, Fairbanks
12. Jack Schultheis, Knik
13. Ralph "Babe" Anderson, Nome
14. Jerry Riley, Nenana
15. Bill Vaudrin, Anchorage
16. Warren Coffin, Noorvik
17. Tom Johnson, Knik
18. Isaac Okleasik, Teller

FINISHING TIMES, 1975

	Days	Hours	Minutes	Seconds	Prize Money
1. Emmitt Peters, Ruby	14	14	43	45	$15,000
2. Jerry Riley, Nenana	14	15	?	39	10,000
3. Joe Redington Jr., Knik	14	15	?	2	7,500
4. Herbert Nayokpuk, Shishmaref	14	20	29	7	5,000
5. Joe Redington Sr., Knik	15	15	23	43	3,000
6. Henry Beatus, Hughes	15	16	20	36	2,500
7. Dick Mackey, Wasilla	16	9	41	30	2,000
8. Ken Chase, Anvik	16	9	43	25	1,500
9. Rudy Demoski, Anvik	16	14	10	17	750
10. Eep Anderson, McGrath	16	15	6	9	350
11. Alan Perry, Anchorage	17	6	1	33	350
12. Ray Jackson, Noorvik	17	9	48	34	350
13. Rick Mackey, Wasilla	18	5	55	39	350
14. Victor Katongan, Unalakleet	18	7	38	15	350
15. Ralph Lee, Naney Lake	19	6	55	10	350
16. Robert Schlentner, Fairbanks	19	7	8	15	
17. Bill Cotter, Knik	19	7	27	27	
18. Chris Camping, Canada	19	8	12	35	
19. Bill Vaudrin, Barrow	19	17	1	7	
20. Darrell Reynolds, Anchorage	20	7	14	17	
21. Richard Burnham, Kaltag	22	13	17	17	
22. Jim Kershner, Chugiak	22	13	17	37	
23. John Ace, Palmer	22	15	15	0	
24. Mike Sherman, Nome	23	0	55	55	
25. Steve Fee, Elmendorf AFB	29	8	37	13	

SCRATCHED

1. Col. Norman Vaughan, Anchorage
2. Edward Bosco, Nenana
3. Hans Algottsen, Dawson City
4. Sandy Hamilton, Alatna
5. Michael T. Holland, Fairbanks
6. Ginger Burcham, Tok
7. Bobby Vent, Huslia
8. Guy Blankenship, Fairbanks
9. Terry McMullin, 70 Mile River
10. Lavon Barve, Chugiak
11. Carl Huntington, Koyukuk
12. Walt Palmer, Chugiak
13. Charlie Fitka, Fortuna Ledge
14. Doug Bartko, Palmer
15. Franklin Paniptchuk, Nome
16. John Komak, Teller

250

FINISHING TIMES, 1976

	Days	Hours	Minutes	Seconds	Prize Money
1. Gerald "Jerry" Riley, Nenana	18	22	58	17	$7,200
2. Warner Vent, Huslia	19	3	42	0	4,200
3. Harry Sutherland, Trapper's Creek	19	4	2	52	3,600
4. Jamie "Bud" Smyth, Fairbanks	19	4	38	19	2,400
5. Emmitt Peters, Ruby	19	5	10	12	1,800
6. Ralph Mann, Montana Creek	19	6	35	34	1,500
7. William Nelson, Ekwok	19	6	36	7	1,200
8. Dick Mackey, Wasilla	19	6	43	6	1,080
9. Tom Mercer, Talkeetna	19	7	0	31	960
10. Rick Swenson, Eureka	19	7	57	27	840
11. Joe May, Trapper's Creek	19	8	8	29	600
12. Don Honea, Ruby	19	8	34	38	570
13. Alan Perry, Anchorage	19	10	53	5	540
14. Ray Jackson, Noorvik	19	10	56	33	510
15. Ken Chase, Anvik	19	10	58	37	480
16. Billy Demoski, Galena	19	11	7	52	450
17. Terry Adkins, Mountain Home, Idaho	19	11	17	4	420
18. Rudy Demoski, Anvik	19	13	27	7	390
19. Jack Hooker, Ovanda, Montana	19	13	33	33	360
20. Ford Reeves, Mt. McKinley Park	19	14	26	36	300
21. Ralph "Babe" Anderson, McGrath	19	18	2	28	
22. Lavon Barve, Chugiak	20	3	31	58	
23. Jerry Austin, St. Michaels	20	4	20	25	
24. Ron Aldrich, Montana Creek	20	7	46	31	
25. Richard Burnham, Kaltag	20	8	6	6	
26. Charlie Fitka, Fortuna Ledge	20	14	10	58	
27. Steve Jones, McKinley Park	20	14	11	31	
28. Clarence Towarak, Unalakleet	20	15	55	25	
29. Alex Sheldon, Ambler	20	16	45	31	
30. William Solomon, Kaltag	21	13	35	25	
31. Allan Marple, Chugiak	21	13	44	48	
32. Peter Nelson, Kotzebue	22	5	45	50	
33. Jon Van Zyle, Eagle River	26	8	42	42	
34. Dennis Corrington, Anchorage & Nome	26	8	42	51	

SCRATCHED

1. Joe Redington Sr., Knik
2. Col. Norman Vaughan, Anchorage
3. Dr. Richard Hanks, Anchorage
4. Trent Long, Chugiak
5. Bob Schlentner, Fairbanks
6. Peter Kakaruk, Mary's Igloo
7. John Giannone, Saugerties, New York
8. Lee Chamberlain, McGrath
9. Oran Knox, Kivalina
10. Mel Fudge, Clear
11. Bruce Mitchell, College
12. Phillip Foxie, St. Michael
13. Steve Fee, Anchorage

FINISHING TIMES, 1977

	Days	Hours	Minutes	Seconds	Prize Money
1. Rick Swenson, Eureka	16	16	27	13	$9,600
2. Jerry Riley, Nenana	16	16	32	5	5,600
3. Warner Vent, Huslia	16	16	44	39	4,900
4. Emmitt Peters, Ruby	16	19	57	2	3,200
5. Joe Redington Sr., Knik	17	1	26	30	2,400
6. Dick Mackey, Wasilla	17	1	35	15	2,000
7. Don Honea, Ruby	17	3	34	34	1,600
8. Robert Schlentner, Fairbanks	17	3	44	59	1,440
9. Ralph "Babe" Anderson, McGrath	17	17	51	57	1,280
10. Jack Hooker, Montana	17	9	5	56	1,020
11. Ken Chase, Anvik	17	11	18	28	800
12. Alex Sheldon, Ambler	17	11	50	18	760
13. Peter MacManus, Ambler	17	12	17	41	720
14. Terry Adkins, Minnesota	17	14	41	42	680
15. Al Crane, Nome	17	16	25	10	640
16. Howard Albert, Ruby	17	17	24	31	600
17. Wm. "Sonny" Nelson, Ekwok	17	18	17	33	560
18. Roger Nordlum, Kotzebue	17	19	25	24	520
19. Rod Perry, Lake Minchumina	17	23	18	18	480
20. Richard Burnham, Kaltag	18	7	18	30	400
21. Stein Havard, Fjestad, Norway	18	15	23	15	
22. Bill Cotter, Knik	18	15	53	46	
23. Rick Mackey, Wasilla	18	16	22	25	
24. Sandy Hamilton, Allakaket	19	2	16	29	
25. Bob Chlupach, Chugiak	19	2	28	6	
26. Charlie Harrington, Knik	19	10	51	23	
27. Eep Anderson, Takotna	20	8	21	33	
28. Jim Smarz, McGrath	20	8	32	16	
29. Duane Halverson, Eagle River	21	4	45	47	
30. Peter Kakaruk, Mary's Igloo	21	6	0	3	
31. Randy DeKuiper, Michigan	21	8	35	47	
32. Dale Swartzentruber, Shageluk	21	16	30	59	
33. Jerry Mercer, Delta Junction	21	15	31	1	
34. Varona Thompson, Kaltag	21	18	0	0	
35. Jim Tofflemire, Oregon	22	4	53	20	
36. Vasily Zamitkyn, Ayak Island	22	9	6	6	

SCRATCHED

1. Don Montgomery, Lima, Ohio
2. Tom Mathias, Michigan
3. Ray Jackson, Noorvik
4. Rudy Demoski, Anvik
5. Rick McConnell, Soldotna
6. Bob Watson
7. Dr. Ron Gould, Clear
8. Franklin Paniptchuk
9. John Ace, Palmer

10. Dinah Knight, Minneapolis, Minnesota
11. Jerry Austin, St. Michael
12. John Hancock
13. William Solomon, Kaltag

FINISHING TIMES, 1978

	Days	Hours	Minutes	Seconds	Prize Money
1. Dick Mackey, Wasilla	14	18	52	24	$12,000
2. Rick Swenson, Eureka	14	18	52	25	8,000
3. Emmitt Peters, Ruby	14	19	28	32	6,000
4. Ken Chase, Anvik	15	0	2	0	4,000
5. Joe Redington Sr., Knik	15	3	14	58	3,000
6. Eep Anderson, Takotna	15	3	1	51	2,500
7. Howard Albert, Ruby	15	3	40	59	2,000
8. Robert Schlentner, Fairbanks	15	5	57	54	1,800
9. Jerry Austin, St. Michael	15	6	33	16	1,600
10. Alan Perry, Kasilof	15	10	13	25	1,400
11. Sonny Lindner, Johnson River	15	12	3	3	1,000
12. Ron Aldrich, Montana Creek	15	12	17	11	950
13. Peter MacManus, Ambler	16	1	26	53	900
14. Bob Chlupach, Willow	16	3	44	54	850
15. Ron Tucker, Fairbanks	16	4	29	43	800
16. Terry Adkins, Cheyenne, Wyoming	16	5	11	25	750
17. Harry Sutherland, Trappers Creek	16	5	53	27	700
18. Richard Burnham, Kaltag	16	7	10	34	650
19. Susan Butcher, Knik	16	15	40	30	600
20. Varona Thompson, Kaltag	16	16	40	30	500
21. Joe Garnie, Teller	17	2	1	54	
22. Jerry Mercer, Delta Junction	17	2	1	57	
23. Charlie Fitka, Fortuna Ledge	17	16	28	38	
24. Ernie Baumgartner, McGrath	18	5	9	53	
25. Jack Goodwin, Talkeetna	18	6	4	0	
26. Rick McConnell, Soldotna	18	7	37	34	
27. William Solomon, Kaltag	18	9	28	1	
28. James Brandon, Ekwok	18	12	12	12	
29. Shelley Vandiver, Anchorage	19	15	7	8	
30. John Wood, Chugiak	19	15	7	27	
31. Ray Gordon, Rock Springs, Wyoming	19	15	14	52	
32. Gary Campen, Kaltag	21	2	25	4	
33. Col. Norman Vaughan, Anchorage	22	3	29	41	
34. Andrew Foxie, Stebbins	22	3	29	44	

SCRATCHED

1. Roger Roberts, Takotna
2. Duke Bertke, Anchorage
3. Mike Demarco, Fairbanks
4. Bill Rose, Palmer
5. Babe Anderson, McGrath

William "Sonny" Nelson of Ekwok, who had paid his entry fee and was ready for the 1978 Iditarod, was killed in a plane crash coming into Anchorage for the race. The pilot and all but two of Nelson's dogs were also killed. Al Crane of Nome drew a number for Nelson and that bib was reserved for him.

FINISHING TIMES, 1979

	Days	Hours	Minutes	Seconds	Prize Money
1. Rick Swenson, Eureka	15	10	37	47	$12,000
2. Emmitt Peters, Ruby	15	11	19	7	8,000
3. Sonny Lindner, Delta Junction	15	14	17	32	6,000
4. Jerry Riley, Nenana	15	19	29	44	4,000
5. Joe May, Trapper Creek	16	1	9	15	3,000
6. Don Honea, Ruby	16	2	21	41	2,500
7. Howard Albert, Ruby	16	7	26	40	2,000
8. Rick Mackey, Wasilla	16	11	0	1	1,800
9. Susan Butcher, Wasilla	16	11	15	32	1,600
10. Joe Redington, Wasilla	16	11	04	1	1,400
11. Gary Hokkanen, Eureka	16	16	57	5	1,000
12. Terry Adkins, Cheyenne, Wyoming	16	19	45	16	950
13. Dick Peterson, Chisana	17	3	37	37	900
14. Ken Chase, Anvik	17	4	43	7	850
15. Ernie Baumgartner, McGrath	17	4	47	48	800
16. Mel Adkins, Willow	17	4	54	23	750
17. Bob Chlupach, Willow	17	6	23	19	700
18. Victor Katongan, Unalakleet	17	7	35	6	650
19. Keith Jones, Ambler	17	9	16	8	600
20. Patty Friend, Chugiak	17	9	47	16	500
21. Brian Blandford, Nome	17	16	4	54	
22. John Wood, Chugiak	18	2	20	35	
23. Ron Aldrich, Willow	18	8	10	31	
24. Eep Anderson, McGrath	18	11	33	33	
25. Myron Angstman, Bethel	18	19	22	32	
26. Walter Kaso, Talkeetna	18	22	23	40	
27. Jim Rowe, Nome	18	22	29	43	
28. Steve Vollertsen, Takotna	19	1	25	40	
29. Rick McConnell, Anchorage	19	6	57	57	
30. Rome Gilman, Chugiak	19	13	1	43	
31. Bud Smyth, Fairbanks	20	0	42	14	
32. Bill Rose, Palmer	20	1	2	38	
33. Steve Adkins, Willow	20	1	31	48	
34. Cliff Sisson, Soldotna	20	4	36	53	
35. Ron Brinker, Wasilla	20	4	37	9	
36. Del Allison, Willow	20	8	23	23	
37. John Barron, Palmer	20	9	26	6	
38. Karl Clauson, Wasilla	21	12	8	29	
39. Jerry LaVoie, Anvik River	22	8	23	44	
40. Gayle Nienhueser, Anchorage	22	9	14	53	
41. Richard Burmeister, Nome	22	12	57	37	
42. Jon Van Zyle, Eagle River	22	13	50	50	
43. Jim Lanier, Anchorage	24	6	44	18	
44. Ron Gould, Clear	24	7	25	50	
45. Don Montgomery, Lima, Ohio	24	7	27	11	
46. Prentice "Harry" Harris, Fairbanks	24	7	37	9	
47. Gene Leonard, Finger Lake	24	9	2	22	

SCRATCHED

1. Mark Couch, Palmer
2. Kelly Wages, Fairbanks
3. Lee Gardino, Chugiak
4. Isaac Okleasik, Teller
5. Terry McMullin, Eagle
6. Herbie Nayokpuk, Shishmaref
7. Clarence Towarak, Unalakleet
8. Joe Garnie, Teller

FINISHING TIMES, 1980

	Days	Hours	Minutes	Seconds	Prize Money
1. Joe May, Trapper Creek	14	7	11	51	$12,000
2. Herbert Nayokpuk, Shishmaref	14	20	32	12	8,000
3. Ernie Baumgartner, McGrath	15	9	9	59	6,000
4. Rick Swenson, Eureka	15	10	12	29	4,000
5. Susan Butcher, Eureka	15	10	17	6	3,000
6. Roger Nordlum, Kotzebue	15	10	34	14	2,500
7. Jerry Austin, St. Michael	15	13	57	13	2,000
8. Walter Kaso, Talkeetna	15	15	42	32	1,800
9. Emmitt Peters, Ruby	15	16	14	7	1,600
10. Donna Gentry, Skwentna	15	16	39	6	1,400
11. Marc Boily, Fairbanks	15	17	3	46	1,000
12. Joe Garnie, Teller	15	17	55	24	950
13. Larry Smith, Dawson, Yukon Territory	15	18	1	37	900
14. Bruce Johnson, Atlin, British Columbia	15	18	22	7	850
15. Rudy Demoski, Anvik	16	9	35	56	800
16. David Olson, Knik	16	9	52	51	750
17. Terry Adkins, Cheyenne, Wyoming	16	10	56	16	700
18. Libby Riddles, Nelchina	16	13	58	34	650
19. Harold Ahmasuk, Nome	16	14	44	11	600
20. Henry Johnson, Unalakleet	16	15	28	27	500
21. William Bartlett, Willow	16	16	12	46	
22. Martin Buser, Switzerland	17	6	50	5	
23. Jack Goodwin, Talkeetna	17	7	7	16	
24. Dee Dee Jonrowe, Bethel	17	7	59	24	
25. Ken Chase, Anvik	17	8	32	14	
26. Bruce Denton, Juneau	17	13	29	1	
27. Clarence Shockley, Trapper Creek	17	13	29	29	
28. John Cooper, Ambler	17	14	18	6	
29. Michael Harrington, McGrath	17	14	29	36	
30. Marjorie Ann Moore, Wasilla	20	7	1	17	
31. Eric Poole, Trapper Creek	20	9	14	20	

32. Douglas Sherrer, Takotna	20	9	38	22
33. Ron Cortte, Unalakleet	22	3	7	28
34. John Gartiez, Anchorage	22	18	5	50
35. Norman Vaughan, Willow	24	9	19	25
36. Barbara Moore, Nome	24	9	25	45

SCRATCHED

1. Bill Boyko
2. Jan Masek
3. Ed Craver
4. Eugene Russel Ivy
5. Larry Cogdill
6. Robert E. Neidig
7. John Eckels
8. Steven R. Conaster
9. Duke Bertke
10. Varona Thompson
11. Fred Jackson
12. John G. Barron
13. Dick Peterson

14. Lee Gardino
15. Donald Honea Sr.
16. Babe Anderson
17. Don Eckles
18. Frank Sampson
19. Warner Vent
20. Sonny Lindner
21. Joe Redington Sr.
22. Dick Mackey
23. Alton Walluk
24. Bruce Woods
25. Gerald Riley
  Disqualified, Landon Carter

FINISHING TIMES, 1981

	Days	Hours	Minutes	Seconds	Prize Money
1. Rick Swenson, Eureka	12	8	45	2	$24,000
2. Sonny Lindner, Johnson River	12	9	33	22	16,000
3. Roger Nordlum, Kotzebue	12	9	42	13	12,000
4. Larry "Cowboy" Smith, Dawson City, Yukon Territory	12	10	22	46	8,000
5. Susan Butcher, Eureka	12	12	45	24	6,000
6. Eep Anderson, Takotna	12	14	8	37	5,000
7. Herbie Nayokpuk, Shishmaref	12	22	17	45	4,000
8. Clarence Towarak, Unalakleet	13	1	48	4	3,600
9. Rick Mackey, Wasilla	13	3	58	7	3,200
10. Terry Adkins, Cheyenne, Wyoming	13	7	32	4	2,800
11. Duane Halverson, Trapper Creek	13	13	55	19	2,000
12. Emmitt Peters, Ruby	13	14	14	49	1,900
13. Jerry Austin, St. Michael	13	14	40	38	1,800
14. Joe Redington Sr., Knik	13	15	19	2	1,700
15. Harry Sutherland, Trapper Creek	13	18	2	7	1,600
16. Joe Garnie, Teller	13	18	17	35	1,500
17. Gary Attla, Fairbanks	13	22	1	37	1,500
18. Donna Gentry, Skwentna	13	22	20	20	1,400
19. Martin Buser, Switzerland	14	2	47	23	1,200
20. Libby Riddles, Nelchina	14	6	27	43	1,000
21. David Monson, Unalaska	14	14	44	4	
22. Bruce Denton, Juneau	14	22	5	13	

23. John Barron, Big Lake	14	23	57	0
24. Gene Leonard, Hayes River	15	0	32	14
25. Bob Martin, Wasilla	15	0	45	9
26. Neil Eklund, Shishmaref	15	3	44	9
27. Mark Freshwaters, Ruby	15	3	45	37
28. Jeff King, McKinley Park	15	7	2	47
29. Steve Flodin, Chugiak	16	1	52	14
30. Gary Whittemore, Cantwell	16	4	13	6
31. Dee Dee Jonrowe, Bethel	16	5	5	43
32. Sue Firmin, Flat Horn Lake	16	5	5	56
33. Mike Storto, Germany	16	11	37	57
34. Dan Zobrist, Nenana	17	3	28	43
35. Dennis Boyer, Wasilla	17	16	28	0
36. Jan Masek, Anchorage	18	3	44	44
37. Burt Bomhoff, Anchorage	18	5	22	58
38. Jim Strong, Hope	18	6	30	30

SCRATCHED

1. Frank Sampson
2. Harold Ahmasuk
3. Robert Ivan
4. William Webb
5. Ernie Baumgartner
6. Gordon Castanza
7. Douglas Sherrer
8. Bud Smyth
9. Ted English
10. Wes McIntyre
11. Willie French
12. Clifton Jackson
13. Bill Thompson
14. Jerry Riley
15. Myron Angstman

FINISHING TIMES, 1982

	Days	Hours	Minutes	Seconds	Prize Money
1. Rick Swenson, Manley	16	4	40	10	$24,000
2. Susan Butcher, Eureka	16	4	43	53	16,000
3. Jerry Austin, St. Michael	16	4	52	11	12,000
4. Emmitt Peters, Ruby	16	5	6	42	8,000
5. Dave Monson, Dutch Harbor	16	5	13	24	6,000
6. Ernie Baumgartner, McGrath	16	5	17	3	5,000
7. Bob Chlupach, Willow	16	5	26	46	4,000
8. Don Honea Sr., Ruby	16	6	41	0	3,600
9. Stan Zuray, Tanana	16	6	44	0	3,200
10. Bruce Denton, Juneau	16	13	11	22	2,800
11. Rick Mackey, Wasilla	16	13	30	47	2,000
12. Herbie Nayokpuk, Shishmaref	16	14	8	21	1,900
13. Dean Osmar, Clam Gulch	16	14	54	54	1,800
14. Terry Adkins, Montana	16	15	37	47	1,700
15. Joe May, Trapper Creek	16	15	43	23	1,600
16. Marc Boily, Fairbanks	16	17	54	55	1,500
17. Joe Redington Sr., Knik	17	8	25	45	1,500
18. Ed Foran, Anvik	17	9	9	29	1,400

19. Guy Blankenship, Fairbanks	17	9	13	22	1,200
20. John Stam, Galena	17	9	18	18	1,000
21. Alex Sheldon, Ambler	17	9	24	46	
22. Mitch Seavey, Seward	17	10	27	0	
23. Glenn Findlay, Sidney, Australia	17	11	57	53	
24. John Wood, Chugiak	17	12	39	46	
25. Babe Anderson, McGrath	17	21	12	2	
26. Jim Strong, Hope	18	17	15	36	
27. Ron Cortte, Fairbanks	18	17	17	59	
28. Larry "Cowboy" Smith, Dawson, Yukon Territory	18	23	9	23	
29. Dean Painter, Grayling	19	3	5	6	
30. Ken Chase, Anvik	19	4	1	45	
31. Steve Gaber, Bethel	19	4	23	32	
32. Rose Albert, Ruby	19	4	54	53	
33. Jan Masek, Anchorage	19	10	13	24	
34. Chris Deverill, Anchorage	19	12	45	0	
35. LeRoy Shank, Fairbanks	20	12	43	31	
36. Steve Flodin, Chugiak	20	13	0	0	
37. Frank I. Brown, Fairbanks	20	14	54	59	
38. Mark "Bigfoot" Rosser, Fairbanks	20	16	5	27	
39. Bill Yankee, Juneau	20	22	2	45	
40. James Cole, Nome	21	5	53	42	
41. Richard Burmeister, Nome	21	6	29	0	
42. Rick Tarpey, Seward	21	7	18	30	
43. Eric Buelow, North Pole	21	14	48	28	
44. Rome Gilman, Chugiak	24	0	23	47	
45. Jack Studer, Nome	24	14	54	54	
46. Ralph Bradley, Girdwood	26	13	59	59	

SCRATCHED

1. Michael Harrington, McGrath
2. Norman Vaughan (77 years old), Anchorage
3. Steve Haver, Fairbanks
4. Sue Firmin, Anchorage
5. Smokey Moff, Nome
6. Bill Rose, Palmer
7. Gary Whittemore, Cantwell
8. John Barron, Yentna River

FINISHING TIMES, 1983

	Days	Hours	Minutes	Seconds	Prize Money
1. Rick Mackey, Wasilla	12	14	10	44	$24,000
2. Eep Anderson, Takotna	12	15	50	36	16,000
3. Larry Smith, Yukon Territory	12	20	19	56	12,000
4. Herbie Nayokpuk, Shishmaref	12	22	04	28	8,000
5. Rick Swenson, Manley	13	02	49	46	6,000
6. Lavon Barve, Wasilla	13	03	00	49	5,000
7. Duane Halverson, Trapper Creek	13	04	42	00	4,000
8. Sonny Lindner, Johnson River	13	05	28	20	3,600
9. Susan Butcher, Manley	13	10	25	32	3,200
10. Roger Legaard, Norway	13	11	33	45	2,800

11. Joe Runyan, Tanana	13	12	39	34	2,000
12. Guy Blankenship, Fairbanks	13	12	59	00	1,900
13. Dave Monson, Anchorage	13	14	08	54	1,800
14. Sue Firmin, Flat Horn Lake	13	17	28	52	1,700
15. Dee Dee Jonrowe, Bethel	13	18	10	25	1,600
16. Howard Albert, Ruby	13	22	11	39	1,500
17. Bruce Denton, Juneau	14	00	37	07	1,400
18. Dave Olson, Knik	14	03	35	29	1,300
19. Emmitt Peters, Ruby	14	03	36	20	1,200
20. John Barron, Big Lake	14	05	44	30	1,000
21. Neil Eklund, Nome	14	10	32	03	
22. Burt Bomhoff, Anchorage	14	12	23	20	
23. Roxy Woods, Rampart	14	15	56	16	
24. Walter Kaso, Talkeetna	15	05	00	53	
25. Eric Buetow, North Pole	15	08	06	39	
26. Jim Strong, Hope	15	10	07	54	
27. Ken Hamm, Bethel	15	10	15	15	
28. Vernon Halter, Unalaska	15	10	40	17	
29. Shannon Poole, Trapper Creek	15	13	10	56	
30. William Hayes, Dutch Harbor	15	15	15	15	
31. Walter Williams, Aniak	15	23	17	34	
32. Christine O'Gar, Trapper Creek	16	00	19	05	
33. Ted English, Chugiak	16	00	37	29	
34. Bud Smyth, Fairbanks	16	09	34	20	
35. Ron Brennan, Bethel	17	00	42	57	
36. Wes McIntyre, Ninilchik	17	10	49	39	
37. Ken Johnson, McGrath	17	11	12	06	
38. Steve Rieger, Anchorage	17	11	13	01	
39. Connie Frerich, Delta Junction	17	11	16	26	
40. Ray Dronenburg, Barrow	17	12	31	51	
41. Gary Paulsen, Minnesota	17	12	38	38	
42. Ed Forstner, Knik	18	06	62	16	
43. Mark Nordman, Minnesota	18	17	54	34	
44. Dick Barnum, Fairbanks	18	23	59	59	
45. David Wolfe, Anchorage	19	04	28	40	
46. Leroy Shank, Fairbanks	19	15	07	54	
47. Robert Gould, Fairbanks	20	00	42	29	
48. Fritz Kirsch, Wasilla	20	01	34	24	
49. Steve Haver, Fairbanks	20	12	55	56	
50. Ron Gould, Fairbanks	20	13	12	05	
51. Pam Flowers, Willow	20	13	12	54	
52. Norman Vaughn, Anchorage	21	02	21	16	
53. Norm McAlpine, Anvik	21	02	44	22	
54. Scott Cameron, Palmer	21	04	36	41	

SCRATCHED   DISQUALIFIED

1. Terry Adkins	5. William Cowart	9. Doug Bartko	1. Les Atherton
2. Bob Bright	6. Ken Chase	10. Jan Masek	
3. Alex Sheldon	7. Russell Ivey	11. Beverly Jerue	
4. Clifton Cadzow	8. Hal Bartko	12. Gene Leonard	
		13. Saul Paniptchuk	

FINISHING TIMES, 1984

	Days	Hours	Minutes	Seconds	Prize Money
1. Dean Osmar	12	15	7	33	$24,000
2. Susan Butcher	12	16	41	42	16,000
3. Joe Garnie	12	17	18	48	12,000
4. Marc Boily	13	4	52	51	8,000
5. Jerry Austin	13	5	59	53	6,000
6. Rick Swenson	13	7	4	21	5,000
7. Joe Redington, Sr.	13	8	43	11	4,000
8. Terry Adkins	13	13	54	43	3,600
9. John Cooper	14	0	22	24	3,200
10. Larry Smith	14	1	57	44	2,800
11. Vern Halter	14	3	55	19	2,000
12. Burt Bomhoff	14	7	49	18	1,900
13. Rusty Miller	14	8	44	17	1,800
14. Mark Freshwaters	14	10	31	10	1,700
15. Bob Chlupach	14	10	31	12	1,600
16. Ed Foran	14	11	27	41	1,500
17. Emmitt Peters	14	15	8	0	1,400
18. Rick Armstrong	14	16	55	30	1,300
19. Ray Gordon	14	18	43	32	1,200
20. John Barron	14	22	54	34	1,000
21. Jim Strong	15	7	16	7	
22. Bob Toll	15	9	23	23	
23. Eep Anderson	15	11	0	54	
24. Gordon Castanza	15	11	5	55	
25. Ron Cortte	15	13	18	38	
26. Jerry Raychel	15	13	57	29	
27. Diana Dronenburg	15	15	29	49	
28. Sue Firmin	15	19	9	15	
29. Rick Mackey	15	19	9	23	
30. DeeDee Jonrowe	15	19	18	13	
31. Dave Olson	15	19	30	0	
32. Gary Whittemore	15	20	44	14	
33. Eric Buetow	16	0	56	29	
34. Frank Buttine	16	8	3	7	
35. Karl Skogen	16	8	3	19	
36. Calvin Lauwers	16	12	50	0	
37. Dan Cowan	16	12	35	2	
38. Francine Bennis	16	13	40	3	
39. Rick Adkinson	17	3	23	19	
40. Jim Lanier	17	5	49	22	
41. David Sheer	17	8	53	5	
42. Steve Peek	17	10	58	55	
43. Fred Agree	19	7	41	7	
44. Ed Borden	19	9	43	17	
45. Bill Mackey	19	9	43	33	

SCRATCHED

1. Ted English	11. Larry Dogdill
2. James Cole	12. Brian Johnson
3. Jan Masek	13. Miki Collins
4. Dave Aisenbrey	14. Steve Gaber
5. Gene Leonard	15. William Thompson
6. Ray Dronenburg	16. Mel Adkins
7. Gordon Brinker	17. Bob Sunder
8. Connie Frerichs	18. Darrel Reynolds
9. Don Honea, Sr.	19. Vern Cherneski
10. Lolly Medley	20. Ron Brennan

DISQUALIFIED

1. Guy Blankenship	2. Armen Khatchikian

FINISHING TIMES, 1985

	Days	Hours	Minutes	Seconds	Prize Money
1. Libby Riddles	18	0	20	17	$50,000
2. Duane Halverson	18	2	45	36	30,000
3. John Cooper	18	6	59	33	20,000
4. Rick Swenson	18	7	29	24	15,000
5. Rick Mackey	18	14	44	54	13,000
6. Vern Halter	18	14	55	26	11,000
7. Guy Blankenship	18	16	16	39	9,500
8. Herbie Nayokpuk	18	17	20	0	8,000
9. Sonny Lindner	18	18	33	33	6,500
10. Lavon Barve	18	19	25	4	5,500
11. Tim Moerlein	18	21	10	56	4,500
12. Emmitt Peters	18	23	21	22	4,000
13. Tim Osmar	18	23	43	43	3,750
14. Jerry Austin	19	3	32	43	3,500
15. Terry Adkins	19	22	51	49	3,250
16. Roger Nordlum	19	23	51	15	3,000
17. Glen Findlay	20	1	34	33	2,750
18. John Barron	20	3	21	22	2,500
19. Raymie Redington	20	3	38	19	2,250
20. Burt Bomhoff	20	3	59	17	2,000
21. Jacques Philip	20	5	0	21	
22. Bob Bright	21	2	34	27	
23. Peter Fromm	21	2	34	33	
24. Steve Flodin	21	5	8	4	
25. Warner Vent	21	5	31	54	
26. Ron Robbins	21	5	40	25	
27. Kazuo Kojima	21	6	12	12	
28. Nathan Underwood	21	6	54	0	

29. Betsy McGuire	21	7	7	15
30. Kevin Saiki	21	8	4	9
31. Earl Norris	21	9	38	0
32. Kevin Fulton	21	9	39	0
33. John Coble	21	10	13	0
34. Alan Cheshire	21	10	21	0
35. Victor Jorge	21	10	25	0
36. Fred Agree	21	11	25	36
37. Claire Philip	21	11	35	37
38. John Ace	21	21	1	1
39. Rick Armstrong	21	21	1	2
40. Monique Bene	22	3	45	45

SCRATCHED

1. David Aisenbrey
2. Terry Hinsley
3. Susan Butcher
4. Ted English
5. Jan Masek
6. Joe Redington, Sr.
7. Fred Jackson
8. Victor Katongan
9. Gary Paulsen
10. Ray Dronenburg
11. Joseph Mailleille, Sr.
12. Terry McMullin
13. Dennis Towarak
14. Ernie Baumgartner
15. Rudy Demoski
16. Norman Vaughan
17. Armen Khatchikian
18. Scott Cameron
19. Chuck Schaeffer

DISQUALIFIED

1. Bobby Lee

2. Wes McIntyre

FINISHING TIMES, 1986

	Days	Hours	Minutes	Seconds	Prize Money
1. Susan Butcher	11	15	6	0	$50,000
2. Joe Garnie	11	16	1	11	30,000
3. Rick Swenson	11	23	59	43	20,000
4. Joe Runyan	12	2	11	31	15,000
5. Duane Halverson	12	2	27	51	13,000
6. John Cooper	12	3	28	3	11,000
7. Lavon Barve	12	4	17	55	9,500
8. Jerry Austin	12	10	15	1	8,000
9. Terry Adkins	13	0	22	29	6,500
10. Rune Hesthammer	13	4	20	0	5,500
11. John Barron	13	4	27	45	4,500
12. Guy Blankenship	13	7	12	29	4,000
13. Tim Moerlein	13	7	40	31	3,750
14. Bob Chlupach	13	10	32	13	3,500
15. Jerry Riley	13	14	36	49	3,250

16.	Vern Halter	13	15	29	29	3,000
17.	Gary Whittemore	13	20	37	23	2,750
18.	Ted English	13	23	1	26	2,500
19.	Nina Hotvedt	14	6	20	41	2,250
20.	Rick Atkinson	14	6	21	21	2,000
21.	Rusty Miller	14	11	4	54	
22.	Peter Sapin	14	11	17	42	
23.	Frank Torres	14	16	43	15	
24.	Paul Johnson	15	0	8	6	
25.	Martin Buser	15	0	53	56	
26.	John Wood	15	4	29	42	
27.	Dan MacEachen	15	5	9	14	
28.	Jerry Raychel	15	7	9	14	
29.	Raymie Redington	15	7	12	24	
30.	Mike Pemberton	15	7	44	37	
31.	David Olesen	15	9	44	15	
32.	Steve Bush	15	9	55	31	
33.	Kari Skogen	15	10	52	49	
34.	Gordon Brinker	15	15	20	31	
35.	Bobby Lee	16	10	34	3	
36.	Ron Robbins	16	15	3	19	
37.	Dave Scheer	16	15	3	58	
38.	Gordy Hubbard	16	16	44	44	
39.	Matt Desalernos	16	19	22	59	
40.	Alan Cheshire	16	21	9	57	
41.	Ray Lang	16	22	39	2	
42.	Roger Roberts	16	22	53	2	
43.	Allen Miller	17	5	41	37	
44.	Armen Khatchikian	17	8	12	29	
45.	Don McQuown	17	15	59	49	
46.	Mike Lawless	18	1	20	52	
47.	Mark Jackson	18	11	1	34	
48.	Joe LeFaive	18	18	7	24	
49.	Peter Thomann	18	18	7	34	
50.	Pat Danly	19	0	38	21	
51.	Bill Hall	19	0	38	48	
52.	Bill Davidson	19	0	55	55	
53.	Scott Cameron	19	19	51	27	
54.	Stan Ferguson	19	21	42	58	
55.	Mike Peterson	20	13	42	21	

SCRATCHED

1. Abel Akpik
2. John Anderson
3. Frank Bettine
4. Roger Bliss
5. Ron Brennan
6. Joe Carpenter
7. William Cowart
8. Jim Darling
9. Ray Dronenburg
10. Don Honea
11. Fred Jackson
12. Rick Mackey
13. Jan Masek
14. Earl Norris
15. Joe Redington, Sr.
16. Douglas Sheldon
17. John Stam
18. Norman Vaughan

FINISHING TIMES, 1987

	Days	Hours	Minutes	Seconds	Prize Money
1. Susan Butcher	11	2	5	13	$50,000
2. Rick Swenson	11	6	25	43	35,000
3. Duane Halverson	11	8	27	51	27,500
4. Tim Osmar	11	11	11	27	20,000
5. Jerry Austin	11	12	16	5	15,000
6. Joe Runyan	11	13	13	48	12,000
7. Lavon Barve	11	20	15	22	11,500
8. Ted English	11	22	23	3	10,000
9. John Cooper	12	0	14	14	9,000
10. Martin Buser	12	2	26	28	8,000
11. Joe Garnie	12	3	24	24	7,500
12. Guy Blankenship	12	5	11	10	7,000
13. Jerry Riley	12	6	59	0	6,500
14. Diana Dronenburg	12	9	13	18	6,000
15. Stephen Adkins	12	9	30	30	5,500
16. Matt Desalernos	12	9	31	40	5,000
17. Harry Sutherland	12	11	25	11	4,500
18. Robin Jacobson	12	14	35	30	4,000
19. Bruce Johnson	12	17	15	0	3,500
20. Jacques Philip	12	18	27	53	3,000
21. Sue Firmin	13	2	57	11	
22. DeeDee Jonrowe	13	2	58	15	
23. Terry Adkins	13	4	6	21	
24. Gary Whittemore	13	4	56	24	
25. Herbie Nayokpuk	13	10	27	47	
26. Claire Philip	13	10	33	33	
27. Gary Guy	15	4	35	14	
28. David J. Olesen	15	4	46	13	
29. Dan MacEachen	15	8	33	15	
30. Kazuo Kojima	15	8	53	17	
31. Bruce Barton	15	9	24	22	
32. Dick Mackey	15	13	28	22	
33. Joe Redington, Sr.	15	14	13	12	
34. Dennis J. Lozano	15	15	29	28	
35. John Nels Anderson	15	18	6	46	
36. John Coble	15	18	14	50	
37. Michael V. Owens	15	18	39	49	
38. Roger Roberts	17	10	32	42	
39. Pat Danly	17	11	2	22	
40. Bill Chisholm	17	11	16	28	
41. Henry Horner	17	11	28	10	
42. Caleb Slemons	17	12	33	39	
43. Mike Lawless	17	13	30	0	
44. Roy Wade	17	15	21	51	
45. John T. Gourley	18	4	51	49	
46. Don McQuown	18	12	34	35	
47. Matt Ace	18	12	45	38	
48. Brian Johnson	18	23	32	23	

49. Andre Monnier	18	23	35	30
50. Rhodi Karella	19	9	1	1

SCRATCHED

1. Peter R. F. Thomann
2. Rick Mackey
3. Raymie Redington
4. John Barron
5. Burt Bomhoff

6. Gordy Hubbard
7. Libby Riddles
8. Gordon Brinker
9. Joe LeFaive
10. David Aisenbrey

Carolyn Muegge, Tony Burch, and Norman Vaughan were withdrawn from the race by officials because they did not comply with a rule that required them to be in Unalakleet within five days after the winner had reached Nome. They continued nevertheless and finished the trail. The rule has since been eliminated.

FINISHING TIMES, 1988

	Days	Hours	Minutes	Seconds	Prize Money
1. Susan Butcher	11	11	41	40	$30,000
2. Rick Swenson	12	2	10	9	21,000
3. Martin Buser	12	4	21	46	16,500
4. Joe Garnie	12	9	21	39	13,200
5. Joe Redington, Sr.	13	3	25	28	9,000
6. Herbie Nayokpuk	13	3	26	44	7,200
7. Rick Mackey	13	14	43	29	6,900
8. Lavon Barve	13	15	22	42	6,000
9. DeeDee Jonrowe	13	16	29	6	5,400
10. Robin Jacobson	13	17	19	48	4,800
11. Jerry Austin	13	19	6	3	4,500
12. Jan Masek	13	22	18	3	4,200
13. Lucy Nordlum	13	23	47	31	3,900
14. Jacques Philip	14	0	2	43	3,600
15. Bill Cotter	14	1	33	18	3,300
16. Tim Osmar	14	1	49	16	3,000
17. Dan MacEachen	14	2	46	11	2,700
18. John Patten	14	3	57	6	2,400
19. Harry Sutherland	14	4	16	56	2,100
20. Matt Desalernos	14	5	1	36	1,800
21. Bill Hall	14	5	49	7	
22. Darwin McLeod	14	6	1	6	
23. Horst Maas	14	7	11	11	
24. Ted English	14	8	52	23	
25. Jerry Raychel	14	9	17	9	
26. John Barron	14	9	54	24	
27. Duane Halverson	14	11	19	55	
28. Peter Thomann	14	12	38	45	

29. Conrad Saussele	14	21	24	20
30. Burt Bomhoff	14	21	46	45
31. Frank Teasley	15	6	42	51
32. Peryll Kyzer	15	12	30	48
33. Ken Chase	15	12	54	20
34. Babe Anderson	15	13	6	49
35. Ian MacKenzie	17	6	45	45
36. Mike Tvenge	17	8	1	59
37. Mark Merrill	18	1	29	14
38. John Suter	18	1	50	50
39. John Gourley	18	6	52	30
40. Jennifer Gourley	18	6	54	12
41. Peter Kelly	18	7	6	41
42. Tim Mowry	18	7	21	41
43. Matt Ace	18	7	34	6
44. Gordon Brinker	18	7	44	7
45. Lesley Anne Monk	19	13	22	55

SCRATCHED

1. Tim Moerlein
2. Terry Adkins
3. Joe Runyan

4. Brian Carver
5. Ray Dronenburg
6. Norman Vaughan

DISQUALIFIED

1. Stan Ferguson

**OFFICIAL 1982 RULES & INTERPRETATION
IDITAROD TRAIL INTERNATIONAL SLED DOG RACE**

DITAROD TRAIL COMMITTEE, INC

1   RACE START-DATE/TIME/PLACE/WEATHER
The official starting date and time for the 1982 race will be March 6, 1982 at 10:00 A.M. The official starting place will be Anchorage, Alaska, unless otherwise designated by the Iditarod Trail Committee. The race will be held as scheduled regardless of weather conditions.

> *Each year the starting date and time will be determined by the Iditarod Trail Committee. Each year the official starting place will be Anchorage, Alaska. The starting place may be changed by the Race Marshal and Judges because of weather and/or trail conditions.*

2   COMMON START/LATE START
For elapsed time purposes the race will be a common start event. Each musher's elapsed time between Anchorage and Nome will be calculated using 10:00 A.M. on Saturday March 6th as the starting time. Any musher who cannot leave the starting line in the order drawn will be started after the musher who drew last place has left. Any team that cannot leave the starting line within 60 minutes of the last team's departure will be disqualified.

> *Common start event means that although teams will leave the starting line at two minute intervals, each team's official starting time will be regarded as 10:00 A.M. Make-up time will be clarified in Rule 3.*

3   24-HOUR STOP
One mandatory 24 hour stop will be required during the running of the race. The stop may be at any checkpoint at the driver's choice. The checkpoint checker must be notified by the musher that he is taking the 24-hour stop and the checker must note. Time begins upon notification. The starting time differential will be compensated for during each team's mandatory 24-hour layover so that each team has equal trail time. Every musher must personally sign in at each checkpoint before going on. A musher is not officially checked in until he has all the required gear.

> *It is the intent of this rule that the 24-hour stop be taken when it is the most beneficial to the dogs. If a musher loses a required article of gear between checkpoints, he cannot sign in at the next checkpoint until he has acquired and replaced the lost item. Starting time differential will be equalized for each musher when he takes his 24-hour stop. The Iditarod Trail Committee will give each musher the required time information prior to leaving the starting line. It is the musher's responsibility to comply with all parts of all rules.*

4   ENTRY FEE
The entry fee will be $1,049.00, payable on or after July 1, 1981. The entry fee must be received by the committee or postmarked by midnight January 15, 1982. Any entry fee received otherwise will be refunded and the musher will not be permitted to participate. Receipt of the $1,049.00, fee will constitute the musher's intent to enter the race and further acknowledges that the musher agrees to concur with each and every rule as stated. Upon written request, $1,000.00 of the entry fee will be refunded up until the required food shipment date, February 19, 1982. After February 19, 1982, no part of the entry fee will be refunded. Rookie

mushers must submit with their application, the recommendation of two known dog mushers or dog mushing organization as a reference to be reviewed by the Iditarod Trail Committee. The Iditarod Trail Committee reserves the right to reject any or all entries.

The entry fee will provide trail work, distribution of initial feed requirements and supplied from main points, return of dropped dogs to main collection points, purchase of Blazo and distribution along the trail, and provide each official finisher with the Iditarod Mushers Association patch. A "rookie" means a musher starting the Iditarod for the first time. Rookie mushers will receive notice of their acceptance or rejection within thirty (30) days of application. The Iditarod Trail Committee will receive mailed entry fees at Pouch X, Wasilla, Ak. 99687.

5   AGE
Driver must be a minimum of 18 years of age.
Self-explanatory.

6   TRAIL COMMITTEE MEMBERSHIP
All drivers must be members in good standing of the Iditarod Trail Committee.
Five classes of membership are available in the Iditarod Trail Committee. Each musher, before acceptance of his entry fee, must be a current member of the committee.

7   DOG MINIMUMS
Mushers must start the race with no less than seven (7) dogs and no more than eighteen (18). Mushers must finish the race with no less than five (5) dogs on the towline. Dogs may not be added to a team after the start of the race.
It is the intent of this rule that all dogs will either be on the towline or hauled in the sled and not led behind the sled.

8   SLED
Each musher has a choice of his own sled, subject to the condition that some kind of sled or toboggan must be drawn at the option of the driver.
The sled or toboggan must be capable of hauling any injured of fatigued dogs and the required equipment.

9   HARNESSES
Harnesses must be padded.
Self-explanatory.

10   ONE MUSHER PER TEAM
Only one musher will be permitted per team and that musher must complete the race with that team only.
Self-explanatory.

11   SWITCHING OF DOGS
Switching of dogs between mushers will not be permitted after the teams have officially left Anchorage.
If there are any dogs exchanged between drivers following the issuance of tags and acceptance of the dogs for the race by the trail veterinarians, it must be cleared with the race official prior to leaving the starting line.

12   TEAMS TIED TOGETHER
Two or more teams may not, in any way, be tied together except to assist another musher in trouble at some immediate location. Any teams so involved must notify officials at the next checkpoint along the trail.
It is the intent of this rule that a musher will not be penalized for helping another musher in imminent danger for his life.

13   SUBSTITUTES
Once a musher leaves the starting line no substitutes will be permitted to replace him.
Self-explanatory.

14   TREATMENT OF DOGS
THERE WILL BE NO CRUEL OR INHUMANE TREATMENT OF DOGS. DECISIONS OF THE RACE
VETERINARIANS, ACTING IN CONJUNCTION WITH THE RACE MARSHAL SHALL BE FINAL.
Self-explanatory

15   CLEARING THE TRAIL
Mushers setting up camp must clear the trail of their dogs and gear.
*This rule means that a musher must select a campsite far enough off the trail so that his dogs cannot swing
into the trail.*

16   TAMPERING
No musher may, without permission, tamper with another musher's dogs, food, or gear.
*Dog food left behind and dog food from scratched and disqualified mushers becomes the property of the
Iditarod Trail Committee and will be used at the discretion of the race officials.*

17   OUTSIDE ASSISTANCE
No musher may receive outside assistance between checkpoints unless an emergency is declared
by the race marshal, or so ruled.
The intent of this rule is that a musher receives no outside assistance. Period.

18   MOTORIZED VEHICLES
In no case will a musher accept assistance from any type of motorized vehicle.
Self-explanatory.

19   PACING
Pacing will not be permitted in front of a team by any vehicle.
Self-explanatory.

20   KILLING OF GAME ANIMALS
In the event that an edible game animal, i.e. Moose, Caribou, Buffalo, etc., is killed in defense of life
or property, the musher must take measures to salvage the meat for human use and report the incident
at the next checkpoint.
*This means that a food animal must be gutted and reported at the next checkpoint. The Iditarod Trail Committee
will make arrangements for further salvage. Any other animal killed in defense of life or property should
be reported.*

21   LITTER
LITTER OF ANY KIND may not be left on the trail. Camps must be cleaned up before moving.
THE TRAIL WILL BE KEPT CLEAN!
*The Iditarod Trail is a National Historic Trail and continued use of this trail for the race relies upon compliance
of this rule.*

22   CHECKPOINTS
Official checkpoints for the 1982 race will be:

1. Anchorage*	10. Nikolai	19. Kaltag
2. Eagle River****	11. McGrath	20. Unalakleet
3. Settlers Bay****	12. Takotna***	21. Shaktoolik
4. Knik****	13. Ophir	22. Koyuk
5. Rabbit Lake	14. Cripple	23. Elim
6. Skwentna	15. Poorman (Rough Ridge)******	24. Golovin***
7. Finger Lake	16. Ruby	25. White Mountain
8. Rainy Pass	17. Galena	26. Safety Roadhouse*****
9. Rohn Roadhouse	18. Nulato	27. Nome**

*   No feed drop. No dog drop.

**   Feed optional, regular shipment.

***   Feed optional at musher's risk, expense and arrangement. No dog drop.

****   No feed drop. Dog drop.

***** Feed optional, regular shipment. Dog drop.

****** Feed drop. No dog drop.

Self-explanatory.

23   MANDATORY GEAR

Each musher must have in his possession at all times the following items:

1. Proper cold weather sleeping bag.
2. Hand axe.
3. One pair of standard snow shoes with bindings.
4. Any promotional material that the musher has been asked to carry to Nome by the Iditarod Trail Committee.
5. Eight booties for each dog either in the sled or in use and in the sled.

> *It is the intent of this rule that mushers have these items in their possession at all times. However, in the event of accidental or unavoidable loss along the trail, the musher will be allowed to replace the missing item(s) at the next checkpoint BEFORE checking in.*

24   MANDATORY FOOD

Amusher may not leave a checkpoint without the following items in addition to the items listed in Rule #23:

1. One day's food for each dog with a minimum of two (2) pounds per dog.
2. One day's food ration for the musher.

> *Self-explanatory.*

25   PROMOTIONAL MATERIAL

The Iditarod Trail Committee reserves the right to require that every musher carry not more than ten (10) pounds of promotional material over the trail.

> *Self-explanatory.*

26   SHIPPING OF FOOD

A minimum of four (4) pounds per dog per checkpoint, plus musher's food must be shipped to all feed drop checkpoints by February 19, 1982. The Iditarod Trail Committee will receive and care for this feed. A name of the person to send this feed to will be provided to each musher. Any additional feed not shipped by this date through the Committee will be the responsibility of the individual musher.

> *Self-explanatory.*

27   INJURED, FATIGUED OR SICK DOGS

All injured, fatigued or sick dogs may be dropped at a designated dog drop. Each dropped dog must be left with two day's food and a reliable chain or cable.

> *Mushers are responsible to provide the chain or the cable, collar, and proper amounts of food for dropped dogs. A proper amount of food is two (2) pounds per day per dog.*

28   SHIPPING DROPPED DOGS

Mushers will pay for the transportation of their dropped dogs back to home. As dogs are dropped at various checkpoints they will be moved to the closest dog collection area at Anchorage, McGrath, Galena, Unalakleet or Nome. The dogs will be shipped home from the dogs lots at the discretion of the race marshal or official veterinarians. Prior to the start of the race all dogs will be marked with tags provided by the Iditarod Trail Committee for the current year.

> *Mushers will be responsible for advising the checker of the desired destination for a dropped dog.*

29 EXPIRED DOGS

Any dog that expires on the trail for any reason must be taken to the next checkpoint or checkpoint just passed, if musher deems it to his advantage timewise. An autopsy will be performed on all expired dogs by a veterinarian.

Self-explanatory.

30 DEMAND FOR FOOD AND SHELTER

A musher may not make demands for food or shelter along the trail.

31 CARE AND FEEDING OF DOGS

All care and feeding of dogs between checkpoints will be done by the mushers only. Only mushers may assist one another between checkpoints. Additionally, no planned help is allowed throughout the race, including checkpoints. Incidental help at checkpoints is permitted. At non-checkpoints a musher may accept hospitality for himself only.

It is the intent of this rule that the musher take care of his own dog team and gear.

32 HAULING DOGS

A musher may not allow any of his dogs to be hauled by another team. A musher's dogs hauled in his own sled must be hauled in a humane fashion.

Self-explanatory.

33 UNMANAGEABLE TEAM

Outside assistance will be allowed only if a team is unmanageable.

Whether a team is unmanageable will be ruled upon by the race marshal in each separate instance.

34 LOOSE LEADERS

There will be no loose leaders; all dogs will be in the team or on the sled.

All dogs will be fastened in the team or properly secured on the sled.

35 LOST TEAM

In the case of a lost team the team will not be disqualified if the driver regains control of the team, provided that the team and driver completed the entire race trail and complied with the rules including checkpoint requirements. All teams must follow the trail as marked.

As long as the team and driver continue on the trail when separated, the driver may continue on when regaining control, refer to Rule #31. Mushers may recieve assistance from another musher in recovering their team. It is the intent of this rule that all teams follow the trail as marked.

36 SPORTSMANSHIP

All mushers will conduct themselves in a civil and sportsmanlike manner during the entire racing event.

The race depends on the assistance of hundreds of volunteers who help out through their own generosity. A musher's conduct is a direct reflection on the Iditarod Trail Committee and the public reputation of the event. The entire racing event includes the awards presentation in Nome and all money winning teams are expected to attend.

37 RACE MARSHAL AND VETERINARIANS

The race marshal and official veterinarians will have absolute authority over the dog teams. Their judgement as to withdrawal of a dog or dogs from the race or any other condition relative to dog care on the trail will be final.

38 DRUGS

No injectable, oral, or topical drugs which may suppress the signs of illness or injury to the dogs may be carried or used by the musher. Iditarod Race Veterinarians have the authority to collect urine samples at any point after the official starting of the race. Veterinarians have the authority to collect both blood and urine samples immediately after the finish line in Nome. It will be the musher's responsibility to assist the Race Veterinarian in the collection of these samples.

THE IDITAROD TRAIL COMMITTEE WILL SCREEN FOR DRUG USAGE.
The following drugs are prohibited:
1. Analgesics (pain relievers), prescriptive or non-perscriptive.
2. Anti-inflammatory drugs including corticosteroids, anti-prostaglandins, salicylates and DMSO. The EXCEPTION to this rule will be the use of topical corticosteroids for use ONLY in TOPICAL FOOT OINTMENTS.
3. Nervous system stimulants.
4. Cough suppressants
5. Diuretics
6. Muscle relaxants
7. Antihistamines
8. Diet pills

It is the intent of this rule that no drugs or other artificial means be used to drive a dog beyond his natural ability. If, in the view of a Race Veterinarian, it is necessary to use one of these drugs for a dog's well-being, that dog will be pulled from the race.

39 VET CHECK

All dogs will undergo a physical examination before the race starts. The examinations will be performed by local members of the Southcentral Veterinarian Medical Association and-or other certified veterinarians. The location and the time for the examinations will be announced to all participants by the Trail Committee. Any dog that cannot qualify for a certificate of good health may not run the race. All examinations must be done within seven (7) days prior to the start of the race. A musher having his dogs examined other than at the official time and place must submit an official ITC health certificate signed by a certified veterinarian, as proof of an examination. This must be submitted to the Iditarod Trail Committee prior to the last veterinarian check sponsored by the Committee. A competitor in the race will not be considered an official veterinarian. All dogs entered in the race will have a current parvo, rabies and distemper shots and the musher must present proof of such shots at the time of examination.

Proof of rabies shots must come from a liscensed veterinarian or certified technician. Proof must be given to the Trail Committee on all aspects of this rule prior to 9:00 AM, March 3, 1982, the time of the official ITC Vet Check.

40 MUSHERS MEETINGS AND DRAWING

It will be mandatory for all mushers to attend a mushers meeting immediately prior to the mushers' banquet. Failure to attend this meeting will prohibit the musher from participating in the race. The time and place for this meeting will be announced by the Iditarod Trail Committee. Each musher must draw his starting position in person. The drawing for positions will be divided in half. The first half of the total mushers to enter will draw for the first half of the starting positions. The second half of the total mushers to enter will draw for the second half of the starting positions. Applications may be recieved at the Iditarod Trail Committee office in person, by proxy or mail starting July 1, 1981. Mail-in entries will be recorded alphabetically at 1:00 PM each day. Entrants applying in person will be recorded in order of appearance prior to and following mail recording.

Entrants will be divided in half at the time of the drawing. In the event of an odd number of entries, the odd number will be included in the last half of the drawing.

41 CLAIMS

Each musher agrees to hold the Iditarod Trail Committee, the race sponsor(s) and other contributors (that is sponsors and contributors to the race committee as distinguished from the sponsors of the individual mushers) harmless from any claim or demand based on any alleged action or inaction by the musher, his dogs, agents, or others acting in his behalf. The musher also agrees to release the Iditarod Trail Committee, Inc, race sponsor(s), and the agents, and employees from any claim or demand resulting from injury to the musher, his dogs, or his property. Further, the Iditarod Trail Committee has the unqualified and unrestricted authority to authorise the race sponsor(s) to photograph and otherwise collect information about the race and all participants therein and to use such photographs and information for advertising, public relations or other publicity purposes. Each musher shall sign any and all documents as may be requested by the Iditarod Trail Committee to evidence the foregoing. These documents will be executed at the mushers' meeting. Any musher who does not sign the documents requested by the committee will not be allowed to participate in the race.

Self explanatory.

42 MANDATORY STOP AT WHITE MOUNTAIN

There will be a mandatory one(1) hour stop for each team at White Mountain. During this stop each team will be checked by a veterinarian with a race official present.

Self-explanatory.

43 NO-MAN'S LAND

No Man's Land will be considered the land between the Ft. Davis Roadhouse and the official finish line in Nome.

No-man's land is defined as the section of trail where you do not have to relinquish the trail on demand. For the remainder of the race trail it is expected that when a musher calls for trail, it should be relinquished.

44 FINISH

An official finish shall be determined by the nose of the first dog across the line.

Self-explanatory.

45 PRIZE MONEY

The prize money for the 1982 race will be as follows.

1. $24,000	6. 5,000	11. 2,000	16. 1,500
2. 16,000	7. 4,000	12. 1,900	17. 1,400
3. 12,000	8. 3,600	13. 1,800	18. 1,300
4. 8,000	9. 3,200	14. 1,700	19. 1,200
5. 6,000	10. 2,800	15. 1,600	20. 1,000

In the event that less than $100,000 is raised for prize money, the awards will be paid on a percentage basis of prize money available in relation to $100,000.

Self-explanatory.

46 AWARDS PRESENTATION

The awards presentation ceremony at Nome will be held the evening following 72 hours after the first team crosses the finish line. All mushers who have crossed the finish line at the time of the ceremony will be present and the winner will have his lead dog present for recognition.

Self-explanatory.

47 PROTEST

Any infration of these rules observed by a musher may be protested in writing to any race official at the next checkpoint.

Self-explanatory.

48   DISQUALIFICATION AND PENALTIES

Failure to adhere to the published rules will allow race officials to disqualify a musher or levy monetary fines commensurate with the severity of the infraction. This will be a responsibility of the Race Marshal. A disqualified musher will forfeit all placements and monetary values. The disqualified musher may demand an informal hearing before a regularly scheduled meeting of the Board of Directors of the Iditarod Trail Committee, including the race officials. "Race Officials" mean the Race Marshal, appointed race judges and race veterinarians.

A race judge's responsibility is to assist the race marshal and race veterinarians.

49   CENSURE

The Board of Directors may censure a musher for cause, including prohibition from entering future races. The musher so involved may request in writing, an informal hearing before the arbitration board of the Iditarod Trail Committee, within 30 days of the date of censure.

This refers to action taken by race officials and the Board of Directors following the completion of the race.